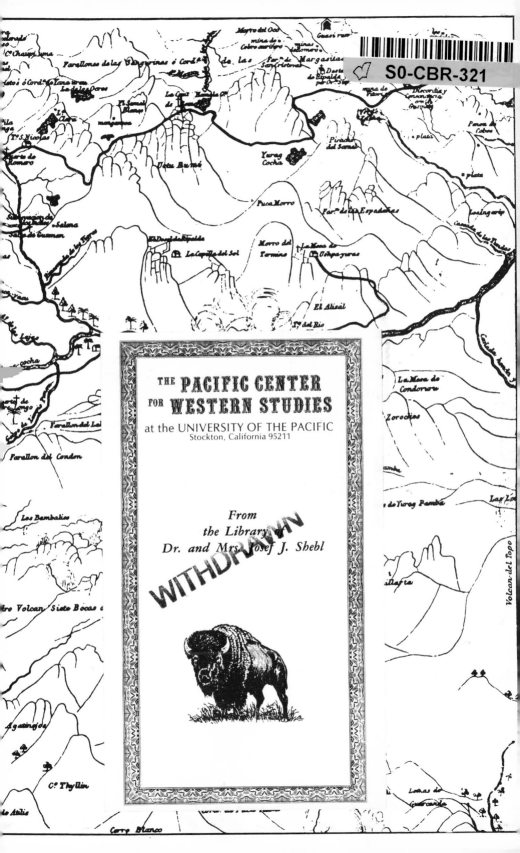

THEY FOUND GOLD

PISCHEL YEARBOOKS, INC.

P.O. Box 36, Marceline, Missouri 64658

By A · HYATT VERRILL

THEY
FOUND
GOLD

The Story of SUCCESSFUL
TREASURE HUNTS

The Rio Grande Press, Inc.

GLORIETA, NEW MEXICO · 87535

©1972
The Rio Grande Press, Inc.,
Glorieta, N.M. 87535

First edition from which this edition was reproduced
was supplied by
Bob Shuhi, Books
Box 136
Bantam, Conn. 06750

Library of Congress Cataloging in Publication Data

Verrill, Alpheus Hyatt, 1871-1954.
  They found gold.

  (A Rio Grande classic, no. 86)
  1. Treasure-trove. I. Title.
G525.V43 1972   910'.453   72-79459
ISBN 0-87380-093-1

A RIO GRANDE CLASSIC
First published in 1936

First Printing 1972

The Rio Grande Press, Inc.

GLORIETA, NEW MEXICO · 87535

Publisher's Preface

We are pleased to present herewith the 86th beautiful Rio Grande Classic. It is the story of treasures sought and treasures found, always and everywhere a fascinating subject. We have hopes ourselves of some day finding a hidden treasure. We don't go looking for one (we haven't time), but we never transplant iris in the garden without wondering if this is the day we dig up a chest of gold coins. The news press reports every now and then that someone digging for fishworms (or some such thing) finds an old tin box full of gold pieces maybe a century old or so. Then what does the lucky boob do? He trots down to the nearest police station with it, thinking maybe that "...honesty pays". In this decadent day and age, such a sap is completely out of touch with reality. If we ever find a hidden treasure, gold or diamonds or rubies or emeralds or great big 35-lb. ingots of pure platinum, we are not going to breathe a word of it to anyone... *not anyone.*

We are reminded of the simple-minded stamp collector who a few years ago purchased and found a printing error on a sheet of commemorative stamps; the sheet had gone through the color press upside down, so the error was a very valuable variety worth a lot of money. Had the finder kept his big mouth shut at least for awhile, he could have realized a handsome profit and the collecting fraternity would have had another truly rare postal item, but he didn't. The jackass brayed publicly about his find, and before he quite realized what hit the fan, the postmaster general ordered the Bureau of Printing and Engraving to deliberately reprint the stamp (with the error) until collectors had all they wanted. So the original sheet of errors was made worthless by too much talk too soon. That the postmaster general acted illegally to produce millions of identical errors didn't bother anyone, including the attorney general at the time and those gamey law "enforcers" at the Department of "Justice". The basic idea was to use the whole force of the government to prevent a citizen from making a bit of money because the government was careless. A nice illustration, really, of two wrongs making a right.

Hunting for treasure has occupied millions of people since time began. The aboriginal occupants of the Western Hemisphere appreciated gold as an ornamental metal about as fast as did those of Europe, Asia and Africa. The history of the world--of mankind--is replete with accounts of secret treasures and lost mines. When the Europeans came to the New World in search of El Dorado, they found tons of the lovely element in the form of jewelry, tableware, weapons and religious objects. The Spanish conquistadors sent treasure back to the king of Spain on fleets of great galleons, keeping four times as much for themselves. The New World became a treasure house for the crowned heads of the Old World. The riches of the West Indies made Spain (and subsequently Portugal) the wealthiest of nations and, in turn, the mistress of the Seven Seas.

But, as we said, all the gold from the New World never got to the Old World (until the Democrat party got going full blast with what they are pleased to call "foreign aid"). The conquistadors by the king's charters were allowed to keep four fifths of all they found, and they did (and human nature being what it is, probably a lot more). Legends of treasure in the Western Hemisphere have grown like weeds in a wet garden. When Hernando Cortez tried to get his men out of Tenochtitlan, they were so laden with treasure they could hardly walk or use their weapons. In the ensuing carnage of *noche triste* (June 20, 1520), dozens of soldiers were driven into the canals and the lake by the angry Aztecs where the Spaniards sank to the bottom under the weight of the treasure they carried. Millions in gold and gems are still there, we are told, covered now by modern Mexico City.

But even when the stately galleons were loaded to the gunwales with treasure, at Vera Cruz, there was no assurance the ships would get to Spain. The waters of the Gulf of Mexico, from Florida to the Yucatan peninsula, were known as the Spanish Main. Not only did frequent and massive hurricanes take their deadly toll of ships, but so did pirates. There are doubtless untold millions in ancient Spanish treasure lying barnacled and silt-covered in the dappled, sun-kissed bays and coves of the continental shoreline from Panama to Key West. Tropical storms, pirates, lost galleons and uncounted treasure is the stuff of myth and legend as well as documented truth, but which is which after the passage of a few hundred years?

Author Verill, beginning on page 245, recounts a number of "Authentic Unrecovered Treasures in America". On page 265, he sets forth a "List of Treasures Actually Known to Have Been Recovered or Salvaged in Recent Years". This book was first published in 1936; some of the treasures he describes have probably been found and salvaged since then. Even as we write, a private enterprise corporation off Padre Island has been bringing up treasure which Texas is trying to grab as "state property". But by and large, author Verrill's research remains largely intact today just as it was in 1936. Hence, this book still has, largely, the validity it had when it was first published 36 years ago. Did Verrill write of legend, or of fact? Why not follow his clues yourself; it might be you to prove that he wrote fact, rather than legend.

But if you find treasure, for Pete's sake keep quiet about it!

In our recent memory, newspapers in the United States carried wire service accounts of a British treasure hunter who after many years of diving and underwater search off the coast of England, did indeed find the wreck of a treasure-laden Spanish galleon. With great difficulty, the poor fellow brought up quite a lot of marvelous gold artifacts, plate and coins--which naturally included a lot of publicity. The British government thereupon claimed the entire find, and brought suit in the courts to obtain possession of it. When the treasure finder realized he would lose his case no matter what the law said, he put everything he had brought up from the watery grave in a boat, took it all out to sea and dumped it back into the ocean. "If the government wants it so bad," he later told the judge, "then let them go find it, just like I did."

We rejoice at such spirit, while we deplore the lack of discretion that brought it to pass. We are on the side of the treasure hunter; what we think of a greedy and confiscatory government is not a fit subject for public print. The "system" is a monster which, even as we write, is turning viciously on those who created it and allowed it to grow to such obscene and malignant proportions. It is later, we think, than we all think.

Author Alpheus Hyatt Verill was a professional scientist and avocational treasure hunter who wrote whereof he knew. He was born in New Haven, Conn., on July 23, 1871. His graduate work was done at the Yale School of Fine Arts, where he studied Natural History and illustration. At the age of 24 he was an accomplished artist; he illustrated the Natural History Section of the 1896 edition of *Webster's International Dictionary*. In 1902, he invented the autochrome process (color) photography which has come such a long way since then.

Author Verrill was a member of a number of professional ethnological expeditions between 1920 and 1953. During 1933 and 1934, he was the organizer of the expedition on which this book is based--an effort to locate and salvage sunken treasure ships off the coast of Yucatan and Central America. In 1940 he founded the Anhiarka Experimental Gardens and Natural Science Museum near Lakeland, Fla.--the name being that of an Indian village discovered on the same site years earlier by Hernando de Soto.

During his active professional years, author Verrill organized or accompanied extensive explorations in Bermuda, West Indies, Guiana, Central America and Panama. From these adventures, he wrote 105 books on natural history, treasure hunting and travel. He published his last book, *The Real Americans,* early in 1954; he died on November 14th of that year, and lies sleeping at Chiefland, Fla.

When we decided to reprint this title, we got in touch with our treasure-hunting authority friend Karl von Mueller at Exanimo Hacienda in Segundo, Colo. At our invitation, he wrote the Introduction following these pages. Friend von Mueller publishes extensively in the treasure hunters' field of interest; his major work and best known (the world over) is the *Treasure Hunter's Manual,* frequently published in new and updated editions. If there is anything one wants to know about prospecting or treasure hunting, as he says, "...call the old man". At his interesting spread in Segundo, near Trinidad, he works a placer mine which enables him to sell small vials of raw gold to visiting tourists. If you get into southern Colorado, and you're interested in lost mines and buried treasure, call on the old man. He's a walking, talking, amiable, convivial bear of a man; a veritable animated encyclopedia on the subject of treasure and gold prospecting.

We have reprinted three other books on this subject, all of which have been exceptionally popular and much in demand. One and two, *Lost Mines of the Great Southwest* and *Lost Mines and Buried Treasure Along the Old Frontier,* both by John Mitchell (not the husband of Martha), and *Black Range Tales,* which is less specific about lost mines and more specific on cowpoking. We have also published a book not on lost gold mines or buried gold treasure, but on the rare gemstone Turquoise. The book has an extraordinarily self-explanatory title: *Turquois; A Study of the History, Minerology, Geology, Ethnology, Archeology, Mythology, Folklore and Technology,* by Joseph E. Pogue. Turquoise is buried treasure, too...

We are most receptive to suggestions for books about lost mines and buried treasures now out of print but worth reprinting. We invite our readers to send us suggestions; anyone suggesting a title will get a copy free if we reprint it...even if 50 readers suggest the same title; all will receive a complimentary copy. What better advertising could we get?

We might mention, in passing, that author John C. Cremony in his book *Life Among the Apaches* (which we recently reprinted, $10.00), describes a ledge of nearly pure silver ore he found in the Guadalupe Mountains of west Texas and eastern New Mexico. He described the find quite nicely; he was, he wrote, on his way from New Mexico to mid-Texas (San Antonio?) shortly after the civil war. We think a treasure hunter would not have much real difficulty in re-locating the outcropping. From Cremony's description, we ourselves deduce that the location is in or near what is now the undeveloped Guadalupe National Park. If memory serves without a lot of research, Cremony never returned to his discovery--so it should still be there, somewhere.

And whether there's real treasure there or not, it's a corking good book to read anyway.

Robert B. McCoy

La Casa Escuela
Glorieta, N.M.
September 1972

Introduction

The locating and analysis of good, basic treasure literature has always been a problem for the beginning and amateur treasure hunter. In fact, some perfectly obvious treasure leads are often overlooked or inadvertently ignored by the amateur treasure hunter because he looks only for word-pictures which usually do not exist.

The modern stampede to the world of buried and hidden treasure was first triggered by the *Treasure Hunter's Manuals* that we published in the late 1950's and early 1960's These books provide every facet of information that a treasure hunter needs to succeed. Prior to this time--in the early 1950's--a periodical known as the *Treasure Hunter's News* was published from Phoenix, Ariz., and it provided some good, sound, basic information. But it was never able to get its circulation much over 1,500 subscribers, so in 1955 it was absorbed by the National Prospector's Gazette. The Gazette went on to publish sound, solid information on treasure hunting as well as prospecting, and its articles were prepared in plain, non-technical language.

Finally, in 1964, we set up the Exanimo Establishment in Weeping Water, Nebr., to provide a multitude of services for the amateur treasure hunter, as well as the professional. This was the pioneer organization in the treasure hunters' field, and it originated such new services and terms as "...call the old man," where anyone could get honest, experienced information merely with a telephone call. Free technical bulletins, news letters and information flyers were among other services not commonly obtainable to the treasure hunter. Many of today's dealers got their start by following the Exanimo Establishment style and format.

During this phenomenal rise in public interest in treasure hunting, dozens of authors prepared hundreds of articles and books. Some of this literature was valuable, and some of it worthless. Often, the worthless information was merely rewritten material, with unsupported information added to make it seem different. Some items were outright fabrications.

Knowing this, and being fully aware of the scores and scores of lost mine and treasure yarns--and their origins--most full time treasure hunters were appalled at the avalanche of unreliable but published information. Still, it all served a useful purpose. It kept the bumbling beginner busy with things that did not exist; it allowed the professional to work without the distraction of separating myth from reality. We do not denigrate the beginner with these remarks; those with a genuine interest keep on until they pass the learning stage and get into the "doing" stage. Others who get into the game have only a fleeting interest; they're here today, and gone tomorrow. The transient amateur treasure hunter can work real mischief, from the professionals' point of view.

There has always been a need for basic source material on treasure hunting, and far too few publishers have known (or cared) what the avid seeker really needed. Nor have these publishers seen fit to locate and publish suitable material. When The Rio Grande Press reprinted the two John D. Mitchell books *(Lost Mines of the Great Southwest; Lost Mines and Buried Treasure Along the Old Frontier)*, they were filling a huge breach in the literature of buried and hidden treasure. The Mitchell books are good basic source books, and many of the modern treasure stories were first brought to light by John Mitchell.

When we discovered The Rio Grande Press planned to reprint this book, we were among the first to encourage it. There are at least ten basic treasure leads in this book, and if a good researcher would pursue some of these leads, he might easily develop three or four times as many. All stories of treasure provide leads to other stories of treasure; it's a sort of self-perpetuating thing. But one has to be able to separate the real from the unreal; the legend from the truth.

In our frame of reference, what "basic source" material means is, essentially, the first report or the most complete report on a lost mine or a hidden treasure. This gives rise to offshoots of the report or the story. As the story goes the rounds of the fraternity, it gains strength in the re-telling; like a snowball rolling down hill, the myth grows around a nugget of truth. Thus, hundreds or thousands of treasure enthusiasts get to searching for the caches described. The full-time professional treasure hunter will spend days in a library searching old books for a virgin lead rather than spend an hour reading some gussied-up version of some tired old story that's been around for years.

We think this book contains basic source material. The geographical area is the Western Hemisphere, rather than the Great American Southwest, but then, treasure is where you find it. The author was one of the most reliable ever to write about lost and hidden treasures, and he wrote from field experience, not from research. You know the scholarly definition of "research"? Lifting material from one book is plagiarism; lifting from many books is "research". Writer Verrill went into the water, the jungles, the ruins himself; what he writes about is genuine and authentic. Thus this work can provide the serious researcher with many clues to hidden treasures. It may not be possible for most of us to follow the expeditions made by Mr. Verrill in fact, but we can in fancy; the author writes well, with gusto and with charm. His work is interesting, even if it doesn't make anyone instantly rich. It is a first rate book for anyone; it is especially and particularly a first rate book for the treasure hunter.

It is a sound three-way investment for the treasure hunter; (1) it is a good book, (2) it is a good treasure book and (3) it offers leads to those treasure hunters who can get up and go.

So, by golly, get up and go!

Karl von Mueller

Exanimo Hacienda
Segundo, Colo.
March 1972

A SKETCH MAP
OF
TREASURES FOUND & UNFOUND
MENTIONED
IN THE PAGES OF THIS
BOOK

PIRATE BELLAMY'S   OAK ISLAND
    BASE   TREASURE.
        CASCO BAY TREASURE.
SMUGGLING   "WHIDAW"   SS PORTLAND.
SLOOP
NEW YORK   PRIVATEER "DEFENCE."
    FRIGATES
    "HUSSAR" & "LEXINGTON."

PRIVATEER "DEBRAAK."

WRECK OF "MERIDA."
SS "CENTRAL AMERICA."

BILLY BOWLEGS'
    TREASURE.
SUNKEN SCHOONER   PALM BEACH.
WITH RICE MILLIONS
OF GOLD.   "SANTA MARGARITA."
BRADEN CASTLE
    TREASURE FOUND HERE.
GASPARILLA'S   GORDA CAY SPANISH GALLEON.
    TREASURE.   NASSAU.
BAHAMA BANKS.   14 SUNKEN GALLEONS.   PIRATE TURNLEY'S
        TREASURE.
BLACK CAESAR'S   TREASURE FOUND IN HIS CAVERN.
    TREASURE.   TREASURE JETTISONED BY SPANIARDS IN 1628.
            CUBA.   GREAT INAGUA.
THE INCA'S TREASURE.   DON CARLOS III.   KING CHRISTOPHE'S
THE TREASURE   TREASURE.
THAT WAS FOUND   14 SUNKEN GALLEONS
& LOST.   SANTO   (PHIPPS' TREASURE.)
        DOMINGO   CAYO LEVANTADO.
    JAMAICA.
        BOBADILLA'S
    SUNKEN CITY   SHIP WITH THE
    OF PORT ROYAL.   "GOLDEN PIG."
            NEVIS.
GOLDEN BOARS OF THE   SUNKEN CITY
    MAYAS.   OF JAMESTOWN.
            DE GRASSE'S   DOMINICA.
            WARSHIP SUNK HERE.
                CURACAO.
LOST MINE OF   SAN BLAS
    TITUNA.   ISLANDS.   SANTA LIMA CONCEPCION.
GOLD INCA   MORGAN'S   SUNK HERE.
    GRAVES.   PIRATES LOST TREASURE.
COCOS IS.   TREASURE   "SAN PEDRO DE ALCANTARA."
    TREASURE.   GALLEON
        LAKE   SPANISH SHIPS
        GUAYAVITA   SUNK BY MORGAN.
        EL DORADO'S
        TREASURE.

    TREASURE SHIP
    WITH BALLAST.
    DRAKE'S TREASURE.   VALVERDE'S
    PLATE IS.   TREASURE.
TREASURE OF GOLDEN HIND.

GALLEON   TODOS SANTOS.
        THE HOLY GARDENS
CHANCHAN   ATAHUALPA'S
BIG FISH   TREASURE
TREASURE.   NEAR HERE.
LIMA   PILLPERU
TREASURE.   PUMA HANAMAR   LAKE TITICACA'S
        TREASURE.   LOST TREASURE.

        TIAHUANACO.

SS "SAKKARAH"
WITH $330,000.

By A · HYATT VERRILL

THEY
FOUND
GOLD

The Story of SUCCESSFUL
TREASURE HUNTS

G · P · PUTNAM'S SONS

New York

TO

*The army of romantic and adventurous souls
who follow the lure of treasure hunting,
this volume is dedicated by their
fellow treasure hunter—*

THE AUTHOR

Treasure Hunter

I have hunted for galleons 'neath tropical seas,
I have dug and have delved under hoary old trees
For treasures that rumor declared had been hid
By Blackbeard or Morgan or bold Captain Kidd.

I have studied the cyphers of countless old tomes,
With the crosses and figures, the skulls and crossbones.
I have followed the rainbow o'er mountains and plains
With never a doubloon to pay for my pains.

I have searched amid ruins and burial mounds.
I have disinterred mummies, and hundreds I've found.
But no gems or jewels have yet been revealed,
Nor hoards of vast riches my labors unsealed.

I have read all the volumes, I know all the lore
Of gold that was hidden on every wild shore.
I have tramped through the jungles along the faint trail
Of the ancient Gold Road, but only to fail.

I have hunted for riches in tombs and in graves.
I've followed the lure through dark, dismal caves.
Though up to the present, no treasures I've won,
In my questing for gold I have had lots of fun.

Table of Contents

(ix)

CONTENTS

(x)

(xi)

CONTENTS

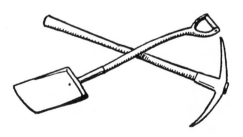

List of Illustrations

(xiii)

Introduction

FROM time immemorial, and in all lands, men have been hunting for treasure. In fact it would scarcely be an exaggeration to state that somewhere, someone is engaged in treasure hunting every hour of every day in every year. And this being the case it is not at all surprising that now and again some hidden, lost or sunken treasure is found and recovered.

But unlike other successful exploits, successful treasure hunts are not as a rule blazoned to the world. For many and obvious reasons the lucky ones usually reveal little or nothing, and as a result, one hears far more of unsuccessful than of successful treasure hunts, which is perhaps the principal reason why the average person regards treasure hunters as visionary impractical beings, and treasure hunts as futile as searching for the pot of gold at the foot of the rainbow. But this viewpoint does not prevent them from being keenly interested in tales of treasure and treasure hunts. Perhaps there is no one subject in the line of literature which holds a greater lure and arouses a greater interest than that of treasure, and regardless of race, station, sex or age, human beings, or at least a large proportion of human beings, find a real thrill and fascination in stories of lost, buried or sunken treasures.

Just why this should be so is difficult to explain. The mention of a few millions in gold stored in a bank vault will cause no comment, no particular interest or reaction. But speak of a fraction of the amount buried in the sands of some lonely isle, or lying in the rotting hulk of some Spanish galleon at the bottom of the sea, and the keenest interest is at once aroused, although in all probability there is about as much chance of helping oneself to the one as to the other.

Even the most practical, hard-headed business and professional men often get a tremendous "kick" out of lost treasure and treasure hunting, and I have known a number of men who would never dream of investing a few hundred dollars in a business deal that was not certain to pay profits, but who would almost clamor to put thousands into a treasure hunt.

It is not always the lure of riches that attracts, for the multi-millionaire is as often bitten by the treasure hunt bug as is the poor man. Neither is it the hope of getting something for nothing, for treasure hunts cost money, and a lot of it, as even the rankest amateur realizes. Hence we can only assume that there is something about hidden or lost treasures that appeals to the streak of romance and adventure that most of us possess.

But quite irrespective of the whys and wherefores of the almost universal interest in treasures and treasure hunting, the fact remains that it is an ever fascinating theme, regardless of whether or not the treasures have been found. For that matter, the most thrilling, romantic and interesting tales often deal with the unsuccessful searches.

In this book I have not attempted to include all or even a small portion of known treasure hunts, successful or not. To do so would require not one but many volumes, and, moreover, the stories of treasure hunts of past centuries, and of past decades for that matter, have been told and retold and published in numerous books, until the treasure loving public is as familiar with the feats of Sir William Phipps and other famous treasure hunters as with the adventures of Robinson Crusoe or Christopher Columbus.

Neither have I included all of the more recent treasure hunts, either successful or otherwise, for many of these are wholly devoid of romance, adventure or story interest, and come more properly under the head of wrecking or salvaging jobs than treasure hunting.

But there have been many recent treasure hunts, in several of which I have taken an active part, which hold a deal of romance, much high adventure, abundant thrills and great human interest, as well as drama, tragedy and, not infrequently, humor also, and the stories of the more outstanding and noteworthy of these will be found herein.

Also, let me assure my readers that all of these tales are fact and none fiction, although for sundry and obvious reasons I have, as a rule, used fictional names for the persons mentioned, other than historical characters.

And I hereby wish to disclaim all responsibility for the statements of values of treasures found or unfound, unless verified by official, documentary or historical records. I have no desire to be blamed by some future treasure hunter who, after reading my book, discovers a treasure

(xvii)

and finds only a mere million dollars' worth of gold where he had been led to believe several millions had been buried.

Finally, let me remind one and all that treasures are very much like fish in a way, for just as the biggest fish is always the one that escapes from the hook, so the biggest treasures are those which still remain undiscovered. Perhaps that was the reason why the Spaniards called the fabulously vast treasure of Chan Chan the "Peje grande" or Big Fish, for it never yet has been found.

THEY FOUND GOLD

ⵊⵊ

The Blockade Runners' Treasure Safe

THERE have been many more treasures found than is generally supposed, for, as a rule, a person who finds a hoard of gold or silver, coins or jewels, seldom broadcasts the tidings to the world at large. There are many reasons why the lucky finder prefers to keep the matter quiet. In many countries the governments claim the lion's share of treasure-trove found within their boundaries or their territorial waters, and the person who has spent time and money in searching for a treasure, and who does all the work and takes all the risks, is naturally averse to handing the officials a large percentage of his find. Also, as treasures are usually found—if found at all—in wild or remote districts, there is always the danger of bandits, hijackers or other scoundrels helping themselves to treasures if it becomes noised about that they have been found. So if treasure hunters fail to report a successful end to their quest it must not be assumed that their hunt went unrewarded. Occasionally, however, some fortunate treasure hunter tells some friend of his luck, or some member of the party or expedition talks, and the truth leaks out. And

(1)

sometimes, also, when returning treasure hunters suddenly and inexplicably adopt a mode of life not at all in keeping with their former financial status, one may put two and two together and make a fairly certain four, as one might say. It is rather strange, too, that in very many instances the really successful treasure hunter is the amateur at the game, some fellow who is by no means a treasure hunting addict but who, quite accidentally, gets wind of some hoard of riches and by merest chance or luck secures the treasure.

This was the case with the man who, about a year ago, won a small fortune on a treasure hunt of barely two weeks' duration, and thereby once again demonstrated the fact that truth is stranger than fiction, and also that "to him who hath shall be given," for Mr. Dudley, as we may call him, was already a very wealthy man. In fact if he had not been wealthy he never would have found the treasure. And by the same token, if he had not been aiding and abetting a violation of our laws the treasure would in all probability still be resting among the corals and the sea-fans on the bottom of the ocean in the Bahama Islands.

Like so many, in fact the majority of us in the pre-repeal days, Mr. Dudley had his bootlegger. And when, on one occasion, the purveyor of illicit wet goods asked his best customer for a loan of five thousand dollars with which to purchase a plane in which to run cargoes of liquor from Bimini and Grand Bahama to Florida, and eloquently described the immense profits of such a venture—if discreetly conducted—Mr. Dudley quite willingly advanced him the required sum.

To Dudley the investment was merely a "flyer," a

gamble, and when a short time later, the man announced that the federal officers had seized the plane and cargo Dudley waved aside the loss of his five thousand as of little consequence.

"Hard luck!" he remarked. "But I took the risk so let's forget it."

"I'm not sure you couldn't get your money back with interest," declared the bootlegger. "When I was flying across the Bahama Bank I spotted an old wreck. It looked mighty good to me, and every one down there tells stories of blockade runners that were sunk with treasure during the Civil War. I've got a sort of a hunch that the wreck I saw is one of them. But I guess you wouldn't be interested enough to put up the cash to find out."

"Is that so!" the other exclaimed. "It strikes me it might be a lot of fun going down there to that old wreck. Do you know—" he chuckled—"ever since I was a kid I've been crazy over treasure hunting yarns. What would it set me back to have a try at it?"

A few days later the Dudley yacht slipped quietly from the New York harbor bound ostensibly on a southern cruise. In addition to the owner and his bootlegger friend there were two deep sea divers aboard, and under the schooner's hatches was a complete diving equipment. It was not so simple a matter to locate the wreck as the treasure hunters had supposed, for viewing the banks from the air and searching the same area in a small boat are two very different matters. Moreover, the flying bootlegger had only a general idea as to the location of the wreck he had sighted. But he had noted the exact course he had followed, which reduced the search to a definite and restricted area, and back and forth the small

(3)

boats cruised, their crews peering through "water glasses" at the coral reefs and sea-gardens with their strange multicolored growths. Fishes of brilliant blue, green, scarlet, orange, as gorgeous as butterflies, swam lazily among the purple and golden sea-fans, the waving lavender sea-plumes, the crimson sea-feathers and giant cup sponges. Sea anemones two feet or more in diameter spread magenta and mauve tentacles from crevices between the orange, scarlet, green and yellow corals. Huge vermilion crabs and peacock-spotted crawfish scuttled from sight as the boats' shadows fell across the reefs. Giant maroon-colored starfish dotted the sandy areas between the reefs, immense queen conchs moved ponderously about upon the sea floor, and always there were the sharks, sinister monsters constantly cruising, like pirate craft, about the reefs. Twice the searchers felt sure they had found the wreck when rusty, coral-encrusted anchors and rotting timbers were sighted. But each time the bootlegger shook his head and declared they were not his wreck and that the latter was still clearly distinguishable as a ship's hull. And then one day a shout from one of the boats and the frantic waving of a red flag brought the others hurrying alongside. There, thirty feet below the surface, with its shattered bilges resting upon the jagged coral, was the remains of what once had been a small steam brigantine. The wreck had been located, every one was excited, and the divers immediately busied themselves with preparations to descend and explore the old hulk. Carefully the yacht was jockeyed into position and securely moored fore and aft as close to the wreck as was safe. Diving gear was brought on deck, the air pump rigged and tested, tackle overhauled, and the divers'

(4)

heavy ladder was lowered overside. Aided by his assistant, the master diver donned his suit and, as helpless as a baby in the stiff cumbersome costume, waited while the heavy bronze collar was fitted about his neck, the lead-soled shoes were buckled on his feet and the canvas overalls were drawn over his legs. Then, clambering clumsily over the ship's rail, he descended the ladder until his head was on a level with the bulwarks. About his waist was strapped the belt with its lead weights, the life line was adjusted and secured under his arm-pits, and, thrusting a cake of chewing gum into his mouth, he bent to receive the grotesque helmet and adjusted the valves to his air hose as the pump began to clank. And here let me pause to explain that chewing gum is a very essential matter in deep sea diving, the movement of the jaws in mastication and the saliva produced preventing danger of injury to the ear drums. At last, with the helmet locked in place, with air hose and life line cleared and held by the tender, the assistant tapped upon the copper helmet to signal all was ready, the diver signaled all well, and releasing his hold upon the ladder sank slowly through the clear water with a silvery stream of bubbles rushing upward from the escape valve of his head piece. Reaching the bottom, he signaled for a crowbar to be lowered, and tense with excitement, Dudley and the others watched his every movement as he secured the bar and moved, like some strange sea monster in a "slow motion" picture, toward the wreck. What would he find? Was the old sunken hulk empty or was there a treasure chest, a store of golden and silver coins or other valuables hidden among the sea-fans, the sponge growths and the stag-horn coral?

Slowly, exasperatingly, deliberately, the misshapen

figure moved about the wreck, poking with his bar, prying loose a rotten plank, wrenching away a mass of sponge or coral, and raising a smoke-like cloud of sand and silt which almost concealed him from the watchers above.

Over and about the old wreck he climbed, until at last he dropped from sight among the skeleton-like timbers of the hull. Slowly the minutes passed, and then, once more the weird figure appeared and signaled for a rope and tackle to be sent down.

"He's found something!" exclaimed Dudley. "Something he wants to send up!"

The assistant diver spat over the rail. "Sure has," he agreed as he lowered the coil of rope and tackle to his mate below. "But that ain't sayin' it's treasure," he added. "Maybe just a old gun or a cask of rum or somethin'."

The bootlegger laughed. "Don't know but what that might be called treasure," he observed. "Liquor that's been down there ever since that ship was wrecked ought to be pretty well aged and high priced, I'd say."

Again the diver vanished in the wreck, to reappear presently and signal for those above to pull him up. "Don't know what I've made fast to," he said as his assistant removed the helmet and weighted belt, and the diver climbed aboard and shuffling across the deck seated himself on the hatch. "Maybe it's what you're after and then again maybe it's just a case of cargo," he continued. "Might as well haul her up and find out."

Slowly the slack came in, the rope tightened under the strain of the electric hoist, and up from the maze of rotten, shattered timbers and twisted iron work came a squarish object covered with weeds and sea growths.

(Williamson Underseas Photo)

A DIVER EXAMINING AN OLD TREASURE WRECK IN THE
BAHAMAS

Speculation ran high as it came nearer and nearer the surface, until at last it was lowered, dripping, upon the schooner's decks. As full of excitement as any boy, the owner of the yacht seized a hammer and commenced knocking off the accumulation of coral. "It's metal!" he fairly shouted, as a section of corroded rusty iron was revealed. Seizing hammers, hatchets and crowbars, the others attacked the covering of coral. "It's a chest all right," announced the diver.

"Or a safe," exclaimed Dudley.

"Pretty near rusted through," declared the bootlegger. "Let's knock a hole in it and see what's inside." As he spoke he struck the metal a resounding blow with the crowbar, a gaping jagged hole was torn in the corroded iron, and out from the rent poured a flood of dull-yellow coins.

"Gold!" shouted Dudley, dropping on his knees. "Gold sovereigns, as I live!"

Shouting, laughing, excited, the men crowded about, picking up the coins, examining them, clinking them together. Gold! Minted British sovereigns! Treasure!

"Here, bring a bucket, some one," cried Dudley. "We'll gather up this money before we lose some of it in all this muck. Then we'll rip the safe wide open; there must be a lot more inside."

With the coins safe in the bucket, the men fell to work, and with hammers and bars tore away a large section of the salvaged safe, to reveal a mass of gold and silver coins and the remnants of sodden, rotten, canvas bags.

"Holy mackerel!" exclaimed the diver. "I never seen such a heap of money in my life. Must be pretty near a million dollars in there."

(7)

"Million nothing," declared the bootlegger. "A million dollars in gold is close to a ton."

"Well, this old tin box wasn't no lightweight, judgin' by the strain on the hoist," commented one of the crew. "What do you say, Mr. Dudley?"

"Don't ask me. All I can say is it's a lot of money, and most of it British, dated in the sixties. Guess it's a blockade runner's safe all right."

"Hey, what's this?" demanded the bootlegger who had thrust his hand into the safe and was examining a sodden, pulpy, grayish mass he had extracted. Then:—"Damned if it isn't money, too!" he cried. "Paper money!"

There was no doubt of it, although the once crisp Bank of England notes were reduced to pulp and were utterly worthless.

With the first wild excitement over, the men fell to work, filling buckets with the coins until the safe was empty. ·

"Bet we're the only men who ever handled gold sovereigns by the bucketful," grinned the bootlegger as he mopped his forehead and gazed at the galvanized iron buckets filled with the minted coins.

Dudley chuckled. "It's going to be some job to count them," he remarked. "Come on, boys, let's get busy and find out how much treasure we've got." When at last the coins had been counted and their values added up there was a grand total of something over eighty-eight thousand dollars. Dudley slapped the bootlegger on the back. "Dan, old man, that five thousand I put into your plane was the best investment I ever made!" he declared. "Pretty near eighteen hundred per cent profit isn't bad!"

The bootlegger grinned. "Thank Uncle Sam, not me,"

he said. "If those prohibition guys over in the Glades hadn't grabbed my plane we wouldn't be here with near ninety grand right now."

Dudley chuckled. "You're dead right, Dan," he agreed. "And here's one time when I'm strong for enforcing the dry laws."

The assistant diver rubbed the stubble on his chin and spat into the sea. "Just the same," he observed reflectively, "it's a damn shame about all them wads of bills. Hell, I'll bet they was worth more'n all this hard money, and just nothin' but slops now. Why the blazes didn't them blockade runners have a watertight safe?"

⊥⊥

Billy Bowlegs' Blood-Stained Treasure

OF all the pirates who, in the early part of the nineteenth century, infested the Gulf of Mexico and the neighboring seas, the most cruel, ruthless and probably the most successful, was Billy Bowlegs. Just who he was or whence he came, no one ever knew. But there was no doubt that he was English—or at any rate British—and when he first appeared in New Orleans, in 1810, he went under the name of William Rogers. Seemingly an honest and law-abiding man, he bought a small plantation about seventy-five miles from the city, married a Choctaw Indian woman and, in due course of time, became the father of four sons and two daughters.

Obviously, however, neither family ties nor a planter's life could satisfy Rogers' restless and adventurous spirit, and leaving the estate to be cared for by his dusky spouse and his half-breed offspring, off he went on his new career. Joining the Lafitte Brothers at Batavia, he became a member of that famous band of smugglers and outlaws and rose high in the estimation of the Lafittes. And when the quixotic Frenchmen enlisted their services on the American side during the Battle of New Orleans, and for so doing received pardons from the Federal Government, Rogers, or Billy Bowlegs as he was now called, distinguished himself for his reckless bravery. But his association with the Batavians had taught him a few things. There was more money to be made dishonestly than by honest means, he had discovered; human lives, he had learned, were a rather cheap commodity after all, and danger and battle had become an obsession. So with the breaking up of the Batavia colony, friend Rogers, instead of returning to his family and plantation, decided to turn smuggler on his own account. Gathering together a few of the Lafittes' henchmen, and acquiring three small vessels, he established himself on the shores of unfrequented Santa Rosa Sound. Here, in the maze of bayous, creeks, islands, swamps and hidden coves, with an abundance of fish and game, Rogers and his gang were safe from the long arm of the law and carried on a lucrative smuggling industry.

But, before very long, it occurred to the resourceful Billy Bowlegs that there would be a far greater profit in smuggling contraband into the States if the cost of purchasing the goods were eliminated; and as the only means of thus reducing overhead was to take possession of what he required without regard to the rightful owners' consent, he decided to combine piracy with smuggling. To Rogers and his shipmates all vessels were fair prey regardless of their nationality, although Spanish ships were his specialty, owing to the fact that they carried richer cargoes than those of France, Holland, England or the United States. Even at that late day vast quantities of bullion and gold and silver currency were being shipped from Mexico, Panama and elsewhere in Spanish America to Spain, and incredibly rich pickings were to be had for the taking. To be sure, the taking was not such a safe or easy matter. The plate ships were always convoyed by powerful heavily-armed frigates, and the ordinary type of pirates who infested the Gulf and the Caribbean gave these convoys a wide berth. But this did not mean that Billy Bowlegs had the field all to himself. On the contrary, he had a very serious competitor in the self-styled King of the Pirates, the famous Gasparilla, the ex-nobleman of Spain, José Gaspar, who had established his headquarters at Charlotte Harbor.

On more than one occasion the King of the Pirates and Billy Bowlegs very nearly came to grips; but as there was a certain amount of honor among these thieves of the sea, and an unwritten law that dog did not eat dog, as one might say, the two scourges of the Gulf managed to ply their trade without flying at each other's throats, and, eventually, they became quite fast friends as pirates go, for each recognized in the other the one quality both admired and respected—bravery. No one ever accused Gasparilla of being a coward, and whatever his short-comings may have been Billy Bowlegs did not know the meaning of the word fear. Also, both pirate chieftains were absolutely ruthless and cruel, and as utterly regardless of human life as ravening wolves. Both thoroughly believed in the axiom that dead men tell no tales, and while the Spaniard's Latin temperament and amorous and sentimental nature led him to spare female captives (whom he added to his harem) even though he murdered every man who did not join his forces, Billy Bowlegs spared none, and never permitted a man, woman or child who fell into his clutches to live to tell the tale.

For this reason no one can say with any degree of certainty how many ships or what cargoes were taken by this last of the Gulf pirates. But judging by the number of ships which vanished, and the fact that in a few short years he amassed an immense fortune, he must have been most successful in his nefarious career. But the heydey of piracy was nearing its end. Being no fool, Billy Bowlegs realized that the days of piracy were rapidly drawing to a close and that, with the United States Government bent on exterminating the pirates, and with British and American warships scouring the seas in search of the corsairs, it was about time he retired from business. In fact, he had held on long after his compeers had retired or had met with their just deserts. His erstwhile friend, Gasparilla, had ended his spectacular career by dramatically wrapping a piece of chain-cable about his body and leaping into the sea rather than be taken prisoner and hanged at the yard-arm of an American corvette that had him cornered. But Billy Bowlegs had no intention of committing suicide or being hanged. So, in 1838, the last of the Gulf pirates paid his men their promised shares, bade them farewell and God speed, and busied himself caching his blood-stained loot in secret hiding places. The bulk of his fortune he buried on the northern shore of a sandy island. Then, on the neighboring mainland, he cached his minted coins in two separate hoards. But as he did not wish to disturb these extemporized safe deposit vaults except in case of some unforeseen emergency, he retained a few hundred thousand dollars in specie aboard his ship, a trim and speedy little schooner ninety feet on the water line, twenty-two feet in beam, drawing six feet of water and armed with eighteen guns.

For a few years thereafter, Billy Bowlegs, resuming

the name of Rogers, led an honest enough life as far as any one knows. He made no more voyages to unnamed destinations, there were no lost ships whose disappearance could be charged to the account of the notorious Billy Bowlegs, and honest merchant skippers thanked God and the American navy for having driven the pirates from the waters of the Gulf of Mexico. But like so many others of his profession, Rogers could not resist the call of the sea. He pined for the excitement and din of battle and the thunder of guns. He lusted for blood and murder, mutilated fellow men and women, and regardless of the peril, or perhaps because of it, he decided to have one more fling at piracy. No one knows, no one but his crew ever knew, what took place on this last cruise or what ships he took and scuttled with all on board. But obviously he had lost none of his skill as a pirate, for in a few short weeks his ship's hold was laden to the hatches with sacks of hand-picked gold ore, chests of gold, and silver coins and bullion. He had not acquired his loot without a struggle. A number of his spars had been shot away, there were canvas-stopped holes in his schooner's hull, great jagged gaps showed in her bulwarks, her canvas was riddled and torn and she was leaking badly from round-shot wounds below her water line. But she was still afloat and seaworthy, and despite her crippled spars and patched rigging she could still show a clean pair of heels to any craft of her size in the Gulf of Mexico. Billy Bowlegs had satiated his desire for bloodshed and excitement and loot, and satisfied with the outcome of his last cruise, he headed for his lair on the western coast of Florida. But his luck, or the evil genius which had watched over him, had deserted him. A British sloop-of-war appeared upon the horizon, and knowing that a vessel in the condition of Rogers' had been in no honest venture, the British commander instantly gave chase.

It was no weather for a partially crippled ship to crowd on sail with safety; there was a gale of wind blowing; a heavy sea was running, and Billy Bowlegs realized that to attempt to outrun the warship under such conditions would be hopeless. But his intimate knowledge of the coast stood him in good stead. A few miles ahead he knew of a good harbor, a large bay protected by a bar which the warship could not cross, but with enough water to enable the light-draught schooner to enter.

Piling on every stitch of canvas which his spars could stand, the pirate drove off before the howling gale which was steadily increasing and piling up a tremendous sea which was breaking in a smother of foam upon the bar.

Although the schooner raced across, yet she struck bottom more than once as the breakers dropped her, and at each shock, rigging and top-hamper went by the board, while green seas washed her from bow to stern, carrying away deck-houses and fittings, and drowning several of the crew. But she still floated when at last she reached the calm surface of the lagoon inside the bar, and anchor was dropped beyond reach of the enemy's guns.

The British, however, were not to be cheated of their prey so easily, and, backing his yards, the corvette's commander lowered away boats filled with armed bluejackets and marines who pulled for the crippled schooner. Then, to prevent his vessel and her precious cargo from falling into the enemy's hands, Rogers hurriedly stripped her of what he could and scuttled her in four fathoms of water.

Tossing a few supplies into the long-boat, the pirates made for the shore and took to the woods.

With the schooner at the bottom of the bay, and her crew concealed in the jungle, the British gave up and sailed away. When at last they had vanished beyond the horizon, Billy and the twenty-seven survivors of his crew came from their hiding places, built shacks on the beach, and busied themselves salvaging what they could from their scuttled vessel. With neither divers nor equipment it was impossible to recover the treasure, even had there been time to do so. But friend Bowlegs had no idea of abandoning his sunken loot, even if he did possess a fortune in treasure already. His plan was to build a good camp, leave two of his trusted officers in charge, and make his way to Louisiana where he would sell his plantation, secure the necessary equipment, and returning to the cove with his family, he would make his home there until he had salvaged the cargo of his schooner.

It may seem strange that a man who had salted down more riches than he could ever need did not charge off the schooner and her cargo to profit and loss, and return to civilization for good and all. But Billy Bowlegs Rogers was not only an exceedingly avaricious scoundrel but miserly, and it was not in his nature to leave a million or more resting in shoal water without making an effort to get it.

In due course of time his plans were accomplished, and in a small sloop Rogers and his family set sail for the bay. But only four men were there to greet him. One was Pedro, the Spanish mate, another was Jim Kelly, the bo's'n, and the other two were Spanish seamen. Of the other twenty-one, some had been killed by hostile Indians, some had deserted and some had died of fever.

Thus short of men, all Bowlegs' efforts to recover his treasure proved fruitless, and when his wife died of fever he gave up, and moving to the other shore of the bay he built a log cabin and settled down. By 1865, Billy Bowlegs, still dwelling within sight of the spot where his schooner had gone down, was the sole survivor of the piratical crew. Pedro and the two other Spaniards had died years before, and Jim Kelly, who had married, raised a family and had become a respectable citizen, had also passed away. Rogers was by now an old man and his family had grown up. Over seventy and irascible, he flew into a fearful temper whenever his sons suggested making use of their father's hidden treasures and dwelling like civilized beings instead of remaining in the wilderness minus comforts and neighbors. To them such a life was intolerable, and they plotted to help themselves to what they needed. But by some means or another old Billy the pirate got wind of their plans, and cursing them with all the fervency and fluency of his piratical days, he drove his family away, swearing never to see or to speak to one of them as long as he lived—a vow which he kept to the day of his death. But his anathema did not include a favorite nephew. To him Rogers promised a large share of his treasure when he died, and to make certain that the youth would get it, the old man showed his nephew where he had concealed one of his hoards. Moreover, after Billy Bowlegs' death (in 1888 at the ripe old age of 95) the favored nephew secured the treasure and lived comfortably for the rest of his life on his pirate-uncle's legacy, which fact proves beyond question that Billy Bowlegs' treasures were no imaginary or fictional hoards.

Aside from his nephew, the old pirate chieftain had another and even more intimate friend, a man whom he had met while killing cattle in 1878 and who was his constant companion during the last twelve years of his life. Sullen, secretive, avoiding his fellow men, yet the hoary old scoundrel took this man into his confidence and to him related the story of his past and even discussed plans for salvaging the schooner and digging up his buried treasures. Death, however, put an abrupt end to Billy's schemes, and his friend, thinking the old man had been romancing or was a bit "off," and also being without funds or means to make an investigation or search, never attempted to recover any of the sunken or buried treasures. The man, however, is still living and so, also, is a grandson of Billy Bowlegs, and through them the story came to the ears of romantically-inclined treasure hunters who, a short time ago, set out on an expedition to locate and recover the old pirate's cachèd riches and to salvage the treasure-laden schooner.

Just why the old pirate never made any use of the fortune he had won by fire and sword and at cost of countless lives, is a puzzle. But he was a miserly rascal, acquisitiveness had become a mania with him, and, moreover, he had no use for wealth, being a rough old scoundrel content to live in semi-savage style in the jungle. At all events, he certainly never dug up the bulk of his treasure, although from time to time he would visit the spots where he had cached it, in order to satisfy himself that the hoards had not been molested and that the landmarks were still in evidence. Unquestionably, as the years passed and gales and storms altered the sandy shores where the old pirate had secreted his riches, the landmarks changed and such changes were duly noted by Billy who, familiar with the exact locations of his caches, was not misled by drifting sands, by growing brush or by vanishing trees. And as he had no intention of digging up the treasures himself he doubtless chuckled as he noticed how Nature was aiding him in protecting the gold-filled casks and chests from others' hands. No doubt, he thought, even his most intimate friend in whom he had confided could never locate the caches owing to the changes that had taken place. And in this surmise he was right, for when, a year or so ago, the white-bearded old fellow, who alone of all the world held the secret of Billy Bowlegs' treasure-trove, led an expedition to the spot he found himself totally at a loss to identify a single landmark old Rogers had described. Trees, markers—everything had vanished, and over the spot where, so he declared, the treasures must have been buried, many feet of sand had been piled and drifted by the winds of nearly a century.

Hand digging would be hopeless; but the treasure hunters had faith in the old man's tale. Billy Bowlegs' grandson bore him out, the old records substantiated the story, and convinced that the pirate's vast treasure lay under its covering of sand they prepared to return with a steam shovel.

Provided with the means of handling tons of sand, the treasure hunters proceeded to dig where the old comrade of the pirate and the latter's grandson declared the treasures had been buried. Hopes ran high as the great steel bucket bit into the sand, and lifting high dumped its load far to one side. Ton after ton was removed, and when, buried beneath the accumulated sand, the dead trunk of a peculiarly gnarled and twisted oak tree was disclosed,

(19)

every one felt that Billy Bowlegs' treasure was as good as found, for one of the markers mentioned particularly by the pirate was a gnarled and twisted oak tree, the only tree of its kind in the vicinity. Here was proof that they were at the right spot. At any instant the big shovel might reveal a chest of golden coins or a store of bullion. With a rattle and roar the great steel bucket dropped; like some ravenous beast it bit savagely into the sand, and snorting rose with its load. Wild with excitement the treasure hunters crowded about. Exposed by the last scoopful of sand removed, were the ends of old planks forming a rectangle, one of the old pirate's caches, exactly as he had described them to his friend. Seizing shovels the men hurled aside the mass of sand that filled the boarded space, certain that at last their efforts had been rewarded, that Billy Bowlegs' treasure was theirs. But an instant later their hopes were shattered. The cache was empty!

But only for a moment were they disheartened. Billy Bowlegs' nephew, they remembered, had secured some of his uncle's treasure. And no doubt this empty cache was one from which he had taken the contents years before.

So once again the steam shovel puffed and snorted and performed the work of fifty men, and as the sand was removed, another and another cache was uncovered. But, like the first, all had been rifled. At last the treasure seekers gave up in despair. They had found Billy Bowlegs' secret hiding place, but some one had been there before them. Whether they had had the ill luck to stumble on the hoards that the nephew had taken, or whether some one else had discovered the hidden treasures and had made away with them, no one could say. Still only one of the pirate's caches had been found and the old rascal had concealed his loot in three places. But the funds of the expedition were exhausted. They could not search farther, and their treasure hunt came to an end. But they have not abandoned all hope of recovering Billy Bowlegs' treasure. By means of delicate detectors they hope to locate the stores of hidden gold and silver, and are even now planning to return to the spots where the last of the Gulf pirates hid his blood-stained riches.

Neither has any one found the rotting timbers of Billy Bowlegs' sunken ship with her precious cargo, yet beyond a doubt it still rests among the weeds and water plants on the bottom of the bay where the pirates scuttled her so many years ago.

꙱꙱꙱

CHAPTER III

The Treasure-Trove of
Casco Bay

THE mere thought of buried treasures creates visions of tropic seas, palm-fringed keys and the Spanish Main, which is quite natural, for the Caribbean and the tropics were the haunts of the buccaneers and pirates, and piratically-inclined gentlemen and hidden hoards of precious metal and precious stones are ever associated in the public mind. Yet by no means all the sunken, hidden and buried treasures are confined to the favorite haunts of the freebooters and the seas whereon Spanish plate ships sailed and came to grief. And while the rock-ribbed coast of Maine would be about the last place where one might expect to find hidden treasures, yet, if we can believe history and tradition, many a cached hoard lies buried in Maine soil, and more than one Maine treasure-trove has been recovered. To be sure, most of the treasures found in Maine have been comparatively small, scarcely valuable enough to merit being called treasures; but at least one has been wrested from its hiding place which not only was a veritable treasure-trove, but in addition was surrounded with all the mystery, the romance, the tragedy and the secrecy which make tales of treasure and treasure hunting so fascinating.

For generations, from the days of the earliest settlers, there had been a tradition that a treasure was hidden somewhere on Jewell's Island in Casco Bay. The oldest inhabitant could not recall when the oldest inhabitant of his memory could remember who was the originator of the tale. Neither could any one recall when the first seekers for the hidden gold dug and delved for the reputed treasure. But for at least two hundred years people had searched for the treasure, without success. Who had buried the hoard, or what its origin, no one knew; but it was generally agreed that it was pirates' loot and, as in the minds of the islanders, one pirate was as good, or as bad, as another, it was always referred to as "Captain Kidd's Treasure" regardless of the fact that poor, timid, much-maligned Captain Kidd never went near the Maine coast nor possessed treasure to bury.

Being, like many fisherfolk and islanders, somewhat prone to superstition, the people embroidered their tales of the treasure by adding stories of ghostly guardians, spectral pirates and terrifying apparitions which watched over the hoard of gold and frightened away those who sought for it. And as a result, many a treasure seeker sought to checkmate the guardian spirits by employing occult or supernatural means of locating the legendary hoard.

Lambs were slaughtered and their fresh blood was scattered on the areas where it was planned to dig. Charms and talismans of various kinds were used as aids in locating and securing the treasure, and one man even brought a famed mesmerist and a girl subject to the island, his

(23)

idea being that when under a hypnotic spell the young woman could locate the gold. But neither charms, talismans, fresh lamb's blood, divining rods nor a mesmerized maiden resulted in finding a cent's worth of treasure on the island.

And then, one day, a stranger arrived. To be sure, strangers were not so unusual upon an island within sight of Portland as to cause any particular comment; but this particular visitor made no bones of announcing that he had come to Jewell's Island for the express purpose of recovering the traditional treasure and, so he declared, he possessed a chart which showed exactly where the treasure was buried. He had come, he said, from St. Johns, Newfoundland, where, according to his tale, he had obtained the precious document from an aged negro who had recently died. The deceased African, it seemed, had once been the devoted and faithful body-servant of a notorious pirate, who, upon his death bed, had given the chart showing the hiding place of his treasure to the negro. Unable to read or write, and, needless to say, without means, the black man had never attempted to secure the loot; but had safeguarded the chart until, when he in turn was passing away, he presented the map to the man who had befriended him and who had now arrived at the island.

One would have expected that a man having a chart which allegedly indicated precisely where the treasure was concealed, would have lost no time in getting to work to dig it up. But instead of hurrying to secure the treasure, the owner of the precious chart hung about, and volunteered the information that he was awaiting the arrival of Captain Jonathan Chase, the skipper of a

Jewell Island schooner, giving as his reason that Captain Chase was the only inhabitant of the island who possessed an accurate mariners' compass and who could "shoot the sun," both the instrument and the ability being essential to the finding of the treasure.

Naturally tongues began to wag. How did the man from St. Johns know of Captain Chase? Had they once been shipmates or old friends? And why, the people asked one another, hadn't the stranger provided himself with a compass and acquired a knowledge of taking an observation before he started on his treasure hunt?

But no one could find an answer to these logical questions, and no one ever knew whether or not the possessor of the chart had ever before met Captain Jonathan; although from the events which transpired it may be quite reasonably assumed that the two were not strangers.

Once an element of mystery had been injected into the matter, rumor and gossip added more. Captain Chase, it seemed, bore a far from savory reputation. In hushed tones it was noised about that he himself had once been a pirate. Every one knew that he made the greater part of his money by smuggling, and there were lurid tales of strange goings-on in the big rambling house where he dwelt. But as smuggling was not considered in the light of a crime by the islanders, and as the captain when at home led a law-abiding, moral life and regularly attended "meeting," and as he was a hearty, friendly sort, he was regarded in a most favorable light by his fellow islanders.

In due course of time Captain Chase's rakish little schooner came beating up Casco Bay and dropped anchor off the island. And scarcely had the skipper stepped 'ashore and, after the usual greetings, entered his home when the stranger from St. Johns knocked at the heavy oak door and was at once admitted.

What took place within the residence of Captain Jonathan, what was said, no one of course will ever know, although many an islander would have given his or her "eye teeth" as they would have expressed it, to have been able to overhear the conversation that took place between Captain Chase and his visitor from Newfoundland.

There was one thing certain, however: the Captain must have been convinced that the stranger possessed a valuable and trustworthy clue to the hiding place of the traditional treasure, for after a few hours the two men appeared, carrying a shovel and pick, the captain's compass and sextant, and without speaking to any one, they vanished in the woods. Of course no one followed them—the burly captain was not one to deal lightly with snoopers if caught, and the man from St. Johns was not the type to be trifled with either. Hence no one knew where they had gone or how long they were absent, for, oddly enough, no one on the island saw them return. Yet, a few days later, Captain Chase was pottering about his garden as usual and when, in quite a casual manner, neighbors mentioned the stranger from St. Johns, the captain either ignored the matter altogether or made non-committal replies and opined that the fellow's chart wasn't worth a tinker's darn and that, finding he was on a wild goose chase, he'd probably cleared out. But on a small spot such as Jewell's Island a man's movements are pretty well known, especially if he is a stranger, and as nothing had been seen of the Newfoundlander since he had set out with Captain Jonathan, and as he could not have left the island without taking a boat—which he assuredly had not—another mystery was scented by the islanders. And when, shortly after his reappearance, Captain Chase sailed away on another trading voyage, and the man with the chart had not shown up, tongues began to wag with a vengeance. He had not been seen about the island or the village, he had certainly not been aboard the captain's schooner when she had sailed, no small boat was missing, and no one had rowed or sailed him ashore. Every one was soon asking every one else: "What became of the man with the pirate's chart?"

It was a delectable mystery, but mystery soon changed to suspicion, and, the captain being out of the way, the people decided it was high time to do a little investigating on their own account. But even if they found no traces of the missing man they *did* find something else.

On the Southeastern shore of the island was a deep, freshly-dug hole, and in the soft earth and sand at the bottom of the cavity was the rectangular impression left by a chest or box! It was quite obvious to all that some one had dug the hole and had removed a chest from its hiding place, and no one doubted that the chest had contained treasure and that Captain Chase and the man from Newfoundland had been the lucky ones to lift "Captain Kidd's Treasure" from the spot where it had rested so many years. That, in the minds of the islanders, explained everything. It was quite natural, they reasoned, that the stranger should have departed secretly carrying his share of the loot, and unquestionably, they decided, he had left in one of Captain Jonathan's dories, the captain owning a number. And no doubt, they thought, Captain Chase had quietly placed his portion of the treasure aboard his schooner and had sailed away to deposit it in some large town on the mainland.

So, satisfied that they had solved the mystery, and that the long-sought treasure had been found at last, the islanders again resumed their placid lives and forgot all about the man with the pirate's chart. And when, in due course of time, Captain Chase returned, and abandoning the sea, settled down and lived in ease and comfort in his big house, the people accepted his change of life as a further proof that he had found the treasure, and forbore questioning him as to the source of his sudden affluence.

Years went by. Captain Chase passed away, respected as a well-to-do, substantial citizen and the island's wealthiest inhabitant should be. But he had left no will as far as known, he had neither kith nor kin, and when, after due formalities, the properly constituted officials took possession of the deceased captain's home they discovered a number of strange things. Everywhere within the place were secret compartments, sliding panels, underground passages and similar devices such as no honest man would need. But there was nothing of an incriminating nature—other than a goodly store of casks and bottles of liquor, cigars and other goods which had paid no customs duties; and the inconsiderable amount of money that had been left by the dead captain was in ordinary currency.

Captain Chase had been dead and buried for several years, his house and contents had been disposed of at public auction, and the islanders had lost all interest in the tale of the famous treasure and its lucky finders when a hunter made a most exciting and gruesome discovery. In a dense patch of woods not far from the "treasure pit," he came upon a human skeleton lying in a deep and narrow crevice between two ledges of rock.

Years of sun and rain, of snow and ice had left no traces of perishable garments other than a few bits of cracked, rotten leather that had once been boots, and a few fragments of a so'wester. But among the bleached bones were buttons and a silver finger ring that identified the remains beyond all question. The skeleton was all that remained of the man from St. Johns!

That he had met death by violence was obvious, for in the back of the skull, near the nape of the neck, and evidently inflicted as the man had been bending over, was a clean square hole such as would have been made by a blow of a pick. Of course, in the light of this discovery, no one doubted that Captain Jonathan had murdered the stranger when, by the aid of his chart, they had secured the treasure chest. All the known circumstances, as recalled by those who were living at the time, pointed to the crime having been committed. But there was nothing to be done about it. Captain Chase was as dead as the skeleton of the unfortunate man from Newfoundland, and no one knew if the murdered man had relatives, or if so, where they could be located in order to notify them of the discovery of his mortal remains. So the bones were duly interred in the graveyard, not far from all that was earthly of Captain Jonathan, and there the matter ended as far as the islanders were concerned. But for many years—in fact up to the present time—there are hair-

(29)

raising tales of strange noises and mysterious lights seen and heard about the Chase house at dead of night, and all the treasures of all the pirates would not induce any islander to visit the vicinity of the "treasure pit" or the spot where the skeleton was found, after nightfall.

‗‗

The Golden Books of the Mayas

IT was a fascinating story that the little aviator told, a story that sounded more like the pages of a fiction magazine than fact, yet told in such a convincing and simple manner that it had the ring of truth.

It began with the ill-starred Escobar revolution in northern Mexico when the rebels ordered six aeroplanes from a firm in the States. Under the contract, the planes were to be flown across the border by American pilots and delivered to the Escobar forces, and the little aviator who was narrating his amazing adventures had undertaken to deliver one of the planes. But when the miniature flying squadron had landed safely within the rebel lines it was discovered that the Mexicans were two pilots short, and when General Escobar offered seventy-five dollars in gold a day for the services of American pilots, our aviator friend and his buddy jumped at the chance.

For a time all went well; the planes were employed solely in scouting and observing, and the promised salaries were paid promptly. But gradually payments fell off, and when several weeks had passed with no money forthcoming, and with all demands met by profuse apologies and excuses, the two Americans decided it was time to quit. That, however, was easier said than done. Being unfamiliar with the Spanish language they had unwittingly signed papers binding themselves to serve the rebel forces for the duration of the revolution, and to attempt to desert and fly across the border was hopeless, for never were they permitted to take off unless accompanied by a Mexican officer. But at length the two men devised a scheme which they felt might work. The next morning when they were ordered to make a flight the motors missed and sputtered and after tinkering with them for some time without improving matters, the two men informed the commandant that the machines required a complete overhauling. And when this wholly unnecessary work had been ostensibly completed, they declared that a "tuning-up flight" was essential and that to test out the planes with an extra man aboard would be dangerous. Shrugging his shoulders at the seemingly inevitable, the officer gave his consent, and elated at the success of their ruse and thoughts of soon seeing the last of Mexico, the two men took off with fuel and oil tanks filled to their capacity.

Once in the air they separated. Where his friend went or what became of him, our aviator could not say; but as he himself had heard that there was need of an American pilot in El Salvador, he headed southward.

Thousands of feet beneath him the terrain of Mexico was spread like a vast map. Deserts and plains, jungles and haciendas, ranches and cities, mountains and valleys, unrolled like a gigantic panorama, until to the east the coastline and the sea appeared.

Unfamiliar with the country, and fearful of being compelled to make a landing and being instantly seized as a rebel, the fugitive followed the shore, hoping to reach the borders of Guatemala or British Honduras before his fuel was exhausted.

All went well until he had passed Carmen Island off the coast of Campeche, and swinging westward high above the lagoon, he set a course for the boundary.

And then, when safety seemed certain, when the worst of his long flight was over, his engine began to miss.

It was no temporary or minor trouble, but a broken oil line, and he realized that a landing was inevitable. Below him stretched the primeval jungle. To crash among the giant vine-entangled trees meant certain death or worse. Far off on either side he could see the silvery gleam of rivers, but already he had lost much of his altitude, and was too low to glide to either stream.

With tensed nerves and set face he stared at the endless sea of green forest, searching for some spot where there would be one chance in ten thousand of coming down without being killed or crippled. Each second that he dropped his peril increased; the engine was coughing and spitting, and at any instant it might "go dead." Then, when, as he expressed it, he had "kissed the world good-by," he saw a clearing in the heart of the jungle. It was not an open field by any means, but a large rectangular area where there were no big trees, a space that might have been an old clearing grown up to low brush and rank weeds. There was no time to consider the chances; all he could do was to "pancake" the plane and hope for the best. But luck was with him; the plane tore through

(33)

the brush for a few yards, swung sharply to one side, ripped off a wing, and then slowly turned turtle.

Shaken but uninjured, the aviator crawled from under the wrecked plane. But as he glanced about he realized that he might almost as well have crashed in the jungle and finished everything. He was miles—he had no idea how many miles—from the nearest settlements, he had no food other than his emergency rations which would serve for a day; he had no weapons, not even an axe or a machete, and on every side stretched unbroken, uninhabited forest. But standing beside the wreck of his plane was merely wasting time, and securing his electric torch, his emergency ration and the compass, he examined his surroundings, seeking the most open spot at which to enter the jungle. A few yards from where he stood was a low hillock or mound, and thinking the slight elevation might provide a better survey, he pushed through the brush towards it. It was covered with a tangle of weeds and vines, and he shuddered involuntarily as he thought what an ideal spot it afforded for snakes. But in the face of his greater and more concrete peril his inordinate dread of reptiles did not prevent him from forcing his way recklessly up the slope.

Suddenly the ground seemed to open beneath his feet. He shot downward and, amid a shower of earth, stones and leaves, came to an abrupt and jarring stop. Dazed and shaken, he gazed about. He was in an underground chamber or vault, and behind him a flight of stone steps led up to the aperture through which he had fallen. Above his head arched a stone roof, and on the farther side of the room, dimly outlined in the semi-darkness, he could see an immense sculptured idol and a square stone table.

A. MAYA TEMPLE IN YUCATAN

Rising, he stepped toward the great stone god, and as he passed close to the table-like affair of stone he noticed that it was hollowed into a deep trough from which hung curious-looking objects resembling gigantic fish-hooks with discs in place of eyes.

Wondering what they were, he examined them closely, and discovered that, threaded on to the ends resting in the trough, were numbers of square leaves or plates of metal. Scraping away the bat guano that covered them, he was amazed to find the plates covered with incised glyphs and figures. And as he raised the uppermost and exposed the surface of the plate below, he could scarcely believe his eyes. The surface gleamed dull yellow—it was solid gold!

Still unable to credit the evidence of his eyes, he attempted to lift one of the affairs from the trough. But he could barely move it, for the hook-like rod with its attached plates weighed over two hundred pounds! And there were fourteen of the things—fourteen immense hooks, each bearing eleven sheets of beaten, engraved gold!

Abruptly he burst into peals of wild laughter. He was standing beside a fortune, half a million dollars' worth of gold at least, yet of as little value to him as the great stone idol in the shadows. At that moment he gladly would have traded all that precious metal for a square meal, or a gun. Cursing his luck, he dropped the metal back into the trough, and climbing the stairs he plunged into the forest.

Realizing that if he went north he must eventually reach a stream which would lead him to the coast, he headed in that direction. But could he survive long enough to make the nearest river? Torn by thorns, beset by swarms of the terrible *rodederos* or biting gnats of Yucatan, he tramped doggedly on. Without a machete to hew a pathway, he was compelled to make long detours around dense tangles and swampy spots. Conserving his meager rations until he was faint with hunger, and never stopping to rest, he stumbled forward.

For seventeen hours—all through the night—he pushed onward, keeping as nearly as possible to a compass-course, until, almost at the end of his strength, he burst from the forest into a small clearing surrounding a *chicle* camp. The rest was easy. Well fed and rested, and accompanied by a guide, he mounted a mule and rode to the nearest village, whence by packet-boat and steamship, he returned to the States.

Such was the story the little aviator told, strange, fantastic, to be sure, but, paradoxically, reasonable by its very incredibility. Naturally he had tried to interest some one to finance an expedition to return with him to the scene of his discovery and secure the treasure. Among others he approached a fellow aviator—a wealthy young man whom he had met at an aviation school, and who was willing to finance an expedition. But neither he nor his friends knew anything about the tropics or the jungles, none of them spoke Spanish, and none of them possessed any archæological knowledge. For this reason they got in touch with me and asked if I would take charge of the party in return for a share in whatever they found.

Although, when I first heard the aviator's story, I was skeptical, yet as I weighed and measured his statements my doubts began to dissolve. The fellow was absolutely ignorant of archæology or the ancient Mayan civilization, yet he had correctly described the appearance of the almost legendary Maya "books." And he could not have imagined anything of the sort nor could he have read of them, for no book, pamphlet or magazine article describing similar objects had ever been published as far as I could ascertain. Only in rare, almost unknown writings of the old Spanish priests and conquerors was there any reference to the traditional, or supposedly fabulous, golden books containing the secret history of the Maya race and civilization. Nevertheless, it seemed far too remarkable a coincidence that an aviator, crashing haphazard in the Yucatan jungles, should have happened to fall in the exact spot where the most valuable of Mayan treasures had been concealed. Still, truth at times is far stranger than fiction. I knew by experience that amazing coincidences *do* occur far more often than is generally believed, and I decided to secure the opinion of a friend, who is perhaps the best known authority on Mayan objects, before coming to a final decision.

His reply astonished me, for I had rather expected a practical hardheaded scientist would scoff at the whole story. Instead, he wrote to me as follows: "I am convinced of the sincerity of the aviator, and I believe that he has found something there, probably of great interest. ... Of course, we could not take part in the expedition officially, as it would spoil our cordial relations with the Mexican Government. As far as the objects described are concerned they are unique. ... Whether gold or not, they would be of extraordinary archæological value, and I am extremely interested in the proposition. I hope you will be able to help unravel this intriguing problem."

That decided me; I agreed to accompany the treasure

hunters and take charge of the expedition. But there were many difficulties to be overcome and many details to be attended to before we could start. First of all we had to secure a proper boat for the trip. This had to be large enough to accommodate our party and our outfit, staunch enough to weather the gales and heavy seas of the Gulf of Mexico, yet it must be of shallow draught to navigate the lagoons and rivers, and equipped with both sails and motor. Most important of all, we needed a captain and crew whom we could trust and who were of the adventurous type.

At last we found a vessel that seemed to possess all the essential requirements. She was sloop-rigged, forty feet in length, drew four feet of water, had a beam of thirteen feet and was equipped with a fifty horse-power gasoline motor. She had had a varied career;—sponger, rum-runner, fisherman and smuggler in turn; and her grizzled, leather-faced Norwegian owner, who also acted as captain, asked no inconvenient questions.

Then came the matter of outfit—supplies, medical stores, camping outfits, arms and ammunition. But at last all was ready and our search for the Maya treasure began.

We were rather crowded, for eight of us went aboard at Havana, while the aviator, who had gone ahead by steamer, for he was a poor sailor, was to be picked up at Progreso. Our party consisted of the captain, the mate who also acted as engineer, the cook who was likewise the radio operator; Dick, Pete, George, Bob and myself; about as varied an assortment as could have been found. The skipper, a hawk-nosed old fellow who would have made an ideal pirate, but in whose veins the Viking blood

(38)

had turned to water—and very thin water as we later discovered. The engineer-mate, an ex-naval man. Sparks, the ne'er-do-well scion of a wealthy family of note. Dick, young, exuberant, enthusiastic and an amateur yachtsman. Pete, who thought himself a mighty hunter and a dead shot, who constantly read wild west thrillers and was provided with a veritable arsenal of rifles, shot guns and revolvers. Bob, big, blonde and British, a husky young giant who had gone through the World War. George, a well-known author and novelist, a treasure-trove fan, and possessing a tendency towards communism and a dry humor, and finally, myself. With everything in readiness, tanks filled with water, refrigerator packed with ice, extra drums of gasolene on deck, we moved bag and baggage aboard and waited impatiently for the weather to permit us to start, for the Gulf of Mexico in winter is a treacherous sea and on the morning we had planned to leave a howling "norther" was thundering across the Gulf. Mountainous seas came rolling in to burst in up-flung foam and spray above the Malecon, and no ships other than the ocean liners dared venture forth. But the next day dawned clear and sunny, and although the seas were still running mountain-high beyond the Morro we cast off moorings and headed for the harbor mouth. For a few moments, as we reached the open sea, I thought certain that our expedition would end then and there, for it seemed impossible that the *Vigilance* could live through such a sea. Between the waves even the highest buildings of Havana were invisible, and friends ashore told us later that each time we vanished in the trough of the seas they never expected to see us rise

(39)

again. But the little craft managed to survive and even made good time.

By mid-afternoon there was only a moderate sea running, and as we were all dog-tired and it would have been dangerous to attempt navigating the channels of the barrier-reef, we put into Bahia Honda for the night.

A mile or so from the entrance of the great landlocked harbor, a boat came pulling alongside, its occupants two Cubans, one in khaki shirt and trousers, barefooted and bare-legged; the other clad in dirty white, and both wearing heavy revolvers and cartridge belts. He of the khaki introduced himself as a sergeant in the Cuban Army and his comrade as a *soldado,* and explained that they had been fishing, and offered to pilot us to the port in return for their passage. At the port, which consisted of a weather-beaten, ramshackle building that served for a barracks, an even more tumble-down shed that did duty as a warehouse, and a rickety wharf, a group of Negroes and a few slouching soldiers had gathered on the dock. But there was no official to receive us, and we were informed that in order to comply with the law we must go to the "City" ten miles inland, the port being only a landing place. And, looking as if he had been waiting for us ever since we had left Havana, a grinning colored fiend sat in the remains of what once had been a Ford car.

"Good Lord!" I ejaculated when I saw the ancient conveyance. "That's nothing but a wreck."

The chauffeur grinned the wider. "Si, señor," he agreed. "But it's the best wreck in Bahia Honda!"

There was no alternative, so the six of us crowded into the battered tin Lizzie, a ragamuffin cranked the motor, and with a rattle and bang it woke into life. Off we went—

and never have I had such a wild ride! As if ruts, stones, holes, fallen branches and other natural objects were not enough, our maniac driver seemed to take supreme delight in seeing how close he could come to running down stray cattle, by how narrow a margin he could miss barbed wire fences and trees and how fast he could take a corner on two wheels. But eventually, by nothing less than a miracle, we reached the town. It was a miserable apology of a place with horrible streets filled with mud-puddles, with a bare dusty plaza, a church that stood drunkenly awry, sundry unpainted shacks and hovels and with mangy, starving curs, naked black and brown children and repulsive black vultures everywhere. In response to our knocks at his door, the Captain of the Port appeared clad in filthy pajamas. He was a surly looking rascal, black-browed and muddy-skinned, and calmly informed us that if we wished to make entry we must return to the port and there await his pleasure to receive us.

We had thought the up trip a nightmare, but it was nothing compared with the return journey, for another "wreck" having materialized from nowhere, our driver decided to make it a race, and how we escaped death still remains a mystery to us all. Like madmen the two black fiends drove their protesting, rattling, tortured cars; leaping the bowlders and the obstructions, plunging through swamp-holes, crashing through brush, skidding around corners, and yelling like wild Indians. But by the grace of God we reached the port in safety. Eventually, also, the Captain of the Port put in his appearance, quite gorgeously arrayed in spotless white uniform, gold lace and brass buttons, and a peaked blue cap, and accompanied by a bodyguard of half a dozen soldiers in full service equipment including rifles and bayonets. Having glanced over our papers he proceeded to "hold us up" by declaring we had violated several of the Cuban maritime laws, that we were liable to a heavy fine for not having taken on a qualified pilot, etc. In vain I argued that as there was no pilot available we could not have taken him aboard, and that our authority from Havana permitted us to enter and leave any Cuban port without paying dues. Very arrogantly the rascal informed us that the absence of a pilot had no bearing on the case. The law decreed that pilotage was compulsory, but it made no provision for having a pilot. It reminded me of the story of the collegiates who, when driving a car without a windshield, were held up by a traffic policeman, and when they protested that the law did not compel a windshield on a car the cop agreed that might be the case, but reminded them that the law made it compulsory for a car to be provided with a windshield-cleaner, and thereupon handed them a ticket. There was no use trying to convince the Cuban official, but he did admit that as we were strangers and Gringos, and hence ignorant of the law, we probably had not violated them deliberately, and hence he would overlook the fine if we paid him fifteen dollars which was the pilotage fee. Then, as an afterthought, he added that there would be a further charge of five dollars to pay for his services for coming aboard. It was out-and-out robbery we knew, but he had the local section of the Cuban Army to support him so there was nothing to be done but to submit.

At dawn we bade Bahia Honda farewell and heading westward found smooth water inside the reefs, and late in the afternoon dropped anchor in the lee of Jutia Cay. A short distance from us was a dingy, patched Cuban fishing smack, and hardly were our sails furled when a boat put off from her and came alongside. Its occupants were the two blackest, raggedest, dirtiest Cubans I have ever seen,—but they grinned amiably, announced themselves the captain and mate of the *Angel Blanca* (White Angel). Ye gods! was ever a vessel more inappropriately named! And presented us with half a dozen fine lobsters. Naturally this called for a return, and with our visitors puffing American cigarettes, and with friendly relations thus established, the schooner's skipper informed us that the neighboring bay was fairly swarming with the jutias. "Ah, señor, you have but to load and fire—Bam! Bam! Bam!" he cried, gesturing vividly. For the benefit of those who do not know, let me explain that the jutia is a large rodent, weighing twelve to twenty-five pounds, resembling a giant guinea pig in appearance, with the fur of a raccoon and the tail of a rat, and more or less arboreal in habits. As its flesh is most delectable, the dusky skipper's information resulted in immediate preparations for a jutia hunt.

Landing upon the cay in company with the two Cubans who had volunteered to act as guides—and to carry back the bag of jutias—we found ourselves faced by an impenetrable barrier of dense thorny brush and vines. But our guide assured us that farther on there was an opening where we might penetrate to the interior where the gaunt limbs and trunks of dead trees marked the alleged haunt of the creatures we sought. The "opening" proved merely a slightly less impenetrable wall of jungle. But we managed to get through—or rather Bob and I did, for the

(43)

others gave up after the first few yards—and with clothes torn and legs scratched and bleeding we emerged from the entanglement into more open country where a jungle of small trees bordered a dark, dismal swamp filled with dead trees and with swarms of hungry mosquitoes. Slapping at the vicious insects, splashing through black mud, dodging thorn trees, we pressed on; but with no sign of the jutias that were supposed to infest the place. And then, suddenly, an enormous jutia dashed from a thicket ahead. I threw up my gun to shoot, but before I could press the trigger the Cuban near me uttered a yell like a Comanche, and waving his machete rushed after the beast directly in my line of fire. The next instant both man and beast vanished in the brush, whence, presently, the Cuban returned ruefully picking thorns from his bare feet and cursing volubly. And that was the only jutia we saw. Tired and disgusted we tramped back to the boat and vowed never again to believe anything a Cuban told us.

Before sunrise we were again on our way. The day passed uneventfully and just as the sun sank below the western horizon we passed Cape San Antonio light and headed across the channel for distant Yucatan.

A strip of dazzling snow white beach above a sea of liquid beryl, and beyond the beach a wall of malachite-green verdure and waving palms—such was our first vision of Yucatan as we dropped anchor off Holbox Cay (pronounced All bosh). Had it not been for the boats moored close inshore, and the throng of people gathered upon the beach, the island might have been uninhabited, for there was no sign of village or house. Directly the keel of our dinghy touched bottom, a dozen men rushed knee-deep into the water and literally lifted our boat high and dry onto the sand. Then, laughing and chattering, the people crowded about us, as curious as though we had been beings from Mars. And no wonder, for never before had Gringos visited the cay and never before had any of the inhabitants seen an outboard motor. In fact we were the first strangers of any kind who had visited Holbox in more than twenty years!

All were Mayas or partly Maya, spotlessly clean and neat, the men wearing drill trousers, the typical Yucatan shirt—much ruffled and tucked and worn outside the trousers—and high-crowned palm leaf sombreros; the women in the low-cut ruffled and richly embroidered Mayan dresses.

Greetings and introductions over, and with the Alcalde of Holbox leading the way, the procession escorting us marched along a straight sandy path between walls of jungle and nodding palms. Two hundred yards inland and suddenly, unexpectedly, we were in the "town." Perhaps it should not be called that; rather it might be deemed a mere village, for its total population would not number three hundred. But as it is the only settlement on the island, as it is the metropolis and the port as well as the capital, with its essential officials, why not dignify it by referring to it in the fond terms applied by its delightful citizens?

Though its streets were merely thoroughfares of sand, all were named, and although the buildings were all of thatch, all were numbered, all were spotless, and many were painted. There was a tiny plaza, and, quite true to form, on one side was the *alcaldia* and the church. Although the church was a tiny affair, and while neither

(45)

priest nor cleric dwells at Holbox, yet loving care was lavished upon it, and very impressive was the deep reverence the people showed for it. And even if the *alcaldia* was of thatch, yet it was the largest of the buildings and served not only as the seat of government, but also as a schoolhouse and a ballroom as occasion demanded. But there were two things that I missed. I saw no jail, no calaboose, and I saw no one who appeared to be a policeman. In answer to my queries I was told, quite as a matter of course, that neither policemen nor a jail were required. Neither did Holbox possess a lawyer, a doctor, a judge nor even an undertaker.

"Do the people never die—are they never ill?" I asked the roly-poly, brown-faced *alcalde*. For a brief instant he removed the long, crooked cigar from his mouth in order to reply.

"It is a most healthy place—my island," he informed me. "Perhaps it is that we of Holbox eat so much of the fish, *quien sabe?*" he shrugged his shoulders. "And never have we required a *medico*. And only the very young and the very old die, señor."

I glanced about, children barely able to toddle, kiddies of both sexes and all ages, were everywhere in evidence, and in the blazing sunlight, spreading copra to dry, were two men whose snow-white hair and beards spoke most eloquently of age.

"And what, Señor Alcalde, do you consider very young and very old?" I asked him.

He grinned. "Until they can creep about and after they can no longer creep," he replied. Then, indicating one of the ancients busy with the copra, "There, señor, is my great-grandfather. He is one hundred and two, yet he

(46)

still carries his load of wood as well as any one. And there with him is Pablo Gonzales whose ninety-eighth birthday was but last week, and who celebrated by taking to himself a new wife. Ah, a lovely bride, señor; *muy guapa,* and *only* ninety-six!"

Perhaps the most outstanding feature of Holbox and its people is cleanliness, and this is the more astonishing as the inhabitants are engaged in one of the dirtiest of trades, for the sole industry of the people is shark-fishing! I doubt if any other community of equal size anywhere is supported entirely by sharks; but sharks not only provide a livelihood for the three hundred odd inhabitants of Holbox, but enable them to live very well indeed.

To be sure, nobody is rich, but neither is anybody poor. All are independent, all are content and there are no social distinctions, no jealousy. One might think that shark-fishing would be a hazardous occupation; but I was assured by the *alcalde* and others that never in the history of Holbox had a man been killed or badly injured by a shark. "Not that the sharks are not dangerous," the *alcalde* explained, "but because we of Holbox are most careful."

Of course our visit called for a fiesta which lasted until dawn when, accompanied by practically all the inhabitants, we wended our way to the beach, bade farewell to our charming, happy hosts, and boarding the *Vigilance,* set sail for Progreso where we arrived late that night. Next morning we prepared to receive the port officials, but hour after hour passed with no sign of anybody bothering about us. But at last a boat arrived and its two swarthy occupants informed us that we were to go alongside the dock to be received. As we hove up anchor and prepared to get under way I picked up a line with the idea of throwing it to the fellows and giving them a tow.

"No! no, señor!" they cried in unison. "We cannot touch a rope until you have been passed by the *sanidad* (doctor). If we did we would be arrested, fined and cast into prison."

A moment later as I was hauling in the trolling-line, one of the fellows called to me, a broad grin on his face: "The law says nothing about a fishing-line, señor." So, at the end of our trolling-line the boat was towed to shore, thus complying with the letter, if not with the spirit, of the regulations.

We soon discovered that the boatmen were not the only experts at circumventing the maritime laws of Mexico. As we neared the dock a man waved his arms wildly, yelling for us to keep off. Here was a pretty how-do-you-do! One moment we were told to come to the dock; the next we were told not to. But the seeming impasse was solved by one of the assembled officials shouting to us to come alongside a tug moored to the dock. Mexican rules may prohibit a vessel touching the dock until passed by the health-officer and Customs, but they say nothing about mooring to another ship lying at a dock!

We had planned to stop at Progreso only long enough to secure fresh water and provisions and to pick up our aviator, but Fate decreed otherwise, for a norther sweeping down across the treacherous Gulf lashed the harbor into a maelstrom and held us prisoners ashore for three days while the port remained closed to all shipping. Time, however, did not hang heavily on our hands, for there was Merida only a few miles inland, with the amazing ruins of Chichen Itza and other ancient Maya cities and temples within easy reach.

When at last the norther had blown itself out we once more resumed our journey toward the site of the aviator's strange discovery. Stopping in at Campeche we were received as hospitably and effusively as at Progreso and we were asked by the postmaster if we would carry two bags of mail to Puerto Aguada. Anxious to accommodate him, but fearing that it might result in some entanglement in the intricacies of Mexican red tape, I explained that we had cleared for Carmen and that as Aguada was not a port of entry, we could not legally put in there. But he assured me that it was quite all right. "You will be carrying the national mails, señor," he said. "*Si*, I will provide you with an official flag. And you need not land. If you but blow the whistle a boat will come to you from the shore and receive the *correo*."

So, temporarily, we became a mail packet, and by so doing raised as much of a commotion in Mexican officialdom as though we had smuggled a cargo of munitions of war into Aguada.

Leaving Campeche and headed for the Laguna de Terminos we felt that we were "getting warm" as they say in "hunt the thimble," for up one of the rivers that empty into the big shoal lagoon was the wrecked plane and the golden books of the Mayas. But scarcely had we entered the lagoon, having duly delivered the mail to the boat at Aguada, when Fate began to interfere with our plans. Though we were directly in the channel—as plotted on the charts—we went hard and fast aground on a mud flat. Pushing, poling and kedging proving fruitless, so we gave up and settled ourselves to await the rising tide, meanwhile sending Dick and Bob in the small boat to Aguada to secure a pilot. With the Maya *practico* aboard we had no further trouble, until we approached the fringe of mangroves with the mouth of the Candelaria River marked by a primitive lighthouse on a flooded point of land. But here our local pilot came to grief. Like all the rivers of the district the visible mouth of the Candelaria is barely one hundred feet wide and barred by sand banks and oyster reefs between which, somewhere, was a reputed channel. But to find the channel was like hunting for the proverbial needle in a haystack and only after going aground a dozen times did we succeed in entering the river's mouth and drew up to a flimsy bamboo wharf near the lighthouse where a couple of thatched huts were perched on posts above the mud and water among the mangroves. Upon the landing stage two men awaited us, one gray-haired and gray-bearded, clad in heavy woolen mackinaw and canvas trousers; the other, almost as venerable, dressed in a patchwork of odds and ends. That any human beings could exist in such a spot seemed incredible. There was no dry land, no fresh water, no firewood—nothing but stinking mud, sprawling mangroves, hordes of pelicans, ibis and herons, and oysters, growing by millions on the mangrove roots and bed of the stream. But he of the mackinaw, who declared himself to be eighty-four, informed us that he had lived in this spot for sixty years and never had been ill for a single day. By this time our skipper had acquired the pilot habit and as our *practico* from Aguada admitted total ignorance of the river channels, we hired the ancient with the mackinaw, who claimed to be familiar with every bend, shoal, current and twist of the stream. The fact that he was the tender of the lighthouse and that he would be deserting his post did not trouble him in the least. "The light, señor," he informed me, "has been here but thirty years. Before then, for God knows how many years, there was no light. Yet all that time boats came and went. Por Dios, señor, can it not then be spared for a few days? And—," he added as a final argument, "few boats come this way, and those that do know the channel without the light and, of a truth, much of the time I bother not to light it anyway."

Our aviator treasure-finder had assured us that the Candelaria was the stream he had noted just before he had crashed and that he could easily identify the proper place to search because of a conspicuous sharp "S" bend of the stream due south of the spot where he had crashed. But as we chugged up the great river between interminable mangroves and impenetrable jungles, we were unwittingly traveling not nearer but farther from the treasure that we sought. And very soon it became obvious to all that we were on the wrong river.

The aviator insisted that he had not sighted a house, village or even a clearing other than the deserted spot where he had come to earth. Yet along the Candelaria there were clearings galore, houses and settlements, and even two good-sized villages! However, having come thus far, we decided to keep on. Possibly, we thought, the aviator had been farther inland than he had believed, and that the upper reaches of the river might be uninhabited. Anyway, we'd have a look, do a bit of exploring and satisfy ourselves one way or the other before deciding on our next move. But when we were a few miles above the largest settlement—which most appropriately bore the name of Suspiro or "The Last Gasp," our pilot informed us that we could go no farther in the *Vigilance*. Just ahead were rapids—a whole series, hundreds of them. So, running in under the banks, we moored our little ship to a tree, and lowering our dinghy with its outboard motor, I prepared to discover for myself what lay beyond. George, it appeared, had a mortal terror of snakes and firmly believed the Yucatan jungle fairly swarmed with venomous serpents. Pete, too, held back, for he shared George's fear of deadly reptiles.

And as the aviator had already decided that for some inexplicable reason he had made a mistake, and hence took no further interest in the river, only Dick, Bob and myself embarked in the small boat and headed upstream.

The first rapid didn't amount to much, and with little trouble our motor forced the boat through the swift broken water. But the second rapid was an entirely different proposition. Foaming and roaring, the stream came plunging over the rocks with terrific force. But I had had years of experience with tropical rapids, and selecting a chute-like stretch of black water, I shouted to Dick to give the motor full speed and head for it. With a rush we were at it. For a moment the boat hesitated; then slowly, inch by inch, it moved up the liquid slope and emerged in the smooth water beyond. At the third rapid, however, we very nearly came to grief. Despite the full power of the motor, the boat remained stationary in the terrific grip of the current, and even when Bob and I pulled with all our strength at the oars, we could make no headway. Realizing that the struggle was hopeless, I yelled to Dick to slow the motor down and permit the boat to drop back. But I had forgotten to warn him that the eddies and whirlpools below the rapids were more dangerous than the falls themselves. Instead of letting the dinghy drift with the current, until well clear of all danger, Dick opened the throttle and swung the boat about. Instantly we were in the grip of the whirlpool. The dinghy careened perilously, water poured over the gunwale, and she spun like a top. For a moment I thought nothing could save us; but fortunately Dick heard my frenzied: "Stop her!" in time.

He shut off the motor and the boat righted and swung with the current.

But it was a mighty close shave!

Next morning, completely beaten by the series of rapids, and thoroughly convinced that we were on the wrong river, we returned downstream and again moored to the lightkeeper's wharf. After discussing every possible angle of the situation, and cross-questioning the aviator and consulting maps and charts of the district—none of which were anywhere near correct—we decided that our only course was to try the next river. So with our venerable mackinaw-clad pilot at the helm we left the Candelaria and headed across the lagoon for the Chumpum River. But before we sighted the mouth of that stream, another norther came howling down, whipping the shoal water into ugly seas. To be caught in the height of the storm on a lee shore without harbor or shelter would have meant certain disaster, and our only hope was to head across the bay and anchor in the lee of Carmen island. It was lucky for us that we did not delay, for we barely made it.

Green seas broke completely over the decks, the little

ship seemed actually to stand on end at times; and each time she dropped from the crest of a wave she came down with a sickening crash that threatened to knock the bottom out of her. Even with her powerful motor at full speed she made barely three knots in the face of the terrific gale, and six terrible hours were consumed in crossing that eighteen-mile strip of bay to where, at last, we were able to drop anchor in comparatively smooth water. By the next day the worst of the norther was over, and as we were in need of fresh water and provisions, we decided to put into port before returning to ascend the river.

A crowd was awaiting us as we approached the dock at Carmen, and to our surprise we discovered that we had innocently and unwittingly created more commotion and excitement than anything since the last revolution. In fact we had been the cause of a serious controversy between officials that had for a time threatened to disrupt the peace of the district, we had caused official despatches to keep the wires hot between Carmen and Mexico City, and we had very narrowly escaped being chased by an armed force, arrested and thrown into prison! And all because of those sacks of mail from Campeche which we had delivered to the boat at Aguada!

Our stop at Aguada had been reported; the port captain at Carmen had been advised from Campeche that we had cleared for Carmen, and instantly he had gone up in the air, so to speak. He had sent a scathing and denunciatory message to the *commandante* at Aguada in which he accused that official of having violated the law by allowing us to enter the port, and hinted that he was aiding and abetting revolutionists or filibusters, or at the least an American secret mission, to enter Mexican territory illegally. Following this, the irate and excitable port captain had sent a wireless message to Mexico City asking for the arrest and imprisonment of the poor Aguada *commandante*. The latter had countered by wiring to the capital that as we carried mail from Campeche to Aguada, and had had the mail flag, the authorities must have expected us to touch at Aguada, and he quite logically argued that had he not permitted us to enter he would have been interfering with the Government mails. In the meantime, frenzied word had been sent that an "American gunboat"—Ye gods! the *Vigilance* being mistaken for such—had been seen ascending the Candelaria River after kidnaping the keeper of the lighthouse! The excitable natives and the imaginative port captain could think of but one explanation. The Americanos had designs on Yucatan! And the fact that the local press had been filled with hot-headed denunciations of the "Yanquis" in connection with the Lower California episode, lent color to the idea. Thereupon the port captain had been on the point of radioing for a gunboat and a company of soldiers to capture us when an American resident of the town had received word from our "agent" in Campeche informing him that as we had taken out "cabotaje" or coasting papers we had a perfect right to stop at Aguada or anywhere else. Thereupon every one concerned was satisfied. The tempest in a teapot was over. The port captain and the *commandante* exchanged mutual regrets over the misunderstanding. Mexico City was duly notified that a mistake had been made, amicable relations were once more established all around, and when we arrived we were welcomed effusively, and literally with open arms. "But,"

(55)

suggested the fiercely-mustached and pompous port captain, as he patted me on the back and embraced me, "it would be wise if the Americanos did *not* fly their flag on the 'yate' except when entering a port."

Even if all suspicions of our gun-running mission had been allayed, still the romantically-minded Yucatecans could not be satisfied with such tame and everyday reasons as we offered in explanation of our presence, not of course mentioning our search for the Maya treasure. To their minds there must be something far more adventurous to have induced Gringos to voyage so far in such a small boat. And as they knew nothing of the Maya treasure-trove that the aviator had discovered, their active, imaginative minds sought for some sinister and ulterior reason for our being there. As a result, when we were at last ready to sail, our local "agent" informed us that the port captain would not issue clearance papers unless we were accompanied by an officer. Moreover, we were not only required to supply bed and board to the unwelcome official, but were to pay him for his time also. It was crowded enough aboard the *Vigilance* as it was, we had no intention of supporting an officer in comparative luxury and paying him in addition, and with an officer on board it would be impossible to get away with the treasure. Finally, we decided, it was just a new scheme for squeezing a few more dollars from us, and angry and disgusted I hurried off to beard the port captain in his den. As I entered his office he sprang to his feet, welcomed me cordially and patted me on the back like the dearest of friends. And when, still seething, I demanded why he had given such an order, and added that if that was his idea of courtesy we'd clear for Progreso forthwith, he instantly disclaimed all intentions of causing us the slightest inconvenience and actually appeared to be as "desolated" as he claimed to be because I should have misjudged him.

"But, señor mio!" he exclaimed. "I am your friend, your *compadre*, your servant. I kiss your hand, *excelencia*, I obey your slightest wish. I am here to show you and your companions every courtesy, to make everything easy, to render you every service. Of a truth, *amigo mio*, anything within my poor power will I do to make you remember Carmen with nothing but delight. The order—" he chuckled, embraced me and beamed—"the order, señor, was but my little joke. You are at liberty to go where and when you so desire without hindrance, *amigo*. But—" he winked—"I must show my authority at times. Your agent—" he shrugged—"must be made to know his place. He would have you Americanos think that only he can arrange matters. So to him I give the order so that you will come to me and I may thereupon prove my desire to be of service, while your agent may thus know that he is not such a great man as he may think himself. Ah, si, *excelencia*, it is in such manner that we must make small those who feel themselves to be great. Si, of a truth, señor, we must now and then prick the bubbles so that they may burst—Pff! Is it not so, *excelencia?* And now, *mi amigo*, do me the honor to accept my most humble apologies that you have been so inconvenienced. And may you go with God, señor!"

Grinning, I left his presence. There was something very ludicrous in his scheme for calling down the agent by issuing an order aimed at us and which did not affect the agent in the least. In fact it reminded me forcibly of old Blackbeard the pirate who, having pistoled two of his officers, remarked that if he "didn't shoot an officer now and then his crew would forget who he was."

The water over the bar at the river's mouth proved too shallow for the *Vigilance,* so she was anchored outside and we ferried ourselves and belongings ashore in the dinghy and made ourselves at home in the ranch house of a huge estate whose owner had given us letters to his Mexican manager. Here, once again, George's terror of snakes caused him to decide to remain at the ranch rather than tempt Fate in the jungles, and, as usual, Pete followed suit. So, with a grinning, brown-skinned Mayan to serve as guide, camp-boy and man-of-all-work, Dick, Bob, the aviator and myself started up river in hopes of finding the hidden treasure.

As an excursion or a hunting trip the voyage was all any one could have wished. There were no houses, no settlements. Everywhere was jungle containing countless forms of bird-life. Alligators and crocodiles basked on logs beside the banks. There were deer, peccary, jaguars, pumas, ocelot, tapir and wild turkeys in the forests. And, basking in the sunshine upon the tops of the low trees that lined the river banks, were hundreds of gigantic iguanas, dragon-like monsters eight to nine feet in length and striped like tigers with brilliant orange and black.

Possibly iguanas should not be dignified by the name of game; but if any one thinks that these giant lizards cannot provide sport and excitement let him try shooting iguanas with a rifle while standing in a fifteen-foot boat. And to see and hear an eight-foot dragon come crashing down at the report of one's rifle gives one no small thrill. Moreover, the creatures are good to eat, and with three of the big fellows in our boat I anticipated a toothsome stew when we camped for the night. At last, a short time before sundown, we swung around a bend and Encantada was before us, a deserted camp-like dwelling once used as barracks by the *vaqueros* and *chicle* gatherers of the ranch. In its entrancing setting of luxuriant tropical vegetation, flaming flowers, golden fruit-laden orange trees, waving palms and background of virgin forest its name, meaning "The Enchanted," seemed most appropriate. But no sooner had we stepped ashore than we realized how misleading was the name and why the place had been abandoned. Instantly we were enveloped in a perfect cloud of the terrible *rodederos* or day-flying biting gnats of Yucatan. In vain we thrashed about, slapped, brushed, smoked and cursed. They filled our ears, crawled up our noses, blundered into our eyes and drew blood from every inch of our exposed skin. Madly we raced up the steep bank, hoping the pests might be confined to the lowland. But they were as thick if not thicker there, and to make matters worse, they were reinforced by swarms of equally vicious mosquitoes. It was humanly impossible to withstand the united attack, and we dashed for the tumble-down building that had once served as a kitchen, hoping that by kindling a smoky fire we might find relief. But scarcely had we entered when we were in full retreat, for the kitchen was fairly alive with vermin. We were between the devil and the deep sea, so to speak, but sulphur candles and spraying with formalin decreased the flea army in the kitchen to some extent, and to our vast relief we found that the *rodederos* abandoned their offensive in the semi-darkness of the building, while the

(59)

pungent smoke from green leaves had the desired effect upon the mosquitoes.

With sundown, both *rodederos* and mosquitoes vanished, but we looked forward with anything but pleasure to exploring the jungle the next day. In the morning, however, a brisk wind was blowing, and although the jungle teemed with mosquitoes, and we were compelled to cover our heads and faces with improvised nets, to stuff cotton in ears and nostrils and smear our hands and arms with a mixture of vaseline and creosote, we managed to do fairly well. Throughout that day we explored the river, cruising for miles upstream, searching for the aviator's peculiar S-shaped bend by which we hoped to locate the treasure. Time after time we would come to a bend which he declared must be the right one. Landing, we would take compass bearings and hew our way into the jungle with machetes. And such jungles! Never in my forty years' experience in the West Indies, Central and South America, have I seen anything to equal them. It was impossible to move five feet in any direction without cutting a path. Palms with trunks covered with great black spines, wiry bushes armed with crooked thorns, twisted, tangled briars, razor-edged saw-grass, prickly agaves, acacias and cacti, with fallen limbs and leaves, knee-deep vegetable débris and slimy trunks of wild plantains—all formed an almost solid wall, while underfoot the ground was a sea of sticky black ooze in which we sank to our ankles. It was obvious that the aviator, with no machete, could never have forced his way at night through such a barrier, and according to him the vegetation about the ancient clearing was not dense. In fact it couldn't have been, for he had walked through the forest for seventeen hours with no means of cutting a trail. But there was the chance that the character of the jungle might change a short distance from the river, and the only way of determining what lay inland was to hew a way in. It was terrible work, and bitterly disheartening, to toil for hours cutting through the tangle, tearing flesh and garments, in agonies from biting insects, only to find no large trees or open forest.

But so positive was the aviator that we were on the right stream, so certain he seemed of his distance from the coast and river and his compass bearings when he had first found his engine missing, and so sincere in his statements, that despite discouragement after discouragement, despite the fact that he "identified" fully a dozen bends as the right one, we kept at it. But at last, after days of futile, fearful labor, after weary hours of hacking and hewing through the jungle, the aviator was forced to admit that he had made a mistake somewhere, that he was totally at a loss. The river, he argued, when viewed from a boat upon its surface did not look the same as when seen from the air, and also, he pointed out, although he had spotted only one S-bend there were scores which, in all probability, had been hidden from his view by the forest. All our hopes were dashed. The one man who knew or claimed to know the secret of the Mayas' treasure had failed us. And at last, bitterly disappointed and utterly discouraged, we abandoned the search and returned downstream.

We arrived at the ranch to find George tremendously elated. He actually *had* seen a snake! During all the time we had been upriver and in the jungles we had not seen a trace of a serpent, yet here at the ranch, a snake—and a venomous snake at that—had been killed in the kitchen patio. And I still maintain that the little viper wriggled from the jungle and into the patio and sacrificed its life for the express purpose of satisfying George that there really were snakes in Yucatan.

Perhaps it was lucky for us that we did *not* find the Mayan treasure, for when we reached Carmen we were boarded by my friend the port captain and half a dozen soldiers who—with profuse apologies and begging ten thousand pardons—thoroughly searched the *Vigilance* from stem to stern. Evidently they had their suspicions, and had the Mayan treasure been found on board who can say what might have been the result as far as we were concerned? But it was not until we were about to sail, and the port captain had invited Bob and myself to drink a farewell toast in a native liquor which, he affirmed, was compounded of sulphuric acid and gunpowder, and which tasted as if it might have been, that I learned why our vessel had been searched.

During the last ill-starred revolution, an airplane, bearing a fleeing rebel leader and laden with gold coin and incriminating documents, had crashed somewhere within the jungle, and that, so the officials surmised, was what we had been seeking.

Here was an entirely new angle, a new development. By some strange and almost incredible coincidence had two rebel airplanes crashed in the same jungle-covered area? Was our aviator the pilot of the ill-fated plane freighted with revolutionary documents, revolutionist funds and a revolutionary leader? If so, had the little aviator really stumbled upon the underground hiding place of the golden books of the Mayas, or had he invented the tale in hopes of luring an expedition in search of a mythical treasure in order that he might locate the plane and secure the papers for which the Mexican Government would pay a small fortune? *Quien sabe?* as the Spaniards say. It is a mystery we have never solved. Unquestionably, somewhere in the jungle, rests the wreckage of an airplane containing the skeleton of a rebel leader, thousands of dollars in minted gold and paper which, if in the possession of the Mexican Government, would result in many a man facing a firing squad. And possibly, not far distant, the golden books of the Mayas still lie hidden in their subterranean chamber, a treasure whose value is beyond all estimate.

A Treasure That Was Found and Lost

JOHNSON had pored over the old chart until he could shut his eyes and see every detail, every crease and wrinkle of the ancient parchment, every crudely-drawn symbol, every quaintly-formed letter on the pirates' map which had come into his possession by mere chance. That it was genuine Johnson did not doubt. It bore all the earmarks of age, of passing through many hands, and of having been made by a seaman. Neither was there any question of the locality where, according to the old map, the vast treasure looted from the churches of Vera Cruz had been buried. Rough and sketchy as were the outlines and landmarks there was no difficulty in recognizing the island as the Isle of Pines and the mountain as Mt. Columbo. Yet Johnson had searched and searched, tramping slowly, examining every rock, every old tree, every ledge in his efforts to find the markers mentioned and sketched on the old chart; a man's hand clutching a dagger, and a second hand holding a cutlass. It was neither a very easy nor simple matter to search the district, for there were people about and the natives, knowing he was a confirmed treasure hunter, might suspect he was on the trail of some hidden hoard and might dog his footsteps or watch him. Hence he was compelled to carry on his investigations at unseemly hours or very cautiously. It was exasperating, maddening, to have the old chart, to know beyond any reasonable doubt that the treasure was there within an area of a few square rods, and yet be as hopelessly at a loss as to where it was as though he had never seen the chart.

Mentally cursing his luck, Johnson seated himself upon a fragment of rock and idly, as men and boys will do, gave vent to his feelings by hurling stones at the nearby cliffside. Suddenly his jaw gaped, his arm already lifted to heave another rock, dropped to his side, his eyes remained fixed, staring incredulously at the cliff. The next moment he leaped from his seat as if a coiled spring had been released under him and gave a yell that would have been a credit to an Apache warrior. The last stone he had flung had dislodged a mass of moss and clinging plants from the cliff and there, plain on the freshly-exposed surface, was the rudely-cut outline of a human hand grasping a cutlass!

Feverishly Johnson compared the incised marking on the stone with the sketches on the old chart. There could be no doubt of it. By merest accident, by the medium of a carelessly thrown stone, he had discovered that for which he had been searching for weeks past. The rest, he felt, would be simple. By following the directions set down on the map he could locate the second marker and then—the treasure in its hidden cache.

Hastily stuffing the precious parchment into his pocket, he glanced about. Suppose some prying eyes had seen him! It would never do to leave that sculptured hand within plain sight, and having assured himself that no one was near, he busied himself smearing the carving with mud and plastering it with moss.

Then, following the directions of the map, pacing the distances, taking careful note of his compass bearings, he searched for the second marker of the treasure. Presently a puzzled frown wrinkled his forehead, and halting, he gazed about. Something must be wrong, he decided. He had not gone half the distance indicated on the chart and yet before him rose a solid wall of rock, projecting above a rank growth of weeds, brush and tangled vines.

For a space he hesitated, puzzled, wondering. He was positive he could not have made a mistake, could not have misinterpreted the directions on the chart, yet— Possibly, he decided, there was a way to pass around or to climb the rock. Perhaps— Pressing through the growth that concealed the base of the cliff he came within view of the rock and the mass of fallen débris.

The next instant he was on his knees, hurling fragments of rock aside utterly oblivious of bruised and bleeding hands. Half-hidden by the débris of centuries was the dark opening of a cavern, and, just above it, overgrown by delicate lichens but still visible, was the incised outline of a man's hand gripping a dagger!

Confident that the treasure lay within the cave—what a fool he had been not to have grasped the meaning of that heavily outlined area on the chart—he cleared away the accumulation of rock fragments until he could squeeze his body through the opening. It was dark within and he had not provided himself with an electric torch. But he had plenty of matches, and gathering some dry pine branches he made an extemporized torch and by its light examined the cavern. It was not large, scarcely more than a fissure in the limestone, and he took in the entire interior at a glance. But not a sign of treasure, not a cask, chest or barrel was visible. Johnson's heart sank. It was bitterly disappointing, maddening, to find the hiding place of the treasure only to find it missing, removed no doubt by some one years before.

And then, as he was on the point of turning back, he noticed one spot on the floor of the cavern which seemed different from the rest. Here, instead of the smooth water-worn limestone surface, was a large mass of rock, a slab which at first he had assumed had fallen from the cavern roof.

But as he examined it more closely, elation and hope again surged through his veins. The rock bore half-obliterated symbols!

Exerting all his strength, prying and lifting with an improvised lever, Johnson managed to move the rock slightly, enough to reveal a cavity beneath it. With heart beating like a triphammer, he flung himself down and thrust the flickering light into the hole. He could scarcely believe his eyes.

Within the pit were chests, kegs, rawhide sacks and earthen jars. The loot of Vera Cruz was there!

But unaided Johnson could not recover it. And, he realized, even if he could reach it, if he could help himself to the contents of those old chests and casks and jars, he could not carry one tenth, one hundredth of the treasure on his person. There was only one thing to be done. He would conceal the entrance to the cavern as thoroughly as possible, obliterate the marker over the

(67)

spot. Then, returning to the town, he would confide in some trusted friend, return with bars and picks at night, and under cover of darkness cart the treasure away.

But Fate willed otherwise. The next day dawned with a tawny, lowering sky and a West Indian hurricane came roaring, howling demoniacally, from the Caribbean, with the island directly in its path. Trees were torn up and hurled about, houses were unroofed or blown to bits, vessels were wrecked, and scores of the inhabitants were killed or injured by the fiercest, most destructive hurricane that had devastated the island in many years.

Johnson was among the injured and, partially disabled, and with all thoughts of recovering the treasure in the immediate future driven from his mind, he returned to his home in California to recuperate. But he had little fear of the treasure being disturbed before he could go back to the island. It had lain there in the cavern for centuries and the chances were all in favor of its remaining there for centuries more, unless he removed it.

But events transpired which no one could have foreseen. A revolution was sweeping over Cuba, and when at last it had been suppressed hundreds of rebel prisoners crowded the prisons and jails of Havana and other Cuban cities. From time immemorial the Isle of Pines had been used as a prison by the Spaniards, and later by the Cubans, and by scores the captive rebels and other criminals were shipped to the island prison. Soon it was evident that the place could not accommodate them all, and the government ordered a large area of land cleared and surrounded by a high, barbed-wire fence to add to the prison's confines. And when Johnson returned, feeling confident that he would still find the treasure intact, he

(68)

discovered that the cave and its hidden riches lay *within* the prison grounds! However, as there were no rumors of the treasures having been discovered, he still had hopes of securing them. But in order to do so it was necessary for him to obtain permission, and that meant dividing the riches with the officials. Still, half a loaf was better than no bread, and if there proved to be one-half as much treasure as reputed there would be enough to make him a rich man, even if the Government got the lion's share.

Officials, however, and more especially Cuban officials, are not to be depended upon when a matter of easily-gotten riches is concerned.

Assuring Johnson of their coöperation, and explaining that there must be a certain delay owing to official red tape, the smiling authorities lost no time in seeking to find the treasure themselves. And when the allotted time for the necessary permit to be ready had expired, and Johnson called upon the officials, they blandly informed him that he was merely wasting his time, for seven wheelbarrows full of gold and silver had already been taken from the treasure cave!

CHAPTER VI

The Treasure of the Hidden Crater

IN most cases the value of lost or hidden treasures, even if they actually exist, is greatly exaggerated. In the course of a few centuries hoards of thousands of dollars grow into millions as the tales of some cache of treasure are handed down, usually by word of mouth, each narrator adding a little to the estimated value of the riches.

But such is not the case with the lost and hidden treasures of the Incas and their predecessors in Peru, Bolivia and Ecuador. In the first place, it would be next to impossible to exaggerate the values of these ancient treasures, and in the second place, unquestionable records and historic documents prove the almost incredible value of the gold, silver and precious stones actually taken by the conquering Spaniards, and these were but as a drop in the bucket to the treasures the Dons never found or secured.

Although Pizarro and his followers secured nearly twenty million dollars worth of gold as a portion of Atahualpa's ransom, yet fully ten times as much more was being brought to buy the freedom of the captive Inca, but was concealed in the Andes when the carriers learned of the Spaniard's treachery and the murder of Atahualpa.

There is no doubt that, at the time of the conquest, the Incas possessed more gold than all the countries of Europe combined, and while the Spaniards secured stupendous sums, and shipped over half a billion dollars worth of gold and silver to Spain, yet there were even greater treasures which they missed completely. And although four hundred years have passed since then, these incalculable millions in precious metals and precious stones still remain hidden where they were placed so securely by the Indians in the long ago, despite the countless attempts that have been made to find them.

Of all these lost or hidden treasures of the Incas and pre-Incas, none has a more romantic story than that of the treasure of the Incan princess, or as it is more often called, the Valverde Treasure.

Unfortunately, neither the origin nor the history of this vast hoard is known. Although often referred to as the "Inca's Treasure" or as "Atahualpa's Treasure," yet it is certain that it is not the treasure of the betrayed and murdered Inca. But it is equally certain that its hiding place, deep in a remote section of the Andes, was well known to some of the Incan people.

Possibly it may have formed some portion of the vast quantities of gold and silver that were being hurried to Cajamarca to save the Inca; but this is scarcely probable, as the hiding place is far off any known route between Cajamarca and other centers of the Incan Empire.

Far more probably, it was a treasure that was being moved from some deserted and "lost" city in the trans-Andean jungles to Quito or elsewhere, and was hastily

(71)

concealed when word reached the carriers that the
Spaniards were invading the land. No one can say how
many great stone cities may yet lie hidden in the unknown, unexplored area between the Andes and the
Amazon. For hundreds of years Macchu Picchu had been
forgotten and "lost," although it had been occupied by the
Incans under Manco during their heroic but futile struggle
to drive the Spaniards from Cuzco and Peru. And just as
that marvelous pre-Incan city was abandoned because of
constant raids by jungle savages, and its treasures were
transferred to Cuzco, so other equally large cities may
have been deserted by the Incans or pre-Incans.

But regardless of the origin of the treasure, its known
history begins with the story of a humble and penniless
Spaniard named Valverde. As a common soldier he had
taken part in the conquest, and his warlike service over,
he settled down and took to wife an Indian woman. Just
as today a white man who marries an Indian is often
regarded with contempt and is referred to as a "squaw
man," so in Valverde's day his fellow Spaniards scoffed
at him. And this, combined with the fact that he was
abjectly poor, made his life a most unhappy one. Perhaps
he married the Indian woman merely because she was
beautiful and he loved her, and was ignorant of the fact
that she was other than an ordinary everyday member of
her race. On the other hand, he may have known that she
came of royal blood and was an Incan princess, and
thought to better himself by the match. Whatever the
truth may be, when he complained of his unfortunate lot
and became more and more unhappy and morose and she
learned the reason for his discontent, she revealed the
truth and declared that if such matters were all that

troubled him it could soon be remedied and that she would show him how he could become the richest Spaniard in the country and the envy of all men.

Perhaps he thought she was only romancing and laughed at her, but far more probably, being a sensible man and well aware that the natives had knowledge of hidden treasures, he had complete faith in her ability to make good her words. At all events he had sufficient confidence in her to accompany her on a long and difficult trip into the fastnesses of the mountains, following secret trails, climbing the lofty peaks, traversing ridges and dark cañons, until at last they reached the crater of an extinct volcano. A great bowl-shaped valley in whose center was a turquoise glacier lake reflecting the three snow-capped pinnacles soaring upward thousands of feet above the ancient crater. Already Valverde's eyes had grown wide with wonder and his pulses had throbbed, as passing through a marshy patch where a small stream trickled over the pebbles, he had seen raw gold gleaming on the bed of the brook where he had stooped to drink. But his Incan wife had laughed at his excitement over this discovery and had urged him on. And now, crossing the crater, she guided him to a dark cleft in the mountain side—an arched opening like a church door, as Valverde described it, and, picking her way along a tunnel-like narrow crevice she led him to a great cavern. Valverde's breath came in hard short gasps, his senses fairly reeled as his eyes became accustomed to the dim light, for piled within the cave was such a vast treasure as he had never dreamed could exist on earth.

Everywhere, on every side, the dull gleam of gold

(73)

reflected the ruddy light from the flickering greasewood torches the two carried.

Golden statues and idols, plates and vessels of solid gold, bundles of thin golden plumes and sheets of beaten gold, ingots of gold and bags of gold nuggets and dust, golden ornaments, and models of birds, animals and other objects wrought in gold and silver; golden ears of corn with husks and silk of silver; coronets and head ornaments, ceremonial utensils and armlets of gold ablaze with gems, and massive bars of silver filled the cave to capacity—countless tons of the precious metals, millions in treasure. It is a marvel that poor Valverde did not go raving mad at the mere sight of such unlimited riches. But he was an uncommonly sensible and level-headed man, and after the first mad excitement of gazing upon such vast treasures had passed off, he examined the contents of the cavern with an appraising eye, and aided by his Incan Princess wife, selected the objects that represented the greatest value for their size and weight. Then, having collected all that he and his faithful spouse could safely carry with them, they shouldered their loads and retraced their way to the crater.

It was a long hard journey to their home, made all the harder by the weight of their loads. But who would not be willing to stagger onward under heavy burdens when the burdens were of solid gold?

No doubt Valverde's friends and neighbors were properly astonished when the erstwhile poverty-stricken ex-soldier suddenly blossomed out as a wealthy man. But in all probability it did not excite so much wonder and curiosity as such a transformation would arouse today, for all knew that there were Incan treasures hidden away, and in order to profit by his riches Valverde had to dispose of the golden objects and could not keep secret the source of his wealth. But both he and his Incan princess wife managed to keep secret the location of the vast treasure whence came their affluence. Whether or not they were spied upon or followed, history fails to record, but if so those who essayed to learn their secret failed, for over and over again the two journeyed to the secret cavern beside the crater, each time returning with all the precious metal and gems they could carry, until Valverde became the richest man in the country and his wife had thus made good her promise. Yet all that they took from the ancient hoard through many years made no appreciable impression upon the vast accumulation of gold, silver and precious stones in the cave.

Although the Señora Valverde needed no chart to guide her footsteps to the hidden treasure, but like the Indian she was followed trails and landmarks invisible or unrecognizable to her Spanish mate, Valverde realized that should anything happen to her and he were thus bereft of his guide he would be at a loss. So he made a fairly good and accurate map—crudely drawn and out of all true proportion to be sure—with quaintly written notes and directions to aid in following it, although being an ignorant, uneducated man his choice of words and his meaning left much to be desired.

When in due course of time, the wealthy, respected, sought-after and envied Señor Valverde realized that even vast riches could not buy immortality or bribe Death, his thoughts turned to his youth and to Spain. Already his Incan wife had passed away. He had a longing to be buried in the land of his birth, and being a

patriotic Don and aware of the fact that shrouds have
no pockets, he made a will by which he bequeathed his
precious map, together with all treasures remaining in
the cave, to the King of Spain on condition that his body
be taken overseas and properly interred in his homeland.

But when Valverde had breathed his last, and the
King's representatives sought with the aid of the map to
garner the famous treasure, they found themselves hopelessly at a loss. Although doubtless the marks upon the
chart, together with the written directions in the document or "deroterro" accompanying it, seemed plain and
clear enough, yet the searchers discovered that, in reality,
they were most confusing and ambiguous. For much of
the way the route was clear and there was no difficulty
in following the trail; but as the vicinity of the crater
was reached it became more and more confusing. Mainly
the trouble centered about a lofty mountain called Margasitas, for while Valverde's map and directions made it
clear enough that this isolated peak must be passed, yet
there was nothing on the chart nor in the directions to
show just *how* or *where* this feat was to be accomplished.

At last those who had been given the task of securing
the treasure for the Crown gave up in despair. The map
and directions were regarded as useless—many claiming
that Valverde had purposely altered portions of the chart
and had penned false directions in order to mislead any
who might find or steal the documents; in other words,
that they were a form of code which he alone could inter-
pret, and that he had failed to leave the key ere he had
died. Be that as it may, the map became more or less
common property, and again and again searchers set
forth, each feeling assured that he could succeed where

others had failed. Some abandoned their quest after traveling but a short distance, unable to face the rigors of the high altitudes, the cold and the hardships of the trip. But there were others who carried on and reached Margasitas, only to become confused, to lose their way and to return utterly discouraged. And there were many who set forth who never returned, but who perished miserably somewhere in the wild, unknown fastnesses of the Andes. But never a man reached the crater in the shadow of the three peaks where the glacier lake gleamed like a gigantic emerald and beyond the arched opening in the cliffside reposed the vast treasure.

Years passed and Valverde and his treasure map became little more than a tradition. Then, in 1857, Richard Spruce, the famous English botanist, while traveling in Ecuador, heard of Valverde's treasure-trove and at once became interested. From somewhere he secured a copy of the ancient map, and, being an adventurer born as well as an experienced explorer, he determined to have a try for the treasure himself.

Following the marks and directions on the map, Spruce found no difficulty in reaching Margasitas Mountain. But here, like all of those who had preceded him, he became hopelessly confused and at last gave up.

But in a book which he wrote of his travels in South America, he gave a full account of his search and published a copy of the famous map. Moreover, he declared that there was no doubt of the authenticity of the chart, that it corresponded perfectly with the country and the landmarks as far as he had gone, and that, in his opinion, the only reason why he or some other had not succeeded was because of a mistaken interpretation of the directions for passing the mountain.

Even he, however, did not attempt to explain *how* the mountain should be passed nor did he state which particular portion of Valverde's directions had been for so long misinterpreted.

Again years passed and the treasure remained undiscovered, almost forgotten and as far as known unsought for, until the representative of the American Bank Note Company of New York visited Ecuador.

Colonel E. C. Brooks was a practical, hard-headed, matter-of-fact business man—nothing of the imaginative, romantic treasure-hunter about him. A graduate of West Point, he had served in the Army, and at the close of the Spanish War had been made Auditor of Cuba. With Cuba freed and paddling her own canoe, Colonel (then Major) Brooks had retired from the United States Army and had been for several years the South American representative of the Bank Note Company. He was familiar with the various countries and their people, he spoke Spanish fluently, and he was noted for his acumen, his business ability and his caution. In his lexicon there was no such word as "gamble." All of which makes it the more remarkable that Colonel Brooks should have been bitten by the treasure-hunting bug when he read Spruce's book and studied the copy of the ancient map of Señor Valverde.

He was not, however, the type to dash blindly into the mountains on the spur of the moment, and not until he had dug into all the old records, had studied every aspect of the case and had convinced himself that the story of the Valverde treasure was fact and not fiction, and that there was no logical reason why it should not be found, did he decide to add his name to the long list of treasure seekers who had been before him.

Unfortunately, however, he had had no experience in exploratory work and was ignorant of the character of the country he would have to enter, and he set out inadequately equipped and at the very worst season of the year. He was drenched by torrential rains, buffeted by blizzards, faced with difficulties and hardships he could not overcome, and convinced that it was hopeless to proceed under such adverse conditions, he turned back. But he had by no manner of means abandoned his search. On the contrary, he was more than ever obsessed with his idea, for he had studied the map and the directions, and had come to the conclusion that he had solved the puzzle of getting beyond Margasitas. Waiting until the winter season had passed, and provided with waterproof coats and containers, with adequate supplies and with eight Indians, he again started out. And, most luckily for him, as it turned out, before starting on his search he left instructions with a friend to send a relief party in search of him if he failed to return within a specified time.

All went well with the Colonel on this trip, and the party made good time to Margasitas. And we can imagine Colonel Brooks' delight when he proved he had interpreted the directions correctly, and having succeeded in passing the mountain which had baffled so many, he saw three snow-capped peaks gleaming against the blue sky to the east.

Not since Valverde and his Incan wife had followed the trail had any man accomplished this much, and now feeling positive that the treasure was almost within his grasp, and that he would have no difficulty in finding the crater and the lake as described by Valverde, Colonel Brooks hurried on.

Then, for the first time, he noticed the strange behavior of his Indians. All but one were natives of Ecuador, the only exception being a Peruvian Cholo or half-breed, and the Ecuadorean Indians were acting strangely. Had Colonel Brooks had as much experience with Indians and Indian ways as with business men and business ways, he would have understood. For that matter he never would have employed native Indians, for the old gods die hard and although nominally good Christians, civilized, and citizens of the Republic, the Andean Indians still pin their faith on the religions and beliefs of their ancestors. To them, the hidden treasure was an almost sacred thing— the property of semi-divine Incas, and, moreover, they felt certain it had been guarded by a spell or perhaps by evil spirits and that to molest or even approach it was inviting disaster. The fact that Valverde had helped himself and had met with no harm thereby was a totally different matter, for he had an Incan wife who had a perfect right to the treasure. But here was a Gringo, a white man and a foreigner, intent upon robbing the long-dead Incas of their secret riches, their sacred vessels, their ceremonial objects, the images of their gods, their very jewelry and ornaments. Faithful as they might be under any ordinary circumstances, the Indians became more and more nervous and loath to go farther. They hung back, glanced apprehensively about, and tried in every way to induce Colonel Brooks to turn back, declaring that a storm was coming on, that there were fearful perils to be faced and that all would perish if he persisted.

(80)

But Brooks merely laughed at their warnings and their fears, and cursing and berating them in Spanish—which they barely understood—he commanded them to proceed. The trail was easily followed and was precisely as indicated on the old map, and with no difficulty and in a much shorter time than he had expected, the party reached the crater valley at the base of the three peaks and saw the mirror-like lake before them.

Success had crowned his efforts, the Colonel felt sure. Somewhere in the cliffs close at hand was the dark, arched entrance to the treasure cavern, and it would be a simple matter to locate that.

But it was late in the afternoon, all were tired with their long march, and deciding to postpone his search until the next morning, Colonel Brooks ordered his men to pitch their camp beside the lake. And here, again, he made a grave mistake which no true explorer would have made.

Confident that he would be gazing at the long-lost treasure in the morning, Colonel Brooks dropped off to sleep and to dream of limitless wealth.

Frenzied shouts, and the crash of thunder awakened him, and he leaped from his camp bed to find himself knee-deep in water with rain and hail coming down in a perfect deluge. Struggling through the water he dashed from his shelter-tent to find his camp inundated by the rapidly-rising waters of the lake. Flooded by the torrential rain, the bowl-like valley was fast filling with the water pouring down the mountain sides. How far the flood might rise neither Brooks nor his Indians could foresee, but only a narrow strip of dry land remained, and dashing across this they reached a cave-like recess in the mountain side where they were protected from the fury of the storm. With no fire, with teeth chattering, and chilled to the bone by their drenched garments and the cold thin air, they passed the long and terrible hours until dawn. And when at last light showed above the gleaming, ice-sheeted peaks, they found their condition even worse than they had expected. Where a tiny lake had nestled in the bottom of the crater was now a vast expanse of water.

No vestige of their camp remained; clothing, equipment, supplies, provisions—all had disappeared. A few water-soaked garments, a single ham, and some hermetically-sealed foods were the only things they could find. Moreover, the weather had not cleared, and though its first fury had abated, the storm still raged, and sleet and rain were falling steadily. To attempt to retrace their way under such conditions was impossible. It was equally impossible to explore the flooded valley and search for the treasure cave, and to remain in the inadequate shelter of their cave refuge without food or other necessities until the waters receded was as impossible as either.

But hunting for a treasure, even if so close at hand, had lost all interest in the face of such very pressing and imminent danger of starvation. Colonel Brooks' one thought was to conserve what little food they had, and at the first sign of clear weather to hurry back the way he had come.

To make matters even worse the Indians had become sullen and almost hostile. To their minds the flood was the direct result of the white man's attempt to secure the treasure, and although not in the least superstitious, Colonel Brooks could not help thinking how strange it was that his Indians had warned him of the danger of a storm and had declared one was near, although there had been no signs of it.

When the next day dawned, the Colonel found only one Indian remaining. Filled with terror, convinced that the gods of their ancestors were wreaking vengeance upon the white man, they had stolen silently away during the darkness, leaving Colonel Brooks alone with the Peruvian Cholo.

Luckily for them the last storm-torn clouds were drifting from about the mountain tops, a few flecks of blue sky were visible, and the rain had decreased to a drizzle. Gathering their slender supply of food, the two took the last desperate chance of making a forced march back to civilization.

It was a terrible nightmarish journey. Half-starved, chilled to the bone, sleepless and foot-sore they hurried on. They passed Margasitas and gained the high, stone-riddled mountain desert or "puna." Then, down from the Andean heights swept a blinding snow storm, and in the blizzard they lost their way completely.

Only the Colonel's forethought saved them from perishing miserably as they wandered aimlessly about. But just as the two were on the verge of giving up their seemingly hopeless struggle, they saw men in the distance, and a few minutes later, were safe with the relief party that had been sent out.

Of all those who had sought the vast treasure of the secret crater, since Valverde's day, Colonel Brooks alone had passed Margasitas and had actually been within sight of the treasure cave. Yet like all the others, he had failed, and the guardian spirits of the Incans' treasures must have chuckled with unholy glee at his discomfiture.

But he had accomplished much. He had not only verified the accuracy of the old map and the strangely-worded directions left by Valverde, but in addition, he had solved the mystery of passing Margasitas.

Despite all that he had suffered, all he had risked, and his narrow escape from death, the Colonel was anxious to go back, to have another try at finding the treasure of the Incan princess.

Many a time he related the story of his ill-fated trip to me, many a time we discussed the possibilities of taking another expedition to the crater at the foot of the three peaks. But before anything definite could be accomplished his health failed. It would have been dangerous in the extreme for him to have attempted to go on the trip, and he passed away with his one romantic adventure uncompleted.

From time to time since Colonel Brooks' death, rumors of the finding of the crater's treasure have been heard; but in every case so far they have proved unfounded. Small treasures or hoards of gold have been found in the hinterland of Ecuador. Some rich placers have been located; but the vast cache of pre-Incan golden objects and raw gold, hidden in the cave by the crater lake, still remains unfound, untouched, since the last visit of Valverde.

But now, as this book is being written, another expedition is being fitted out in New York to search for the famous long-lost treasure. Primarily it is a scientific expedition, with ethnological collections, surveys and motion picture records of wild life and of Indians its chief objects. But as the scientific work will take it to the vicinity of the Valverde treasure, it is planned to make a serious attempt to recover the riches within the cave. Whether success or failure results remains to be seen. Perchance, before this book is published, the treasures of the crater will be found and the finders will be enriched by millions. But, on the other hand, the secret of the vast hoard of gold may still remain unsolved and the spirit guardians of the ancient treasure may again triumph over modern methods, scientific instruments and the most strenuous efforts of experienced and seasoned explorers.

ᴜᴜᴜᴜᴜᴜᴜᴜᴜᴜᴜᴜᴜᴜᴜᴜᴜᴜᴜᴜᴜᴜᴜᴜᴜᴜᴜᴜᴜᴜ

Hunting the World's Most Mysterious Treasure

IT was a lovely autumn day. There was a tang of frost in the air, but the sun shone brightly, and the scarlet leaves of oaks and maples, the golden foliage of the white birch trees, and the softer browns of beeches and hickory, barely stirred in the gentle breeze. Overhead, vast flocks of wild pigeons winged southward, and wild geese honked as they dropped in V-shaped formation to ponds and lakes.

It was just the sort of day to send one's blood tingling through one's veins, to lure one into the woods or fields with a trusty gun on one's shoulder and a keen-nosed setter at one's heels. A day with air like old wine, when the call of the wild and the lure of adventure were too strong to be resisted—at least by Daniel McGinnis, Anthony Vaughan and Jack Smith, three youths of sixteen or thereabouts, who planned to spend a glorious holiday on Oak Island.

This island—one of many that dot Mahone Bay, on the Nova Scotia coast—was an ideal spot for the boys' outing. It was uninhabited, seldom visited, and its oak and pine forests were the haunt of ruffed grouse, deer and other game, while in its coves and bays geese, brant, ducks, and an occasional swan could be found. So, shouldering their shotguns, with shot pouches and powder horns well-filled, the three youths launched their birchbark canoe and paddled across the bay to the island's shores.

Being young, romantic and imaginative, they experienced a distinct thrill as they stepped ashore on the beach of a little inlet surrounded by the silent forest. Never before had they been on the island; they might almost have been the first human beings to set foot on its shores, and they felt like explorers or discoverers as they glanced about, discussing in low tones where they should start into the woods.

"Let's try over yonder," suggested Jack, pointing to the north. "It's more open over there."

Sure enough, at the spot Smith indicated, there were no large trees but only small secondary growth, and the three started forward.

"Some one must have cleared it here," observed Daniel, as they pushed through the thicket of sweet fern and bracken.

"Indians, perhaps," suggested Tony. "They may have had a village here. I— Hello, look there!"

Near the center of the old clearing was a single gigantic oak standing like a sentinel above the smaller saplings. But it was not the tree itself that had attracted Vaughan's attention. Projecting horizontally from the mighty trunk was a stout limb, the end of which had been sawed or chopped off. And dangling from the stump were the rusty links of a chain.

(87)

THEY FOUND GOLD

For an instant the three youths stood staring, a strange sensation of uneasiness stealing over them. That stout, outjutting branch with its rather suggestive remnant of chain, hinted at a gibbet, and the boys' imaginative minds pictured a ghastly corpse swinging in the wind.

To be sure, in that year of grace, 1795, hanged men were no novelty, even to the youngsters, and they had seen more than one body dangling in chains.

But it was rather creepy and disquieting to think of such things, there in the silent deserted forest, and the three stepped hastily back and glanced apprehensively about them.

Then they made another discovery. Almost directly under the lopped-off branch was a circular depression, about a dozen feet in diameter, in the earth.

The boys drew farther back, for might not the body of the hanged pirate—somehow they unconsciously assumed the victim of the tragedy to have been a pirate—lie under that sunken patch of soil? Then, suddenly, Vaughan darted forward and gave a triumphant shout.

'Treasure!" he yelled. "Buried treasure! That's what it is. Look, here's an old tackle-block. They never hang men with block and tackle!"

Half-buried in the soil and overgrown with weeds and moss, was an ancient weather-beaten ship's block. With bated breaths the three youths dropped to their knees to examine it.

"They must have used a block and tackle to lower their treasure-chests into the hole," suggested Vaughan. "That's what is in here—buried treasure."

"I guess you're right," agreed Dan. "Say, maybe Captain Kidd buried it here." (Like so many others, the boys associated all treasure with the notorious Kidd who never in his life visited Nova Scotia.)

Instantly the three became wildly excited. Here was adventure with a vengeance. Not one of the trio doubted for a moment that a vast hoard of gold was concealed under the oak tree. There was the cut limb, the tackle-block, and the depression in the soil marking the hiding place of the loot.

And any lingering doubts they might have had were dispelled when, on a closer examination of the tree, they discovered the healed scars or furrows made by ropes or chains on the stump, and, on the bark of the trunk, the welts of ancient axe-cuts which appeared to form crude numerals and letters.

All their plans for hunting were, of course, immediately forgotten. They had stumbled on a treasure-cache; that was enough for them!

At that time pirates still ravaged the seas in the West Indies and elsewhere; the story of Captain Kidd was recent history, and, less than one hundred years before, the near-by port of Lunnenburg had been the resort of many a pirate, so, quite naturally the boys took it for granted that the treasure hidden under the oak tree consisted of pirates' loot.

And now that they had discovered the hiding place of pirates' treasure they thought only of digging it up. So, abandoning all other plans, they returned to their canoe with the idea of going home, securing picks and shovels, and hurrying back to the island to secure the riches they felt sure were theirs for the digging.

During their sojourn ashore the tide had fallen and now, as the three approached the canoe they made another discovery. Left exposed by the ebbing water was an immense, old-fashioned, rusty ring-bolt let into the seaweed-covered rock. Here was further proof of pirates having landed on the island, and as the boys searched about they made two additional thrilling discoveries. One was a water-worn coin, the other an old-fashioned boatswain's whistle of silver.

The following day the three youths returned to the island and went to work. Within a few minutes they found they were digging in an old, clearly-outlined circular shaft, about thirteen feet in diameter, in which the marks of picks and shovels could clearly be seen. Wildly excited, now that they were certain they were close to treasures, the three worked madly, and Smith uttered an exultant shout when, ten feet below the surface, his shovel struck some solid object.

Dropping on hands and knees the boys feverishly scraped away the dirt, to disclose oak boards. Not one of them doubted that here was the treasure chest. But when, panting and sweating and toiling their hardest, they pried out the wood, their faces fell. It was no chest, merely a roughly-laid platform or bulkhead of planks, and instead of a hoard of gold and silver, only loose earth lay beneath.

Nevertheless, they were far from being discouraged. The presence of the timbering proved that *something* must be buried in the old shaft, they argued, and again they went to work. Two days later, ten feet below the first layer of boards, the boys came to a second platform of wood. Once more, with fast-beating hearts, they pried the planks free, and once again found only barren soil below.

They had vowed to keep at it, however, until they

reached the treasure or the bottom of the old hole—a pledge impossible for them to fulfill, as they eventually discovered—and more encouraged than depressed by the presence of the second bulkhead, they continued to dig. But when at last, at a depth of thirty feet from the surface, the weary youths found a third oak platform with nothing but earth beneath it, they gave up in despair. Not

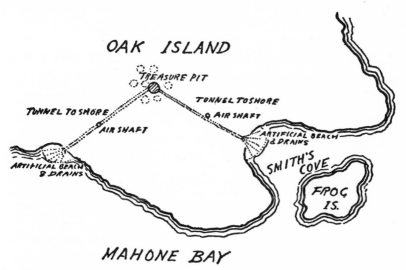

SKETCH PLAN OF OAK ISLAND SHOWING TREASURE PIT, TUNNELS, ETC.

because they had lost faith in their treasure—the very fact that whoever had hidden it had buried it so deeply and had protected it so carefully, convinced the boys that the hoard was a vast one—but because it was impossible for them to go deeper without tackles, winches, buckets and men to help them.

They hated to divulge their secret; but as they now felt convinced that the treasure was great enough to make a dozen men rich, they decided to tell of their discovery and to share their find with whoever would join them in excavating the old shaft. But when they told their tale they found that the villagers were not at all enthusiastic over the hidden hoard. In fact their elders did all they could to discourage the boys. They related hair-raising stories of ghostly apparitions, uncanny lights and mysterious sounds that for years had been seen and heard on Oak Island. They declared that the place was well known to be haunted; that for that reason it was uninhabited, and that no man would consent to set foot on the place, much less touch pick or shovel to earth in search of treasure. So, until 1803, no one visited the spot where the youths had made their strange discovery, and gradually the three almost forgot their treasure search. Then, one day, a certain Dr. Lynd arrived from Truro. Rumors of the boys' discovery of a decade earlier had reached him, and being a romantic and adventurous soul, he decided to have a talk with the three youths. Eagerly, now that the subject was revived, they related every detail, and accompanied him on a trip to the scene of their fruitless efforts.

Dr. Lynd was as firmly convinced of the existence of the treasure as the boys had been, and, hurrying back to Truro, he organized a company and raised abundant capital. Then, with laborers and equipment, he returned to Oak Island and established a camp. Soon the dirt began to fly in earnest. Rapidly the brawny diggers opened up the ancient shaft, and regularly at depths ten feet apart, they found stout bulkheads which required immense labor to remove. Many were of oak, others of spruce; one consisted of some kind of fiber covered with charcoal; another was of putty and sail cloth, while one was of some

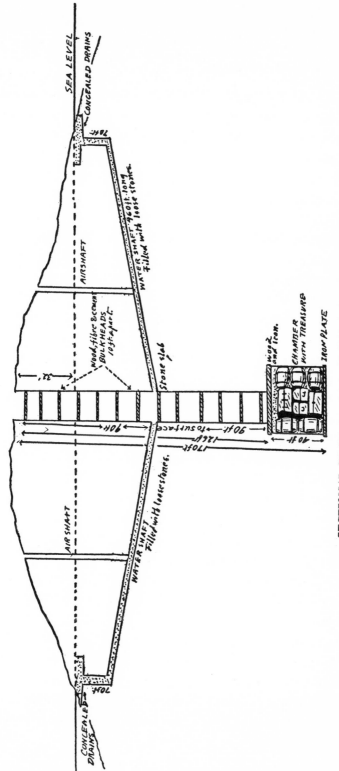

SECTIONAL PLAN OF OAK ISLAND MONEY PIT

cement-like material. And then, at ninety feet below the surface, the laborers came to a flat slab of stone three feet in length by sixteen inches in width, with an inscription in some strange characters cut in one surface.

Most unfortunately, no one with sufficient knowledge was called upon to decipher the lettering which—if correctly read—might have solved this greatest of all treasure-mysteries. But the men were interested only in securing the treasure, which all felt must be immense, and when, after lifting the stone, only earth was found under it, the slab was cast carelessly aside. Smith, one of the trio who had originally discovered the place, took possession of the stone as a souvenir, and built it into his fireplace as a hearthstone. Later it was removed and taken to Halifax where it was used by a bookbinder to beat leather on, with the result that the incised inscription was completely obliterated.

Having gone so deeply, Dr. Lynd did not intend to abandon his search unless positive that there was nothing of value buried there. So he sounded with an iron rod and, at a depth of five feet, struck something solid. Filled with high hopes that the treasure was at last within reach, the men retired fully expecting to lift the riches from their hiding place the next day.

Imagine their feelings of dismay when, upon reaching the excavation the following morning, they found it filled with water to within twenty-five feet of the top!

Every effort to bail out the pit failed, and at last, convinced that the task was hopeless, the first shaft was abandoned and a second started nearby, the idea being that the water in the first pit could be drained into the second by means of a tunnel. Of course, as one may deduce by this, the men lacked all knowledge of engineering. Had they been familiar with even the most elementary laws of physics they would have known that their plan could only result in both pits being filled to the same level —which was precisely what happened. So, once more, the treasure hunt was abandoned. The company's funds were exhausted, no more money could be raised, and the hoard remained as mysterious and as safe as in the beginning.

Twenty, thirty, forty years passed. Smith and McGinnis had grown to manhood, had become old and gray, and finally had gone the way of all flesh. But Vaughan and Dr. Lynd still lived, and to wondering grandchildren they told of their youthful search for the treasure of Oak Island.

By 1849 the story had become merely a tradition or legend; and then, to every one's surprise, another company was formed and once again the vicinity of the "Money Pit," as it was called, hummed with activity. Pumps and methods which, forty years earlier, had been unknown, began emptying the shaft of water until it was clear to a depth of eighty-six feet. And then, just as everybody concerned saw success in sight, the flood came back with a rush and for a time put an end to all work.

The new treasure seekers, however, were men who possessed common sense even if they were not engineers. The most important matter, they reasoned, was to discover whether or not there actually was a treasure in the pit before wasting more time and money digging for it. So drills were rigged up, and they proceeded to bore for the cache as they would for a vein of coal or other minerals. A strong platform was built above the shaft and

(95)

a huge auger-drill placed upon it. Rapidly the drill dropped until it struck the spruce bulkhead which Dr. Lynd had found at a depth of ninety-five feet. Quickly it bored through this, and dropped abruptly for a foot. Then once more it began to bore its way downward, bringing up shavings of oak, until it had penetrated four inches. Then it slowed down, and for a distance of twenty-two inches it moved through loose pieces of metal, bringing up three links of a gold chain.

One may easily visualize the wild excitement that followed this discovery. Here at last was irrefutable proof that treasure was buried in the shaft. Here was actual gold, even if no great value; and where there was *some* gold there must be more. And, so every one reasoned, the loose metal through which they had bored for nearly two feet must be gold or silver coins or jewelry.

Meanwhile the auger was boring its way through oak eight inches thick; then it once more went churning slowly through loose metal for twenty-two inches. More coins, it was obvious, and just as obviously the four-inch layers of oak were parts of oaken chests in which the treasure was contained. Every one was convinced of this most reasonable and logical deduction, and when at last the drill penetrated six inches of spruce and then entered a bed of clay to a depth of seven feet, all concerned felt that at last the bottom of the shaft had been reached.

Moving the drill to one side, a second boring was made. As before, it dug through the spruce platform ninety-five feet down, then dropped eighteen inches and moved with jerky, irregular motions as if working against the side of a barrel or cask, and brought up splinters from staves and some wads of what appeared to be coconut fiber matting.

This continued for six feet when the clay bed was again encountered. Quite plainly there were casks as well as chests in the mysterious shaft.

But, so far as getting at the treasure was concerned, the seekers were as badly off as before, for ninety-odd feet of water separated them from the hoard at the bottom of the pit.

However, the fact that beyond any reasonable doubt the treasure was there, was so encouraging that it was decided to resume work the following summer when a third shaft was dug to the west of the original shaft. But this also became filled with salt water which rose and fell with the tide. The discovery rather pleased the workers than otherwise. If, they reasoned, the seepage was natural, then the men who originally buried the treasure would have been faced with an impossible task, and as it was certain they had accomplished their purpose, it was obvious that the flooding was not natural. In other words, the pirates or whoever the shaft-makers were, must have arranged some sort of a drain or tunnel leading from the sea to the pit designed for the express purpose of flooding the treasure and so protecting it. And although it seemed preposterous that any one should have conceived and carried out such a scheme, it was no more preposterous than that any one should have buried a treasure over one hundred feet below the surface and safeguarded by oak, spruce, cement and putty bulkheads placed at ten foot intervals throughout the entire length of the shaft.

Careful search was made along the island's shores, and, at a spot not far from where the boys had found the ring-bolt, a discovery was made. Here, concealed beneath artificially arranged rocks, was a thick layer of what was thought to be coconut fiber, and beneath this was a bed of small stones not at all like those scattered about the beach. When these rocks were removed the men were astonished to find a series of drains of carefully cut and laid stonework so designed as to lead into a large stone-lined conduit or tunnel.

Of course the proper thing to have done would have been to sink a coffer-dam some distance inland from the shore and so cut off the conduit, or even to have filled the tunnel with stone and cement. But these treasure hunters were almost as lacking in engineering skill as their predecessors of forty years before, and they decided to build a dam *outside* the drains. Possibly this might have served its purpose; but before it could be completed a storm and high tide destroyed the partially finished structure.

Still undismayed, the treasure seekers began to sink a new shaft with the idea of cutting into the conduit and, by letting this pit fill, prevent the water from entering the treasure shaft. But one disaster after another befell. Shafts caved in or were flooded, and finally the men decided to gamble all on one final effort and spent the last of their funds in purchasing a powerful engine-driven pump. But even with this going full tilt the water came in faster than pumped out, just as might have been expected, for the entire Atlantic Ocean was behind the drain. So once more all work on the money pit was abandoned.

Years passed, the shafts sunk by the seekers of decades gone by had gradually become filled with earth and débris; grass, weeds and small trees covered the mounds of excavated material; and only fragments of timbers and rust-covered scraps of metal marked the wasted work of the many who had vainly endeavored to wrest the mysterious treasure from its cache. All those who had taken an active part in former undertakings had died, but there were records in existence, and many persons were living who recalled the past operations and who still owned shares in the defunct Money Pit companies. Moreover, some of these people had not lost interest in the supposed treasure, and eventually a new syndicate was formed, and having acquired all known outstanding interests, the new company resumed work in 1896.

Again the island took on the aspect of a mining camp. Once more the elusive treasure was being sought; and this time all concerned were confident of ultimate success, for there was no lack of funds, and all the latest devices were to be employed. Only one thing was lacking, the one item that always had been overlooked, and yet the most important item of all—a competent, trained engineer.

This time nearly twenty shafts were sunk in a circle about the original pit, and a network of tunnels driven between them, the idea being to locate the underground inlet from the sea and also to drain the old shaft.

Then, after months of labor and the expenditure of thousands of dollars, with no headway having been made, a brilliant idea occurred to some one. Whoever had tunneled for over five hundred feet from the shore to the pit must have had a vertical shaft to admit air and to afford an entrance and exit to the tunnel. All that was necessary to locate the tunnel was to find the vertical shaft! Why hadn't some one thought of this before?

But when, after a search, the shaft was found, it was discovered that it had long since caved in and had become filled with débris. Next, experiments were made to determine positively if the drains on the shore actually admitted water to the money pit. Distinctively colored clays and paints were thrown into the water at the beach and, shortly afterwards, the water in the pit showed the same colors. Then some brilliant genius conceived the idea of blowing up the drain with dynamite, thus allowing the earth and broken stone to choke the conduit. But as might have been expected, this merely made matters worse, and thereafter the water flowed in faster than before. Finally, to cap the climax of their misfortune, the searchers made the astonishing discovery that there was a second subterranean conduit leading from the other side of the island!

By this time the syndicate's funds were exhausted and the ghostly guardians of the mysterious money pit must have chortled with unholy glee as they saw the latest party of discouraged and bankrupt treasure hunters depart. Of course the shareholders in this venture were bitterly chagrined, but there was some compensation, for more had been learned about the hoard and the pit than had ever previously been known. Ever since they had started work they had been making borings which had revealed some most amazing facts. At a depth of one hundred and twenty-six feet the drill had penetrated oak —chips of which were brought up—afterwards striking metal on which it made no impression. A smaller drill was then started to one side and at one hundred and thirty-three feet it cut through a layer of cement covering oak timbers, penetrated a chest, passed through more than three feet of loose metal, and brought up two small objects. One was a gold ring and the other a fragment of parchment bearing portions of written words, only a single syllable of which, a "VI" or a "WI" could be deciphered. These, and the other borings, had proved conclusively that there was a rectangular chamber at the bottom of the shaft, a chamber formed of oak timbers coated with cement and which measured fully forty feet from ceiling to floor, and that within this immense strong box were at least seven chests and several casks filled with loose metal.

Beyond any question whatsoever there really was a vast treasure at the bottom of the money pit. Yet during the hundred and thirty-six years that had passed since the youths first discovered the oak tree and the rotten tackle, despite the many attempts and the expenditure of over one hundred thousand dollars, the only gold ever recovered consisted of three small links of a chain, and a ring—which one of the workmen stole.

But so confident were those engaged in the last venture that the treasure could be recovered, so convincing the evidence of the treasure being there, that several other efforts were made to lift the hoard, but with no more success than before. Then, only two years ago, a really serious and, in some ways practical, attempt was launched. By timbering and boarding the shaft, divided into four sections, and meanwhile keeping down the water by powerful electrically-driven pumps, the searchers worked steadily downward until the depth where the treasure should have been was reached. But there was no sign of the subterranean strong-room, no signs of treasure, although ancient lanterns, abandoned tools and implements were found. Feeling that in all probability they had sunk their shaft to one side of the original pit, the men in charge decided to drive a side tunnel at the level of the treasure as determined by the drills of their predecessors. But again the jinx that seems to guard all hidden treasures interfered with their plans. The tunnel caved in, some of the workmen were killed, and with funds exhausted and winter coming on the searchers abandoned their attempts.

But by now the mysterious treasure of Oak Island had become more or less known to the world at large. Accounts of it had been published in books and magazines, and a syndicate of wealthy New York men was formed to make a thorough investigation with a trained and competent engineer in charge. Throughout the summer drillings, surveys and explorations were made, and the results not only confirmed the existence of the treasure but added more than ever to its mystery. And the boring, which brought up traces of gold and silver, solved the puzzle of why the last searchers had missed finding the underground cache and its contents. During the many years of digging, of flooding and of boring, the bed clay at the bottom of the original shaft had been puddled and softened, and the treasure had gradually settled to nearly twenty feet below its original level. Had the treasure hunters of two years ago gone but a few feet deeper they would in all probability be wealthy men today, and the mystery of the Oak Island treasure would have been solved. But even more amazing than any discovery yet made was the fact that the oak trees on the island were not a natural growth, but were set out in regular order, and, most astonishing of all, there were live oaks there. In no other spot north of Virginia do live oaks exist. So still another mystery is added to the many mysteries of the treasure pit. Who could have planted live oaks in that spot? Who would have imagined that they would grow and would survive the northern winters? But, after all, these puzzles are no more baffling, no more unanswerable than the mystery of who could have buried the treasure on the island. Who could have possessed the ability, the engineering skill, the man power and the time to have devised and carried out such an elaborate, complete, ingenious and efficacious means of safeguarding their buried treasure? Who could have dug a shaft for a depth of over one hundred and fifty feet and connected it with the sea by tunnels over five hundred feet in length? Who could have conceived the idea of those concealed drains? and who could have gone to such prodigious labor as to place more than a dozen layers of planks, timbers, and cement across the shaft at ten-foot intervals?

Countless theories have been advanced as to who buried the treasure and carried out such elaborate and perfectly devised feats of engineering. Even though a few pirates did frequent the vicinity of Oak Island in the early part of the eighteenth century, what pirate ever possessed the knowledge, the ability or the genius to have constructed such a cache for his loot? Not one. And hence we may with practical certainty dismiss the idea that the Oak Island treasure is the loot of pirates. For that matter the pirate theory would have been abandoned long ago had it not been for the fiber found which was hastily identified as coconut husk fiber, a product of tropical lands and thereby associated with the buccaneers and pirates of the Caribbean and the Spanish Main. But samples of the material recently submitted to botanical and fiber experts prove that it is NOT coconut fiber, but some coarse sedge or sea growth which might have come from the marshes of Nova Scotia, the mainland or Europe.

In addition to the pirate theory advanced to account for this most mysterious of treasures, many wild and far-fetched suggestions have been made as to its possible origin. It has even been linked with the Cocos Island treasure filched from Lima, Peru. But those who sponsored this theory overlooked the fact that the Oak Island money pit was known and had been worked on for years before the Lima treasure was taken to sea. Others have claimed that the Oak Island treasure was a Viking hoard, but there is no evidence, not even legendary traditions, that the Vikings, who undoubtedly visited and formed settlements on the coast of Maine, ever possessed any treasures worth hiding. Certainly they could not have amassed a fortune in precious metals during their explorations of the New England coast, and equally certainly there were no settlements, no ships for them to rob at the time of their visit. Moreover, there is obvious evidence that the treasure had not been hidden for very long before the three youths made their discovery, for the trees that had sprouted on the cleared space were mere saplings, the lopped-off branch of the oak had not grown any to speak of, and the fragment of chain and the old tackle-block would have vanished completely in a comparatively short time. In all probability not more than half a century had passed between the time when the treasure was concealed and that autumn day in 1795 when Smith, McGinnis and Vaughan made their discovery. But no one has ever been able to suggest a theory that will fit all the known conditions and facts and will form a reasonable solution to the mystery.

But the truth may yet be known and very soon. The search for the Oak Island treasure has not been abandoned. Even now a company is being formed to make another attempt to lift it, and this time there will be no blunders, no short-sighted, half-way measures. A steel caisson will be sunk, and whatever is at the bottom of the money pit will be recovered.

At any time, even before this volume is published, the mystery of the world's most mysterious treasure may be solved. If so, will the oaken chests and casks be filled with ancient plate and works of art; will they contain the loot of Incans and Aztecs, or will they be found to contain the minted gold and silver coins, the jewelry and trinkets filched—from heaven alone knows where—by some freebooter whose very existence has been forgotten?

ⅼⅼ

The World's Most Sought-
For Treasure

OF all the lost, hidden, sunken and secreted treasures, real or fabulous, probably the most famous—and assuredly the most familiar to the public and the most sought for, is the treasure of Cocos Island. Hardly a year passes—I might almost say a month—without news of another Cocos Island treasure hunt. Yet not one single piece of eight, not a single centavo of the Cocos Island treasure has ever been found by the countless seekers after the island's hidden hoards. No, I must qualify that statement, for the first searchers for the treasure actually found it—as I shall explain later, but the discovery brought death to all but one man, and the sole survivor was glad enough to escape with his life with never a dollar of treasure as his reward.

Although always referred to as the Cocos Island treasure, yet in reality there are at least three distinct treasures concealed on the little Pacific Ocean island; three immense treasures whose aggregate value is beyond all computation, quite aside from the archæological and historical value of the hidden objects which would be many, many times the bullion value of the treasures.

Isolated, uninhabited, out of the track of all vessels,

with no safe harbor or shelter, Cocos Island presented an ideal spot for hiding treasure. In the days when the buccaneers cruised the Pacific and sacked and burned the Spanish towns along the western coast of South and Central America, the freebooters frequently put in at Cocos for fresh water and for a supply of coconuts. For their purposes the island was a "delectable spot," as Lionel Wafer, the buccaneer surgeon-author, called it. "The middle of the island is a steep hill surrounded with a plain declining to the sea," he wrote. "This plain is set thickly with coconut trees; but what contributes greatly to the pleasures of the place is that a great many springs of clear, sweet water, rising to the top of the hills, are there gathered as in a deep basin or pond, and the water having no channel, it overflows the verge of the basin in several spots and runs trickling down in pleasant streams. In some places of its overflowing, the rocky hillside, being perpendicular and overhanging the plain beneath, the water so pours down in a cataract as to leave dry a spot beneath the spout. . . . We did not spare the coconuts. One day some of our men, minded to make merry, went ashore and cut down many of the trees from which they garnered the nuts and drew about twenty gallons of milk. Then they drank the healths of the King and the Queen and drank an excessive quantity. Yet did not end in drunkenness, but so benumbed their nerves that they neither could move nor stand nor could they return on board the ship without help, nor did they completely recover under four or five days' time."

At the time when the meticulous Wafer wrote of the "delectable" features of Cocos Island, and the remarkable effects of imbibing vast quantities of coconut milk, he was surgeon on board of the *Bachelor's Delight* under command of Captain Edward Davis, the famous "extraordinaruly stout" buccaneer, as the chronicler called him. Although less known to posterity and fame than Sharpe, Morgan, Swan, Hawkins and many another buccaneer chieftain, yet the freebooters themselves regarded Davis as the greatest of them all, and he was chosen by them as the leader and commander-in-chief of all Buccaneers in the Pacific. But long before this he had made a name for himself in the Caribbean, and had won notoriety for his strict but fair discipline, his lack of cruel savagery and his humane character, coupled with an almost uncanny knowledge of seamanship and amazing luck at taking rich prizes. Then, in 1683, he decided to try his luck farther afield, and with seventy men, among whom were Wafer, Dampier and Cook, he set sail from the Chesapeake Bay bound on a round-the-world buccaneering cruise. But his ship, the *Revenge,* proved a slow craft, and having captured a swift Danish ship he transferred his men and loot, his equipment and guns to her, scuttled the *Revenge,* and rechristened his new vessel *The Bachelor's Delight.* Rounding Cape Horn the buccaneers sailed along the west coast of South America, sacking the Spanish towns, taking Spanish treasure ships and bringing terror to the inhabitants, until with his ship fairly groaning with accumulated loot, he put into Cocos Island.

Realizing that to continue his piratical cruise with so much treasure in his hold would be risking the loss of riches as well as ship, and being insatiable in his desire for more, Davis decided that he could scarcely find a better spot in which to temporarily cache his treasure.

Having attended to this matter, he careened and cleaned

the vessel and set sail in search of further prizes. Davis, however, had a flair for visiting out-of-the-way spots and doing a bit of exploring as a side line, and putting in at the Island of Plate, he and his shipmates devoted an entire day to dangling tallowed leads over the ship's side angling for the tons of silver coins which Sir Francis Drake had jettisoned when he had found his *Golden Hind* laden with more treasure than she could safely carry. But to men who were accustomed to counting loot by hundreds of thousands of pieces of eight, fishing for stray silver at the bottom of the sea was tame sport, and, having pulled up a thousand or more silver coins, they wearied of the game and again set sail. But again Davis's desire to investigate and explore got the better of him and he had a try at salvaging the treasure galleon, with some ten million dollars' worth of minted silver aboard, which had been wrecked off the Ecuadorean coast many years before. In this he was not successful, but while at the scene he met buccaneer Swan in the *Cygnet,* and the two joining forces, they attacked Guayaquil and took four ships in the harbor. Then off they sailed to Panama, picking up a few stray prizes en route. At Panama they were met by a fleet of buccaneer ships with a total complement of nearly one thousand men, and Davis was unanimously elected admiral of the fleet. For months the buccaneers had a merry time of it, taking ships, sacking towns, making raids on the cities, plantations and mines inland, and accumulating a vast, incalculable fortune in loot, all, or most of which at least, was added to the store already concealed on Cocos Island.

No doubt Davis, as well as others of the buccaneers, filled their private coffers and their sea chests with the

(109)

most valuable and easily transported objects of gold and with precious gems, for Davis, who vanished from the realms of buccaneering, next turned up as a wealthy merchant in the Orient, having received the King's full pardon for his piratical exploits. While he was in the East it happened that Captain Kidd arrived in his *Adventure Galley,* and Davis wishing to return to America, the worthy Kidd took him as passenger for a worthwhile consideration. Without any event of importance occurring, the ex-leader of the buccaneers of the Pacific was set ashore, together with a huge chest presumably containing his fortune, on our Atlantic coast. There he drops out of the picture, having settled down to an easy life ashore and never, as far as records show, having returned to Cocos Island to disinter his buried treasures.

It was more than a century after Captain Davis hid his loot on Cocos and Wafer penned his description of the "delectable spot," that the second treasure was concealed there. At this time the Spanish colonies of South America were in the throes of rebellion. Bolívar, San Martin and Sucre were in the field. Venezuela, Colombia and other countries had been freed from the yoke of Spain, and the liberating army was advancing on Peru. Of all the South and Central American colonies of Spain, Peru was the richest, the most important. For centuries it had been the seat of the colonial government of New Spain. All the coins in use in Spanish America—as well as much of the currency of Spain—were minted in Lima. The mines of Peru and Bolivia (then a portion of Peru) sent a steady, apparently inexhaustible stream of gold and silver flowing into the treasury of the Peruvian viceroys, and Lima, the City of the Kings, was famed as the richest city in the entire world. Its churches were filled with golden and silver holy vessels, gem-studded robes of saints, jewel-encrusted chalices and monstrances, altars and pulpits covered with beaten gold, and in one of the hundred and more churches in the Peruvian capital the supporting columns to the roof were wound with wreaths of golden and silver flowers and leaves adorned with precious stones. Almost as rich as the churches were the hidalgos, the merchants, the mine owners, the planters and the government officials. Many of the citizens were multi-millionaires. It was not unusual for kitchen utensils to be of solid silver, and solid gold table services caused no comment. And in those days a man's wealth was in good solid bullion or currency and not in bonds, stocks, paper or other so-called "securities," which we have learned to our sorrow are far from being secure.

But the Peruvians felt secure enough. Although Callao, their seaport, had in times past fallen to the buccaneers, although Lima had heard the dare devilish British freebooters thundering at the city gates, and had paid heavily in tribute to be rid of them, yet with the completion of the great Rey Felípe fortress at Callao there was small fear of a repetition of piratical attacks or of invasion by a foreign foe, while the massive walls and ponderous gates surrounding the capital were well-nigh impregnable.

But when news came of the amazing victories of the liberators in other Spanish colonies, the inhabitants of Lima became most uneasy and disturbed. The obscure, unknown countryman named Bolívar appeared to possess some occult or supernatural power. With a mere handful of ragged, barefooted or sandaled peasants, poorly armed and equipped, he had defeated the best of Spanish troops, he had taken town after town, fortress after fortress and now, so rumor had it, he was marching southward upon Peru. Moreover, from a mere mob of half-starved peons and farmers his "army" had grown into a large force of thoroughly seasoned, well drilled and splendidly armed men. And when word reached Lima that Colombia and Ecuador had been freed, and that Bolívar with his army of liberation was already over the boundary of Peru, and that Lord Dundonald, having joined the cause of freedom, was sailing northward from Chile with a fleet of war vessels, the people became mad with terror.

In vain the Viceroy and the generals strove to calm the citizens and the priests. They had scant faith in the efficiency of the easy-going, luxury-loving officers and their indolent garrisons.

And even if the rebels found Lima too hard a nut to crack and were defeated and driven off, there would most assuredly be desperate fighting; the fever of freedom would be infectious and would arouse internal rebellion, and there would be death and fire and ruin with looting and destruction. Moreover, with nearly fifty million dollars worth of treasure to be had for the taking in Lima, it was certain that the patriots would make every effort, would exert themselves to the utmost to take the town, for their funds were low and the millions within the Lima mint, the millions in private fortunes and the additional millions in the churches would go far to aid the patriots' cause and place the newly formed republics on a firm financial footing.

There was only one thing to be done to safeguard the treasures, public and private. The Rey Felípe citadel was the most powerful, the most impregnable fortification in

THE LIMA CATHEDRAL. THE TREASURES OF THIS ANCIENT CHURCH
WERE HIDDEN ON COCOS ISLAND

all South America, and within its walls the treasures would be fairly safe. Steadily from dawn until dark, from night until morn, for day after day, plodding burros, sweating porters, pack mules and horses, ox carts and drays plied back and forth over the dusty road between Lima and Callao, transporting the millions in gold, silver and gems from the capital to Rey Felípe. Never in the history of the New World had a greater treasure been gathered together at one place at one time. Every peso's worth placed within the fortress was duly registered and receipts given the owners, and these, still preserved, prove that over thirty-five million dollars' worth of valuables were lodged in the citadel at that momentous period in 1820. And aside from this vast treasure, placed under official lock and key, there were more millions concealed and buried in the fortress by owners who did not even trust the security of vaults and massive walls. Still others, among them the priests, were so filled with dread that they dared not let their riches remain on Peruvian soil, but chartering any ships which happened to be available, they loaded their treasures on board and set sail for parts unknown. Some of these treasure-laden ships arrived safely at their destinations with cargoes intact. Some were never heard from and no doubt foundered at sea or fell to pirates, but among them there was one whose history is well known and whose cargo of riches went to swell the hidden treasures of Cocos Island.

This ship, which was of British registry and was named the *Mary Dear,* was a small merchant brig in command of Captain Thomson, and within her hold was placed the greatest of all the Lima treasures—the precious contents of the Lima Cathedral, the richest church in all America and probably the richest in the world at that time. Never before or since has a pot-bellied little trading brig held such a cargo as filled the 'tween decks of Captain Thomson's ship. Gem-studded golden crucifixes, bejeweled vestments, silver and golden candelabra, chalices worth a fortune each, shrines of gold ablaze with precious stones, rosaries of emeralds and pearls, clerical furniture covered with gold and silver; and bulky chests of minted coin filled the *Mary Dear* to full capacity.

There is a well-known axiom that every man has his price, and while there may be exceptions to prove the rule, few ordinary mortals can successfully withstand the temptation of incalculable riches when placed conveniently within one's reach. No doubt, under all normal conditions, the captain of the brig was a most honest and exemplary skipper as skippers go. He might drive a hard bargain, being of Scotch blood; he might knock his surly, cutthroat seamen about in order to maintain discipline aboard ship, he no doubt hated the Catholics as the devil hates Holy Water, and unquestionably he was not averse to earning many an honest penny by smuggling. But as far as known he had never developed any criminal characteristics until he sailed away from Peru in his ship loaded to her hatches with treasure.

Twelve million dollars in tangible precious metal and precious stones is enough to tempt many a man more godly and more law-abiding than an impecunious merchant skipper, and Captain Thomson succumbed to the temptation. And once the devil had got the worthy skipper in his clutches he saw to it that Captain Thomson became a worthy disciple.

Without the slightest compunction the skipper murdered the Spanish priests and the custodians of the treasure, together with a number of passengers, callously tossed their still warm bodies to the sharks, and thereby was transformed into an out-and-out pirate.

Being a practical and hard-headed fellow he realized that he could scarcely expect to sail boldly into any port and discharge twelve millions in treasure and claim it as his own without most embarrassing questions being asked. For that matter, even to attempt to exchange golden and jeweled church property for coin of the realm would excite suspicion. In other words he was a multi-millionaire unable to profit by his blood-stained wealth. Very probably, had he foreseen this condition of affairs before he committed his crimes, the second and greatest of Cocos Island treasures would never have been hidden on the sea-girt spot. But as it was, Captain Thomson decided that the only course to follow was to cache his loot until circumstances permitted him to cash in on it, and recalling the loneliness and the other advantages of Cocos Island, he squared away and reaching the "delectable" bit of land buried his twelve millions so safely that it remains there yet. Then, as he was obliged to earn a living and to find the wherewithal to pay his men, as he could no longer afford to trade along the coast of Peru, and as he was already a pirate, he decided to cast honest dealings to the winds, and joined as scoundrelly and bloodstained a fiend as ever walked a ship's deck, an infamous Spanish pirate named Benito Benito.

Between them they accumulated a vast amount of loot, and at Captain Thomson's suggestion this was added to the store at Cocos Island and formed the third great treasure which lies buried there.

(115)

But by the year of our Lord, 1821, the law-abiding, honest, sea-going folk had become heartily tired of being killed and robbed by pirates, and the British and American governments decided that strenuous measures should be taken to wipe these gentry from the seas. Thus it came about that the notorious Benito and his ship were captured by the British frigate *Espiegle*. Then, for the first time in his ill-spent life, Benito did the right thing and blew out his brains rather than be taken prisoner and hanged, which was the fitting fate of his crew.

But Benito's partner in piracy escaped. Finding life on the high seas was becoming far too dangerous to his liking, he managed to elude the armed vessels of the United States and Great Britain, and reaching England, settled down under an assumed name.

A quarter of a century had passed since Benito Benito had pistoled himself and Captain Thomson had abandoned the sea, when the former skipper of the *Mary Dear* decided to take a trip to Newfoundland. On the voyage out he became friendly with a Newfoundlander named Keating, and at the latter's invitation took up his residence in the home of his shipboard's acquaintance where the two lived like brothers. For several years Captain Thomson kept the secret of his identity, but at last he revealed the fact that he had been a pirate, that he had served with Benito Benito and that he had a secret which would make them both millionaires. Nowadays, of course, should a friend of several years' standing suddenly announce that he had been a blood-steeped pirate and had millions in treasure cached on a lonely isle, he would either be laughed at as a romancer of the first water or would be clapped into an insane asylum. But at the time when Captain Thomson divulged his past to his friend, piracy and pirates were almost current events, there were plenty of retired freebooters living ostensibly respectable lives ashore under assumed names, and Keating, who had noticed an "air of mystery" about his guest, was scarcely surprised at the latter's disclosures, and listened with interest to his proposition.

Keating, he suggested, should secure a staunch ship with a competent captain and crew; together they would sail to the Pacific, and there the ex-pirate would guide them to the hiding places of enough riches to "buy all of Newfoundland" and leave them wealthy in addition.

As there was little to be risked and much to be gained in the venture, Keating at once agreed and enlisted the services of a friend to supply the vessel and equipment, and induced another friend, a Captain Bogue, to take command. But before the ship was ready to sail Thomson died. This, however, did not interfere with the plans of the treasure seekers, for he had prepared a chart of Cocos Island on which he had indicated the cache of the Lima treasure with explicit directions for finding it.

In due course of time, and without adventure, the ship arrived at Cocos Island and Keating and Captain Bogue, armed with a map, went ashore.

Everything tallied perfectly, and with little trouble the two located the cavern in which Thomson and Benito had concealed their treasures. And as they gazed upon the vast store of precious things they were speechless with amazement. They had been assured that there were immense riches in the cache, but never for a moment had they even dreamed of seeing millions in gold, silver and jewels dazzling their eyes. And now that the treasure was actually within sight and reach it suddenly dawned upon them that they were in much the same dilemma as Captain Thomson had experienced after he had taken possession of the treasure entrusted to his ship. To let the crew of their ship suspect the presence of the treasure would be dangerous in the extreme. They were rough, unprincipled, ignorant seamen, and the sight of gold would in all probability lead to open mutiny and murder. Yet they could not get away with any considerable quantity of the treasure without the crew knowing of it.

Finally they decided to return to the ship and say nothing of their discovery, and to think up some plan for getting away with a portion of the immense treasure. But their manner or their suppressed excitement betrayed them. The men sensed that the treasure had been located and at once became mutinous and unruly, declaring that their officers intended to cheat them of their share in the treasure, and threatening to maroon or kill Keating and Bogue unless they showed them the hoard of riches. It was useless for the two men to plead or argue. The men were inflamed with the thought of treasure, and at last the mate and most of the crew went ashore leaving the captain and Keating under guard aboard ship. But without the chart the hunt was hopeless, and angrier and more dangerous than ever the fellows returned and forced Keating and Bogue to agree to lead them to the cache the following morning. Both the men were convinced that their death warrants were sealed if they remained on the ship. If they showed the crew the treasure the rascals would unquestionably do away with them, and if they failed they would equally surely be killed. So that night they stole away in the whale boat, rowed silently to the shore and helped themselves to all the valuables they could carry. Then, as they pulled away through the surf, the boat was capsized by a huge wave. The captain, his pockets filled with gold and silver, sank like a stone too heavily weighted down to swim; but Keating managed to save his life. He had knotted his coat to form a rude sort of sack to hold his treasure and had placed only a few coins in his trousers pockets. By gripping the overturned boat with one hand he succeeded in emptying his pockets of their burden, and drawing himself upon the bottom of the whale boat clung to it as it drifted out to sea. Two days later a Spanish vessel sighted the capsized boat and rescued Keating who was landed in Costa Rica. Although only half-clad and without a dollar to his name, the ship-wrecked treasure-seeker worked his way across the country and shipped on a trading vessel bound for the States, whence he found his way back to Newfoundland.

Although he was the first and only man actually to have seen the Lima treasure since the day Captain Thomson concealed it in the cave, yet his harrowing experience had completely cured him of treasure seeking for twenty years to come. Then, having heard Keating's oft repeated tale, Nicholas Fitzgerald induced him to take part in another expedition to Cocos. But like Captain Thomson, Keating died before the vessel sailed and left the precious chart to his wife. And as she and the promoters of the search could not agree on the shares of the treasure, if found, the expedition was abandoned. Not until 1894 was another attempt made to wrest the Cocos Island treasure from its hiding place. And this time the expedition, in charge of a Captain Hackett in the ship *Aurora*, was a complete failure. The vessel was buffeted by tempestuous weather, provisions gave out, the crew mutinied, and long before Cocos Island was sighted the ill-starred voyage was abandoned and the expedition returned to Newfoundland.

Since then, innumerable attempts have been made to salvage the treasures hidden on the little Pacific island. Men of all nationalities and in all walks of life have gone treasure hunting to Cocos. There have been practical, hard headed business men, bankers and brokers, rich men and poor men, college students and amateur yachtsmen, sailors and soldiers. Even Sir Malcolm Campbell, the famous racing car driver, has had a try at it, but equally without success.

From time to time there have been rumors that the treasure, or one of the treasures, had been found; but each time it has proved a false alarm. Not long ago a newspaper published a long story of some man who purchased a book on mathematics in a second-hand bookshop in London and discovered, hidden under the lining to the back cover, a map purporting to be that of the hiding place of the Lima treasure and signed by Captain Thomson. But, unfortunately, the person who claimed to have found the map was unfamiliar with the customs of mariners and the illiteracy of the pirate-merchant skipper, for his alleged signature was spelled "Thompson" and NOT Thomson, as it appears on old documents still preserved, and read "Captain of the *Mary Dear*" which immediately branded the map as a fake, for no seafaring man would sign a document as "Captain of the *Mary Dear*" but would write: "Master." Moreover, Captain Thomson was shy on spelling. It was a difficult and painstaking matter for him to write at all, and he invariably spelled the name of his brig *"Mary Dere."*

Equally unauthentic charts supposed to reveal the hiding place of the Cocos Island treasures have bobbed up from time to time, and persons ignorant of the true facts have been fired with the desire to wrest the millions from their caches and have set off for Cocos, only to return sadder and wiser men. In all the long years that have passed since Davis visited "the delectable spot" and Benito Benito and his partner, Captain Thomson, ravished the Pacific, the only treasure that has been found, and kept by the finder, was a Spanish doubloon of 1788 which was picked up by a German named Geissler who dwelt like a hermit upon Cocos Island for over thirty years and constantly searched for the hidden treasures.

It is not at all surprising that all efforts to recover the vast treasures of the island have been failures. There is no question that the vast accumulations of gold, silver and gems are still there, but Mother Nature has hidden them far more effectively and securely than did buccaneers or pirates. Some years after Keating and Bogue gazed upon the treasures in the secret cave, there was a great landslide on the island. A huge section of the "rocky side of the hill, being perpendicular and hanging over the plain beneath," broke away and buried the treasure cavern and the treasures under thousands of tons of bowlders, earth, fallen trees and débris. There it is likely to remain forever unless some one solves the problem of successfully landing a fleet of powerful steam shovels on the surf-beaten shore and methodically digs away the mountain side. And even then, it would be time and money wasted, unless the excavators were in possession of the original map which guided Keating and Captain Bogue to the spot where the Lima treasure was cached.

ֺֺֺֺֺֺֺֺֺֺֺֺֺֺֺֺֺֺֺֺֺֺֺֺֺֺֺֺֺֺֺֺֺֺֺֺֺֺֺ

CHAPTER IX

Salvaging the Spanish Galleon

THROUGH the crystalline waters of the tropics I have looked down upon the remains of a stately Spanish galleon that, laden with treasures, was driven by a hurricane upon the coral reefs three centuries and more ago. In diving suit and helmet I have picked my way among masses of giant corals, exploring the ancient wreck, prying cannon balls and weapons from the marine growth, salvaging utensils and fittings from their centuries-old resting-place, scraping the encrustation from the huge clumsy cannon, breaking up lumps of coral in search of doubloons and pieces of eight. And from the bed of the West Indian seas I have seen the fittings and the contents of the three-hundred-year-old wreck come dripping over the rail of my boat as the divers wrenched them from their resting places and we hauled them upward from the ocean's depths. It is fascinating, thrilling, a strange experience to move about the bottom of the sea where the water is as clear as glass and at a depth of forty feet the sunlight streams downward and illuminates the bottom and the reefs as if under a floodlight. Marvelous are the colors of the living corals— orange, yellow, crimson, mauve, brown, green, scarlet, black and fawn; and endless in their variety of forms. Some are dome-shaped, others like giant mushrooms, some form great flat shelves, others with innumerable branches form veritable jungles; still others are like gnarled forest trees, and everywhere among them are the waving purple and black sea-plumes, the orange, golden or mauve sea-fans, the gaudy sea anemones and the multi-colored growths of bryozoans. In precipices and over-hanging cliffs that tower far above one's helmet, great mysterious blue cañons and caverns open before one. And even more brilliantly colored, more striking than the corals are the fishes. Dazzling blue parrot fish, gaudy graceful angel fish of blue, yellow, orange, black and zebra-striped; butterfly and four-eyed fish, marbled groupers, and scarlet snappers and vermilion squirrel fish, cruel-jawed barracudas and great, gray, baleful-eyed sharks swim lazily about, paying no heed to the strange misshapen being invading their domains.

Probably no human eyes had ever looked upon this sunken galleon since the day she went to the bottom of the sea. No man had ever before gazed downward upon the centuries-old hulk amid the reefs. No human being had seen her since that far distant day when, in the fury of a West Indian hurricane, the plate ships of Spain were hurled to destruction upon the jagged coral fangs, and never a man of the hundreds on board lived to tell the tale of the greatest catastrophe that ever befell the merchant marine of Spain.

It was in the summer of 1637 that the fleet of plate ships—the treasure-laden galleons from Panama, Vera Cruz, Margarita, Colombia, Venezuela and other rich ports of the Spanish Main, gathered in the harbor of

Puerta Plata on the northern coast of Hispaniola. Fifteen treasure ships, carrying a cargo of gold and silver bullion, specie and precious stones, pearls and plate, golden and silver objects from ancient Incan graves and tombs—-a cargo valued at nearly seventy million dollars, formed the fleet; and convoyed by two frigates heavily armed, the flotilla set sail for Spain. Two days after leaving Puerta Plata the fleet was struck by a hurricane and the fifteen galleons and one frigate were driven upon the Silver Shoals, nearly one hundred miles from any land, and went to the bottom with all on board. But one frigate escaped, and crippled and half-wrecked, limped into port and reported the catastrophe. As was customary in those days the admiral in command was court-martialed, and although exonerated of all blame, the proceedings of the court, which are still preserved, give us the facts of the tragedy and the names of the lost ships and a list of the valuables in their holds and strong rooms. Fifty years after the treasure fleet was lost, stout, bluff, old Captain William Phipps located one of the lost plate ships and from it, fished up nearly four hundred thousand pounds worth of gold and silver. Phipps, who numbered the King of England and members of the nobility among his partners, was knighted and appointed Governor of the Massachusetts Colony for his success, and never returned to wrest the "greater parte" of the treasure from the lost galleons. Neither did he, as far as any one knows, leave a chart of the treasure wreck's exact position so that others might profit thereby. But in a single "fly" published at the time of Phipps' triumphant return to England, he gave a very good account of his discovery, while his journal or log records the daily results of his treasure fishing.

(124)

But with no exact position of the wreck recorded, and with no accurate chart with the wreck noted thereon, it seemed a rather hopeless proposition to attempt to locate the wreck or wrecks after three hundred years. And when, two years ago, I was asked if I thought it would be possible to find one of the galleons, I was very doubtful.

Still, treasure hunting at its best is a gamble, and in this case the stakes were high, and with what meager information I could secure the expedition set sail. From Phipps' notes, with both contemporary and modern charts, and here and there in Sir William's journal a chance remark, I had plotted the latitude and longitude where I assumed Phipps had anchored three centuries earlier, and had worked out the position or rather the assumed position of the wreck; little enough to go on to be sure.

In due course of time we arrived at the shoals and cast anchor at the spot I had selected as Phipps' anchorage, or as near it as possible. It was a dangerous place, with threatening green patches of reef showing through the azure water on every side. But it was a calm day, the lapis-lazuli sea lay with scarcely a ripple under a cloudless sky, and only the upflung breakers of the ground swell on the "boilers" broke the line of the horizon.

Never will I forget the sensation we all felt as we approached the first of these coral-heads. Just awash, with the long ocean swell sweeping over them and then receding, leaving the sharp, talon-like corals exposed, they seemed endowed with some malignant purpose—terrible, sinister monsters reaching out hungry hands to grasp our craft and drag the small boat to destruction. Even the most sea-hardened of our men, old sailors that they were, confessed to such a feeling of terror, and all of us actually shuddered with dread each time a surge sucked our boats toward the jagged masses. Very lonely and at the mercy of the sea we felt, too, with our little hundred-foot ship looking very small and insignificant in that vast waste of waters, and we realized fully that should anything happen to the vessel we were all as good as doomed.

So transparent was the water that the bottom at eight or ten fathoms appeared within reach of one's outstretched hand, and with every detail standing out sharply and clearly. Yet the objects upon that floor of the reef-filled ocean were amazingly deceptive. There were great fingers of coral which were the exact counterparts of the timbers and ribs of sunken ships. There were strange sea-growths that looked like kegs and chests, and again and again we felt certain we had located a wreck only to find when we went down in the "hats" (diving helmets) that our "wrecks" were merely natural formations. But we had searched for scarcely an hour when we spotted an anchor. Almost coincidently another of the men found two more anchors, and the next moment a great cannon was seen. Excitement ran high. Here was indisputable evidence that we were above a wrecked ship, and the type of the anchors and gun left no doubt as to the vessel's age. With straining eyes we searched the sea floor for further wreckage, but nothing of the sunken ship's structure was visible. Quickly the air pump was manned, and donning their suits, the divers dropped down. Intently we watched. And then came a surprise. From our boat the two smaller anchors had appeared no larger than ordinary kedge-anchors; but when a diver grasped one and raised it upright the shank extended for more than two feet above his head! It took all our tackle and herculean labor to salvage the smallest of the three; the largest was more than twelve feet in length.

Though they had rested under the sea for nearly three centuries, yet the massive, hand-forged anchors that once had served to moor a treasure galleon of Spain were in a remarkable state of preservation. Beneath the two-inch incrustation of lime the iron was still sound, and a little chipping and cleaning would have rendered them fit for service again.

Next, we attempted to raise the cannon in hopes that it might bear the name of the ship on whose decks it once had been mounted. But the great gun with its ornate breech and oddly-placed trunnions proved too much for our tackle and when within a few feet of the surface it broke away and plunged back to its resting place. So we left the ancient weapon to the fishes and devoted our efforts to tracing the outlines of the wreck and locating its strong room. This was a most difficult task. Nowhere was there a timber of the ship visible. Through the centuries, the detritus from the surrounding reef had completely buried the wreck in fine fragments of broken coral which had become so firmly cemented together by the lime that the wreck was covered with a concrete-like armor nearly two feet in thickness. And such objects as had been upon the galleon's decks or protruded from the cement-like surface, were coated with white lime and appeared like mere irregularities on the ocean's bed or like lumps of coral. Only by striking every object with a crowbar or hammer was it possible to determine which were natural growths and which were portions of the ship.

Inch by inch the divers examined the ocean's floor, and presently up came a bundle of bent and twisted iron work

—hatch bands and chain-plates, toggles and rings, and finally the massive iron sling that had held the "Jimmy Green" or water-sail yard beneath the galleon's bowsprit.

Obviously we had reached the bow of the wreck, and now the divers worked in the opposite direction. From amid a mass of broken coral they salvaged a swivel-gun crutch of steel almost as perfect as on the day it was forged in some smithy in old Spain. In another spot they came upon some irregular black lumps which we at first mistook for iron, but which proved to be cannon powder still capable of burning with a strong sulphurous odor when dried.

However, the forepeak of a galleon is no place to search for treasure, and little by little the divers worked aft—or in the direction I assumed was aft. For a time they found nothing. Then, thirty feet back of the anchors and gun, they came upon more wreckage—chain-plates and standing rigging, iron plates and mast-bands, which convinced me that we were working where once had been the galley and the carpenter's shack abaft the mainmast. Here was a real mine of antiquities, and at each descent the divers salvaged new and surprising objects. There were massive lumps which looked like meteorites, but which, when broken apart, proved to be the remains of kegs of nails. Not a nail remained, but each hand-forged nail had left a perfect mould in the mass of iron oxide and lime which had formed about them. Other material was found which had every appearance of graphite. It could be whittled with a knife, it could be used like a pencil-lead, and I puzzled over it for hours, until I at last discovered it once had been cast iron! Imagine whittling cast iron with a pocket knife!

Here, too, hidden under the limestone crust, was an iron kettle. To one side the divers found a crudely-made, hand-forged, five-pronged grapnel which no doubt had

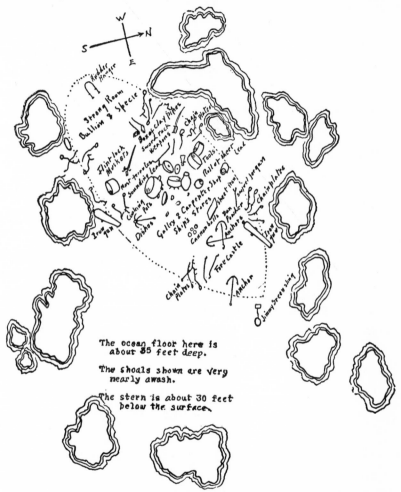

The ocean floor here is about 55 feet deep.

The shoals shown are very nearly awash.

The stern is about 30 feet below the surface.

SKETCH MAP OF THE SUNKEN GALLEON, SHOWING LOCATION OF REEFS, AND OBJECTS SALVAGED

once been in the galleon's longboat. Every moment was filled with intense interest and excitement as we stared downward through our glass-bottomed water buckets, for

(129)

no one could know what the divers might unearth next. And at any instant we might haul up a diver's stout canvas bag filled with gold or silver bars or masses of ancient coins.

And here let me digress to remark that pieces of eight and doubloons and golden onzas buried under the tropical sea for three hundred years are not the bright and shining disks described in fanciful tales of treasure-trove and pictured by imaginative artists. Instead, they were shapeless lumps that no one would recognize as coins, that might easily be mistaken for masses of dead coral. Through the centuries the coins have become firmly cemented together by oxides and lime which, covering the metal, has retained more or less perfectly the form of bags or chests in which they were once contained. And only by their greater weight and by breaking the lumps in pieces with a heavy hammer can one distinguish the ancient coins from coral formations.

Working about the spot where the ship's galley had once stood, the divers salvaged many a strange and totally unexpected object. There were pewter plates, bearing the arms of Spain, on which the coarse fare of the ship's crew had once been served. Three grindstones were found, worn and out of shape from sharpening many a knife and sword and halberd. There were articles and utensils of iron and copper whose original purposes still remain a mystery. There were broken plates and bowls, and wine jars, with blue and yellow designs still clear upon the crackled glaze. There were fragments of the galleon's rails and gun carriages with the wood still well-preserved. We found a pike head as bright as silver (for unwittingly the old Dons used rustless steel forged from iron ore containing chromium) still bearing the gold damascening upon its surface. There were the remains of a tool chest still containing the handles of chisels and other tools, a hammer head, a caulking iron, a hatchet and an adze. We even found the galleon's sounding lead—a rudely-hammered lump of metal weighing about ten pounds, its smaller end perforated by two holes instead of one as modern sounding leads are. More remarkable yet, we secured a portion of the ship's bilge pump, and to our utter amazement found the leather and tow packing of the piston in perfect condition!

From the vanished galley we salvaged the long-dead cook's scouring or Bath brick, and when one of the divers' bar struck metal, and there was a dull gleam of yellow amid the broken crust, every one was on the *qui vive*. But the find proved to be an astonishing, immense copper kettle with huge bronze legs and a long copper spout. Obviously it was an extemporized cooking utensil, for it was built up of sheets of copper of varying thickness riveted together, and with the crudely-cast bronze legs riveted in place. But it was not the workmanship of the thing which drew our interest; it was the fact that there was scarcely a trace of verdigris upon the metal which showed a dull, purplish-black patina, and that it was enormously heavy. Had the legs been of solid gold they could scarcely have weighed more. But the puzzle was eventually solved. The thing was made from copper, probably from Peru, smelted from ores that were rich in silver and gold. Little did the long dead cook dream, as he sweated over the galleon's galley fires, that he was boiling the crew's soup in a kettle containing more gold than he could earn by years of toil. The old pot was a find in

(131)

another way, too. The portion that had been hidden under the crust of lime was filled with loose sand. Obviously, we reasoned from this, the concrete-like coating was merely a floor above sand which buried the wreck, and in this loose material we would find her timbers and her treasure intact.

There were amusing incidents, also. Once a diver brought up some strips of bright shiny metal and remarked that he guessed they were remains of old sardine tins. But if the Dons had used *that* metal for sardine containers—well, the empty tins would be worth more than their weight in gold today! For the strips our diver had found were platinum! Of all the various metals we found, only the platinum had retained its pristine color and brightness. But to the old Spaniards platinum was not a precious metal. They regarded it as almost worthless— "false silver," they called it; too soft for most purposes and of value only for making the cheapest, most ordinary utensils. In all probability the platinum strips on the wrecked galleon had been used for repairing pots and pans!

Slowly the divers worked beyond the site of galley and carpenter's shack. Another great gun was discovered lodged in a jungle of stag-horn coral. Twisted portions of iron work of the mizzen rigging were found, and at last they came upon the massive wrought-iron hangers that had supported the ship's huge rudder. The stern of the galleon had been reached! Beneath the divers' feet, under the corals and the limestone crust, was the lazarette, the floor of the high stern-castle and the galleon's strong room. We felt certain of it, for by now we had fairly well established the wreck's outline and her position on the

SALVAGING A SUNKEN GALLEON

bottom. She was resting wedged between three reefs, her port side jammed against one, and in a sort of small cove or basin surrounded by five coral-heads. It was a dangerous spot in which to work, for in the event of a blow and heavy seas arising the diving boat, moored above the wreck, stood a good chance of being lost. And even in the smoothest weather the swell, surging over the reefs, created a rise and fall, a swinging of the boat that constantly chafed and cut the steel wire cables with which we moored her to the coral heads. But the weather was holding good, and feverishly the divers labored. We were working against time, for the hurricane season was near at hand; each night it blew a half-gale, and in the ever-increasing seas our ship—a converted submarine chaser—rolled horribly (she thought nothing of a 45-degree angle and often did fifty) and each time she rose to a sea the anchor chain, tangled amid the coral, snapped and crashed as if torn asunder. And if it had parted—well, it would have been just too bad for all on board, for on every side and astern the waves were breaking white on countless coral heads.

But dangers to the mother ship or the diving launch were forgotten for the time. Only a foot or two of limestone crust separated us from the treasures in the galleon's hold. We felt that luck had been with us from the start, that we had laid the jinx that seems ever to guard lost and sunken treasures. But we had counted our chickens too soon.

Despite their every effort the divers found it impossible to make adequate headway in getting through the crust. A man under water can exert very little power on a crowbar and cannot strike much of a blow with a sledge, and the crust was not only hard and tough but, in addition, at every blow struck the pulverized material would rise like white smoke, clouding the water and forcing the men to stop work until it had cleared away. A week of this work and we were all convinced that it would be hopeless to continue, that at the rate of progress being made it would be impossible to get into the wreck before the weather forced us to flee for our lives. Drills and dynamite would be required to blast a way into the galleon's hold and strongroom and, as we had neither, we reluctantly decided to abandon our treasure wreck until the following year.

But we had accomplished a great deal. Our forehold was filled with objects salvaged from the three-centuries-old galleon, and now we knew where the wreck was, it would be an easy matter to find it the next time, when with compressed air drills and pavement breakers, sand pumps and dynamite we would return to wrest the treasure from the old plate ship. Also, we had become almost convinced that the wreck we had found was the same which Sir William Phipps had salvaged in 1687. It seemed impossible that there could be two wrecks so similar in their position, their condition and appearance. In his description of the wreck he salvaged he says:

"Yet though we might most dyligenetely make search, naught might be seen of ye galyon save ye grate gunne and somme anklers (anchors), all about beinge whyte marle, until such time as ye dyvvers did discouvere that ye wrack was hydden by ye lyme thereon.

"Such pieces of eight and dollars and halve dollars as were fished were with difficultie counted upon our decks, beinge bound one unto another so that blows with a maule must be struck themme that they should break aparte.

"Ye wrack lyeth within ye compasse of two reefs, wedgette fast atwixt ye twain, with no manner of mastes, nay or stern castle nor poope remainynge, but sank to ye chayne-plates in ye sands and marle. And upon ye forecastle lyeth her grate gunne and anklers, the whych are alle that might be seen from above the sea.

"Notwithstandinge that ye dyvvers did wearie of dyvvinge to ten fathoms, yet they could not make entry unto ye bellie of ye wrack wherein muste lie ye greatest of ye treasure."

It would seem impossible that two of the wrecked galleons should have been so identical in position and in condition—a great gun and anchors on the forecastle the only objects visible from above, wedged between two reefs, covered with white limestone and buried to the rails in sand. Moreover, although we salvaged cannon balls which did *not* fit the large cannon, and also found a swivel-gun crutch, we could find no swivel guns, carronades or bronze cannon; but if our wreck was the same as Phipps' that is easily explained, for he states that he raised ALL the bronze guns on the wreck. To be sure, there were sixteen ships lost—fifteen galleons and a frigate—and Phipps found but one, as did we, and it would seem a remarkable coincidence that we both found the same wreck. But despite our most careful searching we could locate no others in the vicinity, and I came to the conclusion that in all probability most of the doomed ships either became wedged on the reefs, to be broken to bits in succeeding storms, or striking the coral, were carried over and sank in deep water where they can never be found.

But even if our wreck and Phipps' were one and the same, it did not affect our expectations of securing the treasure. Phipps' galleon was identified by the name on her bronze guns, and documents prove that she carried bullion and specie worth fully one million pounds. And as Phipps salvaged barely half that amount, and knew—as he recorded—that the greater treasure still remained in the "bellie" of the galleon, there was plenty left for us.

Neither had our first expedition been lacking in adventure, thrills and sport. Fish swarmed in the sea, and constantly, savage tiger and gray sharks swam slowly about the anchored ship. Whenever time hung heavily on our hands or weather did not permit us to work on the wreck, we amused ourselves by capturing the monsters. Often, as they swam close to the surface, we would shoot them with rifles; but as a rule we either harpooned them or caught them on a hook and line. And believe me, it is some sport with plenty of excitement to haul in a twelve or fourteen foot tiger shark. Yet despite the abundance of sharks, not to mention huge barracuda which are even more dangerous, they never molested the divers in their suits or even when we went down in the "hats" only. At first I assumed that they were frightened away by the rising air bubbles from the escape valves. But later I proved to my own satisfaction that it was the vibration of the motor-driven compressor that terrified them, for often, when sharks and barracuda were present, I have seen them dash madly away the moment the compressor was started and before a diver had entered the water. But the huge groupers that haunted the reefs had no fear of either divers or vibrations. In fact they were a great nuisance, for the moment a diver commenced to stir up the bottom, and uncover worms and other marine creatures, the great, clumsy-looking groupers would appear on the scene, gobbling up the exposed crustaceans and worms, and in their efforts to gorge themselves they would frequently dash between the divers' legs, or bump blindly into them, knocking the men off their feet. And despite blows aimed at them with crowbars, grains thrust into their sides, and being stabbed by the divers' sheath-knives, the groupers never seemed to take the hint that they were not welcome.

Our Second Voyage to the Silver Shoals

WE had learned much by our experience on our first expedition to salvage the ancient treasure galleon. Before we had set out, no one had had the least idea of what condition a wreck would be in after three centuries under the tropical sea, for no one had ever seen such a wreck. I had assumed that it might be more or less overgrown with coral, that few or none of the upper works would remain, that the iron work and fittings would have completely disappeared, and that the hull, during centuries of rotting and being eaten by worms, would be a fragmentary skeleton with ballast, cargo and treasure easily accessible.

Instead, we had found the wreck completely buried in sand and covered with limestone as hard as concrete. Nobody had foreseen such a condition, and hence we had not taken along the proper tools and equipment for salvaging the wreck. But in outfitting for the second attempt we knew just what *was* required, and compressed air-drills and pavement breakers, powerful grappling toggles, and an ample supply of dynamite and detonators were part of the equipment. Also, having learned the impossibility of working while the water was opaque with the powdered lime stirred up by digging through the crust, we added a sand-pump to the outfit. The very latest and best of diving suits, helmets and compressors were purchased, and as I had found the flat-bottomed skiff, which had been our small boat on the previous trip was not a desirable craft for knocking about reefs in the middle of the ocean, I designed and had built three dories of a special style, equipped with outboard motors, masts and sails, and with an open well in the center to enable us to use our water-glasses more conveniently than by leaning over the sides. And although these dories were small— the largest but sixteen feet in length—they proved the staunchest, most seaworthy of craft, and more than once one of them carried nine men through heavy seas from the mother-ship to the wreck and return in safety.

Only one item of the expedition was not what it should have been. That was the salvage ship. I had planned to use a powerful, fully-equipped wrecking steamer; but one of the men interested in the project owned a schooner yacht, some of the financiers were his intimate friends, and nothing would do but to use this vessel. She was wholly unsuited to the work, and had we been provided with a proper ship the results might—in fact certainly would—have been far different and stark tragedy might have been averted.

From the very beginning bad luck seemed to surround the schooner like an aura. She was to sail from New York in March, but the coldest weather ever known swept over New York and freezing rivers and harbor sealed our vessel immovably in the ice where she remained for two weeks. When she finally got clear she was so badly cut and injured by the ice that we were compelled to haul her out and repair her planking in Nassau, with another fortnight's delay. She was supposed to make eight or nine knots under power, but the best she could do was less than six; she was a slow, clumsy sailer, and although a wonderfully buoyant and staunch sea-boat her decks leaked like sieves and each time it rained or when a sea broke over her everything below was treated to a shower-bath. Moreover, she was overcrowded, for instead of the nine men aboard as planned, the owner-captain added three of his friends to the list.

But at last we set sail from Nassau and before a forty-five mile gale, and the heaviest sea in the memory of the oldest local inhabitant, we made the run to Great Inagua in record time. Here we picked up the diving launch and compressor which had been shipped by steamer, and headed for Puerto Plata to obtain fuel and provisions. On our previous expedition we had several times made the run from this port to the anchorage on the shoals without the least trouble, the captain picking up his mooring buoy dead under his bow on the dot. But our amateur yachtsman-owner-captain, who had represented himself as a skilled navigator, as well as his mate, made a sad mess of it. When at last we sighted the coral-heads and reefs we were more than twenty miles to the south of the wreck, and as it was late in the afternoon, there was nothing to do but anchor, for to navigate among the coral at night was unthinkable. Near our anchorage were two large reefs, and suggesting to my chief diver that there might be other wrecks in the vicinity, we launched a dory and made for the reef. Within a few minutes we discovered an immense anchor and several cannon, and all were highly elated and excited at thought of having located a second treasure ship.

Down we went to find ourselves surrounded by wreckage. Everywhere, scattered among the giant coral growths, half-hidden under waving sea-plumes and huge multicolored sea-anemones were cannon, masses of twisted iron work, fragments of huge timbers, massive anchors and hundreds of cannon balls. Also, scattered about among the broken corals and the marine growths, were lumps and masses of white limestone which, when struck by a hammer or bar, revealed many a surprising and unexpected object. Ancient muskets with the flints still in place in the hammers and with the barrels intact although the wooden stocks had long since rotted away, pistols and cutlasses, spike-headed boarding axes, hammers and adzes, a huge iron caulking tool, a heavy spear-shaped boarding pike were pried from their coral beds. We found a dozen blue willow ware plates still neatly stacked, although slightly awry, just as they had been placed in the galley of the wrecked vessel. We salvaged mixing bowls of brown and yellow earthenware, cut glass bowls—badly broken, old-fashioned blown glass bottles, tools and cutlery, several grindstones, and finally the old ship's sounding lead. We had felt confident that we had stumbled upon another sunken galleon with treasure somewhere near, but with the discovery of the sounding lead our hopes were scattered.

Compared to the sounding lead we had found on the old galleon the previous year this was modern. It was well made, octagonal and obviously of comparatively recent date. But the muskets and pistols were flint locks, the cannon and anchors were certainly over one hundred

(141)

years old, and the crockery and glassware proved that the wrecked vessel had lain under the sea for a century or more. Also, it was obvious that she had been no peaceful merchantman but a heavily armed vessel—perhaps a warship, possibly a pirate or a privateer, for scattered about, overgrown with coral, half-buried in the sand and limestone, we found twenty-one guns!

Moreover, it was evident that we did not discover all the cannon that once had grinned from the wrecked ship's ports, for among the countless cast iron cannon balls were many which could never have fitted the bores of any of the guns we found. Also, it was soon evident that to search for any treasures she may have carried was a hopeless task, for the doomed ship had been beaten to pieces against the reef and her remains were scattered over an area fully three hundred feet in length and half as many in width, while everywhere masses of staghorn coral, great brain and mushroom corals and miniature reefs had grown among the wreckage, covering many of the relics under several feet of flinty-hard limestone. But it was great fun searching about, never knowing what one might find next, chipping the encrustations from our finds. And when, on several of the salvaged tools and weapons, we found the Broad Arrow stamped in the metal we knew that the long lost ship was British, while a check up of the articles we had recovered convinced me that she was either a sloop-of-war or a privateer during the War of 1812.

Possibly a more thorough search of the old wreck might reveal a gun or even the ship's bell bearing her name, and thus a mystery of the sea might be solved. But we were after wrecked Spanish galleons, not sunken British war vessels, and hoisting anchor we headed northward towards the spot where we had worked on the previous expedition. But again the amateur navigators erred, and we found ourselves several miles too far north. Eventually, however, we reached a spot where the formation of the reef appeared familiar, and anchored. Launching the dories we headed for the maze of reefs, and within half an hour I once more looked down upon the anchors and cannon of the ancient wreck.

It was a fairly calm and a pleasant afternoon, and fearing we might not have a better opportunity if we waited, we loaded the compressor and the diving gear into the launch, ran her to the position above the wreck, and moored her securely with new steel cables to the coral heads. By the time this was done it was too late to attempt to go down and we returned to the schooner with high hopes of blasting our way into the galleon's strong room the following day.

But that night a terrific gale swept across the shoals. It lashed the sea into a fury, the rain came in a deluge, lightning flashed and thunder roared incessantly. And, believe me, it is no fun to be pitching and rolling in a seventy-five foot schooner in a tropical electrical storm with five hundred sticks of dynamite and as many detonators on board. And it was small consolation to know that if the dynamite *did* explode none of us would ever know it. But the danger of such a catastrophe was not our only worry. At each shuddering pitch of the vessel her anchor chain, snagged on the massive corals, would strain and scream and then, with a crash and jar, would tear free, and each time we expected the cable rather than the coral would part. Nothing on earth could have saved us if the cable *had* given way. On every side the seas were breaking heavily on the coral heads, and before we could have started the motor or got steerage way upon the schooner she would have been shattered on a reef.

But the chain held, the little ship rode out the storm, and toward morning the wind died down and the sea flattened out. And as day dawned and with our glasses we swept the line of reefs a mile distant there was not a sign of our launch visible. Our worst fears were borne out when we reached the spot where she had been moored. The heavy seas, breaking over the reefs, had filled her and there she was, lying on the bottom beside the wreck of the old galleon. All our equipment—our drills, hand-pump, compressor—were at the bottom of the sea. Still there was a chance that both launch and equipment might be salvaged. It would be a herculean, a terrific undertaking, but my chief diver was a herculean, a marvelous man in his profession. We still had the hand-pump, and slipping on his helmet, Dave went down. Presently he came up and reported that the launch appeared to be uninjured and that he believed it could be raised with compressor and equipment intact. Aboard the schooner were six empty oil drums, and by midday we had these over the wreck. Then, lashing timbers across two of the dories to form an extemporized platform from which to work, we prepared to raise our launch and outfit. Everything went smoothly. The drums were filled and sunk, the diver, laboring under most difficult conditions, lashed them securely on either side of the sunken launch, and air was forced into them. Slowly the launch rose toward the surface, the rails appeared above the water, every one felt elated at our success and then, without warning, one of the drums burst a seam, the launch, deprived of the buoyancy on one side, tipped half over, the lashing gave way and down it plunged to the bottom. All the terrific labor had been wasted. And, worse yet, the sinking craft had struck a jagged fang of coral and had torn a huge gaping hole in one side. To salvage the launch would be a waste of time. We realized that our chances of making any great headway on the galleon had been shattered. But there was still a chance to save the valuable power-driven compressor and diving gear. Then followed one of the most remarkable feats of diving ever known. Working with helmet alone, Dave labored for hour after hour beneath the sea, cutting the shaft and connections of the launch motor with a hack saw, unscrewing the six great lag-bolts from its bed, and freeing the big compressor from its fastenings. By using the oil drums as pontoons the machinery was floated, and lashed to the timbers between the dories it was towed through a bad choppy sea to the schooner. And then we came very near having a real tragedy added to our long list of mishaps. Just as the tackle from the schooner's masthead was made fast to the salvaged compressor, one of the oil drums filled, the extemporized raft careened, the timbers cracked ominously, and the dory nearest the schooner began to fill. Even then all might have been well had not one of the amateur sailors lost his head, and whipping out his sheath-knife, cut the lashing that secured the timbers to the dories. Instantly, the dories capsized and the next moment half a dozen men were floundering in the shark-infested sea amid a chaos of splintered, jagged timbers, bobbing oil drums, capsized boats, tangled ropes and lines, and with the suspended compressor rising and falling to

(145)

the roll of the schooner like a ton trip-hammer over their heads. Luckily the men were all expert swimmers. Diving and dodging, they escaped death or mutilation from splintered timbers and the compressor, the racket had frightened off the sharks, and in less time than it takes to tell it some had clambered on board and others had righted the dories and were bailing them out. In the dories had been the hand air-pump, the divers' hose and helmets and other gear vitally important to further diving. We had expected that all of this would have been forever lost— gone to the bottom in thirty fathoms. But when the swamped dories were finally brought alongside, we discovered to our amazement that by some miracle the precious hand-pump, and nearly all the diving gear, had caught under the thwarts and been saved. Only one shallow water helmet and a single length of air hose had been lost!

Handicapped though we were through the loss of our launch and the impossibility of using the power compressor, the pneumatic drill and the hand-pump, yet we were determined to try to salvage something of value from the galleon. Using the two dories with timbers and planks lashed across them for a diver's pontoon, we moored it over the wreck. Then for three days the divers worked like Trojans. Chipping and drilling holes with their crowbars and hand drills they fired several charges of dynamite. And when the cloud of white silt and pulverized coral had settled, down went the divers to see what the blasts had revealed. Rapidly we hauled up load after load of salvaged objects which had been torn loose from the limestone bed by the explosives.

Ancient fire arms and weapons—a bit of armor, broken

dishes, mauls and hammers, axes and halberds, hatchets and sword hilts, torn and twisted fragments of copper and brass, cannon balls and gun flints.

Then, as we gazed downward at the divers and saw one of them bending over a rectangular object with rounded top, excitement ran high, for the thing looked like nothing so much as a treasure chest. And when the diver ran his bar along it and a dull gleam of metal showed, we felt certain our luck had turned and a portion of the galleon's treasure would soon be ours. As we tailed it onto the tackle and the coral-crusted mass came slowly towards the surface, its weight confirmed our hopes, for certainly, we felt, nothing but a chest of gold could be so heavy for its size. Even when it was at last safe upon the platform and we gathered about we felt sure it was a treasure chest. But as we scraped away the white coating our hopes were again shattered. It was lead—four hundred pounds of sheet lead tightly rolled!

Another strange object brought up was a mass of petrified clay pipes. I say petrified, for that was what they were. Originally they had been packed in a metal box, but through centuries under the sea the lime in the water, and the oxide of the metal, had embedded the pipes in a solid rock-like mass from which it was impossible to separate them. There they were—small bowls set at an angle to the stems, rudely ornamented, hand-molded, forming a portion of the rocky formation itself, and looking at first glance like some unknown variety of fossil shells in their bed rock. Another interesting find was a portion of an arms-rack containing the remains of a dozen or more cutlasses. In some the hilts were still well preserved, in others the metal oxides and lime had rendered them as seemingly petrified as the pipes, but the wood of the hilts and of the rack was in perfect condition. Our blasting also disclosed another fact. We had thought the wreck to be resting on a nearly level keel; but we now discovered that she was almost on her beam ends, and in order to reach the lazarette or strong room it would be necessary to blast away practically all of the old hulk and her tons of ballast. Moreover, each time we fired a charge of dynamite immense quantities of pulverized coral and limestone would cloud the water, and settling down, would cover everything with a white blanket. It was impossible to distinguish one object from another under this white coating, and the least agitation—a diver walking about or poking here and there with his bar—would raise a milky cloud as impenetrable as a smoke-screen. Had we been able to use the sand-pump we could have removed this silt easily and rapidly, but without it we were helpless. As it was soon evident to all that to continue blasting under such conditions only made matters worse, and that even if we opened up the strong room we could not find the treasure beneath the silt, we finally gave up. And not any too soon, for when we reached Puerto Plata news of a hurricane had been posted. Luckily it veered, and the schooner reached the States in safety, yet tragedy followed in her wake. Within three weeks after she arrived her owner-captain hanged himself, and a few weeks later my chief diver—a man who had won fame by his unprecedented exploits in salvaging sunken American submarines and had come unscathed through dangers no others dared face—was killed while working in shallow water repairing a bridge abutment in the Cape Cod Ship Canal.

Once more the jinx who guards lost treasures had

triumphed. Only stout Sir William Phipps had been able to snap his fingers at the evil genius watching over the sunken plate ships, and, defying the jinx to do its worst, had sailed away with some of the vast treasures of the Silver Shoals. Yet such is the lure of treasure-trove that even now another expedition is being formed to attempt to secure some of the millions lying amid the hungry coral reefs. Perhaps they may be even more successful than Sir William, or again the attempt may end in a tragedy and the bones of the treasure seekers and the shattered timbers of their ship may be added to those of the long-lost galleons and the hundreds of Spaniards who went down with their ships on that hurricane-torn night three centuries ago.

ⵊⵊⵊ

Dredging the Treasure of
The GOLDEN HIND

THE name of Sir Francis Drake is familiar to every one, and every school child has read in histories of the famous British sea-fighter and his deeds, such as the destruction of the Invincible Armada, and how he insisted upon finishing a game of bowls as the Spanish fleet sailed up the Channel; how he harassed the Spaniards in the New World, and sailing through the Straits of Magellan explored and mapped the Pacific and the islands of the South Seas and was the first to enter the Golden Gate and explore the coasts of California. But comparatively few persons know of red-bearded Sir Francis Drake's exploits as a pirate, or are aware of the fact that "El Draco," as the Spaniards called him, accumulated an enormous amount of loot, such a vast amount in fact, that his famous *Golden Hind* could not carry it all in safety and Drake was forced to throw a good-sized fortune into the sea.

History holds few characters as fascinatingly adventurous, daring and romantic as Sir Francis Drake, and regardless of whether he was a privateer, as the British claimed, or a pirate as the Spaniards considered him, his exploits went far to break the power of Spain and to establish British Dominion in the New World. A marvelous seaman and navigator, as fiery and tempestuous by nature as his ruddy hair and beard would indicate, absolutely fearless, and a born fighter through and through, Drake and his men "synged ye bearde of ye Kynge of Spaine," with right good will and complete success, and in the doing of it proved himself as great a treasure gatherer as he was a fighter.

On the Isthmus of Panama he and his men held up a mule train of bullion, as well as the retinue of the Treasurer of Peru with all the family fortune and jewels, and secured thirty tons of silver, in addition to a large amount of gold and jewels. But, unfortunately for the British, the Spaniards rallied; a large force from Panama was dispatched to attack the raiders and recover the booty, and Drake and his men were compelled to beat a hasty retreat after hurriedly burying fully half of their loot, most of which was dug up by the Spaniards.

Even fifteen tons of silver, not counting a large quantity of gold and jewels, was quite a haul, amounting as it did in Drake's time to nearly half a million dollars, yet it was nothing compared to the treasures which Sir Francis took from the Spaniards a few years later.

Sailing from England with the avowed purpose of seeking a northwest passage around America, and mapping the Pacific islands and the coast of North America, Drake in the *Golden Hind* circumnavigated the world, and as a side line to his explorations made fame and fortune for himself and others by robbing the Dons of the greatest single treasure ever taken by any one ship, either privateer or pirate.

Sailing leisurely up the west coast of South America, Drake quite casually attacked and looted one Spanish town after another. It was really a simple matter, for the Spaniards never dreamed of "El Draco" being in the Pacific and were too amazed and terrified when he suddenly appeared off their shores to offer any great resistance.

The sack of Coquimbo yielded many tons of silver; several Spanish galleons were taken and their cargoes of precious metals were transferred to the hold of the *Golden Hind*, and Drake decided to have a try at Callao, the port of Lima, and the richest town in all Spanish America. It was a lucky day for Drake, for swinging at anchors in the harbor was a fleet of plate ships. No sooner did the Spaniards recognize the *Golden Hind* than they scrambled into their boats and pulled frantically for shore, leaving Sir Francis to help himself to the treasures in the deserted ships.

Picking and choosing while the terrified Dons looked on helplessly from the shore, El Draco transferred the rich cargoes of the vessels to the *Golden Hind;* and a worth-while booty it proved. There were tons of silver bars, hundreds of golden ingots, boxes of specie and chests of plate, gems and pearls, linens and velvets, silks, wines, and a vast store of powder and ball. By the time the entire treasure had been loaded onto the *Golden Hind* she was low in the water, but Drake was not yet satisfied. From a captured Spaniard he learned that the *Cacafuego*, carrying the most valuable of all the plate ships' cargoes, had sailed for Panama two days before his arrival, and hastily cutting the cables of the vessels he had robbed, and setting them adrift, he clapped on sail and started in chase of the treasure ship.

To any one but Drake that long stern chase would have seemed a hopeless undertaking; but Sir Francis knew no such word as fail, and day after day the heavily laden *Golden Hind* sped northward. And as from time to time small coasting craft were overhauled, and by threat of death or worse the British forced their skippers to give information of the *Cacafuego,* they knew that they were steadily gaining on her. At last one day, just as the sun rose over the crests of the distant Andean peaks, Sir Francis's brother, John, aloft at the masthead, sighted the Spanish ship and won El Draco's golden chain as a reward for having first sighted the *Cacafuego.*

At six o'clock that morning the two ships were within cannon range, and as the guns of the *Golden Hind* thundered the Spaniards' mizzenmast came crashing to the deck with all the tangled rigging.

Not a shot was fired in return, not the least resistance was offered by the Spaniards who, no doubt, felt that to sacrifice their lives to protect the King's riches was a tactless thing to do and would avail nothing in the end as Drake was certain to take the ship anyway. Moreover, the captain of the plate ship had never imagined danger near, his guns were lashed fast and not even loaded, and long before they could have been charged and manned the British would have swarmed aboard like fiends from hell and would have spared none.

Drake had expected to find the *Cacafuego* carrying a rich cargo; but even he was amazed to find what a stupendous treasure was within her hold and strong-room. There were tons of precious metals; eighty pounds

(153)

of gold dust, thirteen cases of royal plate, nearly forty tons of silver bullion, three hundred bars of silver and forty-four chests of vessels, Incan images and other objects of gold and silver, in addition to innumerable jewels, the whole amounting to the stupendous value of more than a million and a half dollars.

No doubt the Spaniards were sick at heart as they watched this enormous treasure being transferred from the crippled ship to the *Golden Hind*. But despite their chagrin and their hard luck the Spanish captain still possessed a keen sense of humor. When at length the transfer of the cargo had been completed, and Drake magnanimously released the Spanish crew and their officers and gave them permission to continue on their voyage, the navigator, Nuño de Silva, grinned. "Your Excellency," he remarked, addressing Sir Francis, "I see now that my ship was improperly named. Rather than the *Cacafuego* (Spitfire) she should have been christened the *Cacaplata* (Spit silver)."

Although by now the *Golden Hind* was so low in the water that the seas broke over her midships decks, yet Drake must needs have another fling at collecting treasure, and being conveniently near the town of Guatulco he paid a visit to the port, gathered in a few hundred pounds of currency and a goodly quantity of jewelry and golden ornaments from the citizens, and sailed away for the Island of Cano.

Here he landed his immense treasure, and careened, cleaned and refitted the *Golden Hind,* work which was badly needed before the vessel was in fit condition to proceed on her interrupted voyage around the world.

Perhaps Drake felt that this was as good an opportunity as any to divide the vast loot he had taken, or possibly the men insisted upon seeing their shares doled out and thus learning how rich they had become. At all events, Sir Francis apportioned the currency, using a wash bowl as a measure, and giving each member of his ship's company sixteen bowls-full of coins; and as he could not well hand over silver bars and golden ingots, or the tons of gold for the men to carry in their pockets or pack in their sea-chests, he made a list of all the loot, and duly credited each man with his proper share.

Probably no other ship ever sailed the seas with such a wealthy crew, for every man-jack aboard the *Golden Hind* possessed a fortune. In fact they were altogether too rich, the treasure aboard the ship being far too weighty a cargo for the vessel to carry safely on the long voyage ahead. A portion of it had to be left behind, and although it would have been a simple matter to have buried the excess booty upon the island, the men had become so drunk with riches that money meant nothing to them, and with a glorious disregard for treasure they hoisted forty-five tons of silver and plate from the hold and dumped it into the sea, bellowing with delight and shouting ribald oaths as they watched the shining metal gleam in the clear water as it sank to the bottom of the little bay.

Then off they sailed for home by the longest way around, arriving safely in England in September, 1580.

No doubt, within a few months, the sailors were as poor as ever and were thinking most regretfully of the tons of treasure lying on the bottom of the ocean at far-off Cano Island. But as far as they were concerned it might as well have been on the moon.

Even in those days a man could not throw away forty-five tons of precious metal without causing comment, and word of Drake's exploit was spread far and wide, until mariners on every sea had heard of it and Cano Island was rechristened the Island of Plate, as it has remained ever since.

But it was not until a century had passed that any one thought of trying to recover any of El Draco's jettisoned treasure. It happened that Captain Davis, in the *Bachelor's Delight,* was cruising in the vicinity, and it being Christmas Day, the famous buccaneer decided to celebrate the holiday by dropping in at the Island of Plate and letting his men skylark and enjoy themselves ashore, hunting the wild goats and gathering coconuts. But a heavy swell was running, the small boats could not land, and in lieu of shore leave the crew spent the day fishing for the submerged bullion by means of tallowed leads. Naturally this crude hit-or-miss method of salvaging treasure did not yield very large returns, but it must have been quite thrilling and exciting to drop a line over the ship's side and haul it in with a silver piece of eight or a golden doubloon sticking to the tallow on the lead. Altogether, some fifteen hundred coins were thus salvaged before the *Bachelor's Delight* hove up anchor and sailed away on more profitable business.

As far as known no one ever attempted to recover the fortune in bullion that still rested on the bottom of the sea during the three centuries that followed. Every treasure-seeking enthusiast was familiar with the presence of the treasure and its history, but somehow a mere forty-five tons of silver, worth considerably over half a million dollars even at the depreciated value of the metal, did not appeal as strongly to the imagination as sunken

treasure galleons or buried chests of gold. Yet the chances
in favor of recovering the Plate Island treasure were a
thousand times greater than the chances of finding buried
hoards or salvaging wrecked plate ships. In fact as a
salvaging job it was very simple. The exact spot where
Drake had jettisoned his superfluous riches was known.
It had been confirmed by Davis and his jolly buccaneers
who had fished up some of the coins. The water was comparatively shoal, and the bottom hard sand, and, as one
of my divers expressed it: "a guy could scoop it up with a
garden rake," once it was located.

Yet for some reason or another no treasure hunting
expedition sailed for the Island of Plate. Cocos Island, the
legendary treasures of Old Panama, long lost ships in the
Caribbean, mythical hoards in the Bahamas and elsewhere held their lure, and the jettisoned bullion of the
Golden Hind was passed by.

And then, when the world-wide depression sharpened
men's wits and caused them to rack their brains for means
of garnering every stray dollar, the owner of a rattletrap
little towboat thought of Drake's treasure reposing on the
bottom of the ocean, and only awaiting some one to fish
it up. He was an Englishman, but had lived long in
Spanish America and had made a fairly good living light-
ering and towing in various ports on the west coast of
South America. But his finances were at a low ebb, he
had no money available for the purchase of diving gear
and equipment, and he had no experience in salvaging.
But he was a resourceful chap, and with odds and ends
of junk and the aid of his engineer, a crude sort of
dredge was contrived and off he sailed for the Island of
Plate.

We can imagine with what suppressed excitement and expectation the owner and crew of the little towboat peered over the side as the winches wheezed and rattled and the dripping cable came reeling in and the clumsy makeshift dredge broke the surface of the water.

Swinging it inboard, the men dumped the load of sand, shells and writhing sea-worms upon the decks, and the next instant wild shouts, hurrahs and hysterical laughter startled the dozing sea birds on the island's shores. Embedded in the sand, blackened with age and salt water or green with verdigris, were scores, hundreds, of metal disks; roughly octagonal heavy slugs, irregularly round pieces-of-eight, with here and there a golden doubloon or onza, brown and discolored, but gleaming dull yellow when the patina of centuries was scraped away.

And as the excited men pawed over the mass of sand and muck from the bottom of the sea they disclosed more and more old coins, with an ingot or two of silver and a couple of wrought silver candlesticks.

Again and again the home-made dredge was dragged along the ocean's floor, and each time it brought up silver and bullion, coins and objects of precious metal, until eighteen tons of treasure had been salvaged.

Then, as the steam winch strained and panted and the sheaves squealed and the cable came protesting in, something went wrong. Perchance the dredge caught on one of the heavy silver bars which Sir Francis had cast overboard centuries earlier, perhaps it fouled a rock or a portion of some ancient forgotten wreck. At all events, the cable tautened and strained, the winch groaned and slowed down, and then, with a report like a pistol, the cable parted.

The glorious fishing was at an end. Without the dredge no more of the treasure could be salvaged, and, as all knew, by the time they could reach port and purchase a proper dredge and equipment and return to the island, the officials would have heard of their haul and would have a gunboat on hand to take possession of any further treasure that might be salvaged.

It was a bitter disappointment to be forced to steam away leaving over twenty-five tons of bullion still on the bottom of the sea. Yet no one complained, for after all it is seldom indeed that a towboat crew earns nearly two hundred thousand dollars for a few days' work!

ıı

Digging Treasures from
Ancient Graves

ALTHOUGH the conquering Spaniards secured enormous amounts of gold, silver and precious stones by looting the temples and palaces of the Aztecs, the Mayas, the Chibchas and the Incas, and obtained millions by their treacherous seizure and murder of Atahualpa, yet they actually walked over and erected buildings above far greater treasures than they won by fire and sword and unspeakable cruelties.

Rich as were the living inhabitants of Peru, to whom, however, gold had no intrinsic value, far greater riches had been interred with their dead through countless centuries. As is customary with many races, the Incas and their predecessors, the pre-Incan people, interred a person's most cherished possessions, his regalia and ornaments, his ceremonial objects and his insignia with his body, for they believed in a bodily resurrection and that when the dead rose from their graves they would desire all their earthly possessions. No one can say with any degree of certainty how many thousands of years have passed since the earliest of pre-Incan civilizations existed in Peru. But everywhere, throughout the Andes, on the high plateaus or "punas," in the trans-Andean valleys, on the coastal deserts and the foothills are countless tombs, burial mounds, graves and cemeteries containing incalculable millions in precious metals.

That Peru and the adjacent territories were densely inhabited in pre-Columbian days is proved by the vast numbers of burials of every period or era, and in many places there are layers or strata of graves thirty to fifty feet deep. There are pantheons covering hundreds of acres, large areas of deserts where tens of thousands of bodies were buried, and huge mounds, some several miles in length, over one hundred feet in height and several hundred yards in width which are composed entirely of little cubicles of adobe bricks, each containing a dried and desiccated body or mummy in its burial wrappings. Of course a very large proportion of these ancient mummies are those of the peasantry, the farmers, artisans, fisherfolk, laborers and porters who owned little or no objects of gold or silver, no valuable gems, and whose garments were coarse, plain and poor. But princes and priests, nobles and kings, governors and generals—even the Incans themselves, were mortal and died and were buried in the same cemeteries and mounds as the common people. And in the graves and tombs of these elect are marvelous objects wrought in gold and silver, with here and there a huge emerald, a blazing sapphire, a roughly-cut diamond or a string of priceless pearls.

No one can even guess at the extent of these ancient buried treasures. For hundreds of years the *huacas* * as

---

* In colloquial Spanish any object, such as pottery, vessels, weapons, ornaments, etc., other than textiles, gold and silver and human remains, is called a *HUACO*. Hence the graves or mounds are *HUACAS,* literally the Mothers of *huacos,* and men who dig for *huacos* are *Huaqueros.*

(161)

the graves and mounds are called, have been a source of revenue to the *huaqueros* or grave robbers, and millions of dollars' worth of treasures have been taken from them. Yet the *huaqueros* have made but little visible impression, and for every grave that has been rifled, hundreds remain untouched.

Unfortunately, the grave robbers work secretly and do not broadcast details of their "finds," for theirs is an illegal profession, and in the old days the Crown demanded a *quinta* or fifth of all valuables found; and as a result, priceless works of art and museum specimens have been destroyed or disposed of as bullion. As there are no records of how much treasure has been taken from the burial places in recent years it would be hopeless even to guess at the total value. But in the days of the Viceroys it was a different matter, and in the musty old records and documents we may find entries of the *quintas* paid to the Crown by the more honest *huaqueros*, and in this way we know what amazing fortunes have been obtained from some graves. Thus the one-time Treasurer of Trujillo, Don Miguel Feyjoo de Sosa, in his VERDAD HISTORIA DE TRUJILLO, records the amounts paid into the Royal Treasury as the King's *quinta* or fifth of treasures found in the burial places of Chan-Chan, the ancient ruined capital of the Chimu civilization. Don Miguel says: "In the Royal Account Books it is recorded that Garcia Gutierrez de Toledo, paid, as His Majesty's fifths, on various occasions during the year 1576, fifty-eight thousand five hundred and twenty-seven castellanos in gold from one Huaca not a league from the city close to the road that leads to Guanchaco (Salavery). And in the year 1592, he paid *Quintas* amounting to twenty-seven thousand and twenty castellanos in gold on various figures of fishes, animals, etc. that were taken from the same spot (now known as the Huaca de Toledo). And it is popularly reported, and common knowledge, that what was taken was much in excess of that for which the *quintas* were paid. In the year 1550, the Cacique of Maniciche, Don Antonio Chayuac, who had been baptized a Christian, and was a legitimate descendant of the Chimu king, told the Spaniards of a Huaca near the ruined palace called Regulo, on the condition they would give him a portion of any treasures found, in order that he might use it to alleviate the lot of the aborigines. The sum he received for the treasure was twenty-five thousand pesos, the whole amount being forty-two thousand one hundred and eighty-seven pesos."

As the gold castellano was equal to about five dollars in our currency, lucky Don Garcia must have found treasure amounting to at least $1,213,175 during the year 1576, and $675,550 in 1592, while the treasure disclosed by the heir to the Chimu throne netted the finders the goodly sum of $210,935. And, as the historian observed, we may be quite certain that the finders did *not* report all that they obtained. When we remember that the above records were for but three years out of centuries, and that only a small portion of the graves about Chan Chan have been excavated, we can obtain some idea of the vast treasures that the burial places in this one vicinity must contain. Ever since the Conquest there have been traditions of two vast treasures buried in the Chan Chan mounds; one known as the *Peje grande* or big fish, the other as the *Peje chico* or little fish, and as Señor Gutierrez hit upon

(163)

the latter we may imagine the stupendous value of the still undiscovered "big fish" treasure.

These and many other treasures buried in the deserts and the mountains of Peru were overlooked by the conquerors, which is fortunate for modern scientists and museums, for the present day *huaqueros* have learned that gold, silver and precious gems are not the only contents of the graves which have a market value. A very large portion of the wonderful pottery and textiles, the ceremonial objects and weapons, as well as the gold and silver ornaments and utensils in the great museums, or owned by private collectors, have been obtained from the *huaqueros*. In their search for treasure in the graves, these men annually excavate many hundreds of burials, often without finding a single mummy with anything of intrinsic value. But a large percentage have beautiful textiles, rare or lovely pottery, bronze or wooden weapons, feather ornaments, cloaks or head-dresses; tools and implements, or necklets and bracelets of shells, stone beads or carved mother-of-pearl, all of which are readily sold to the curio shops in Lima and to collectors and museums. But as bootlegging *huacos* is somewhat risky, even if a very remunerative business, many thousands of scientifically valuable specimens are cast aside and left to the mercy of the elements. At practically every mound and in every ancient cemetery in Peru one may see hundreds, thousands, of skulls and dismembered skeletons littering the earth, many with the desiccated skin and flesh still adhering to the bones, and with the hair still attached to the skulls, while everywhere are the fragments of textiles, the broken pottery, the sandals and garments, the mummy-wrappings, slings, pouches and other objects taken from the mummies and cast away by the *hua-queros* in their search for gold and silver. Even in and about Lima it is not unusual to see a modern residence with scattered skulls, scalps, mummy-wrappings and bones within a few feet of the front door, and in cultivating their gardens the residents are as likely to dig up skulls as stones. I doubt if there is another country on earth where the inhabitants dwell happily and contentedly in the midst of countless dead. But no one gives the matter a passing thought, and the people do not appear to regard bodies and bones of men and women a thousand or more years old in the same way as they would regard the cadavers of persons who have died and been buried recently.

Roughly, I should say that not one grave in a thousand contains any precious metal. When, a few years ago, the Avenida Progreso, which connects Lima with Callao, was built, it cut through an immense mound, and for months after the highway was completed the roadsides were littered with human skulls, human bones, mummy-wrappings, broken pottery, wooden implements and other artifacts ruthlessly torn from the tombs and dumped aside by the steam shovels. Fully a thousand of the tombs or cubicles, built of adobe bricks, were thus destroyed, yet in all the work and among all the ancient mummy bundles unearthed, only one or two small objects of gold and silver were found.

Even the most expert and experienced *huaquero,* or the most learned archæologist, is at a complete loss when it comes to knowing beforehand where a worth-while mummy is to be found. It is all a matter of chance or luck, for the graves of the nobility and the priests are

outwardly indistinguishable from those of the husbandmen and fisher-folk; but in certain areas and among certain cultural strata, richly adorned and valuable mummies
are more numerous than in others. Thus, in the Lima
Valley district, it is rare indeed to find a body with anything of value buried with it, whereas at Nasca, and more
particularly at Parakas, nearly every body is wrapped in
wonderful robes and cloaks of marvelous textiles and
feathers, and is surrounded with beautiful pottery and
often with numerous objects of precious metals. On San
Lorenzo Island, silver utensils, vessels and ornaments are
found in more than half of the graves, while richest of all
in gold objects are the graves of the Chimus and Chavins
in northern Peru.

Still it is all a gamble when it comes to digging treasures from these ancient graves. And because it is a gamble
it is fascinating, exciting work, even when one is searching for archæological treasures and gold and silver are of
secondary consideration. As an illustration of how much
of a gamble it is, take my own experiences in Panama. I
had discovered the remains of an unknown prehistoric
civilization and for over a year I had excavated the site
of the long-forgotten temple.

Dozens of graves had been opened, hundreds of sculptured stone altars and monuments and thousands of specimens of pottery had been secured, and over ten acres of
the area had been dug and examined foot by foot, yet
the only gold I had found was on the tips of a beauti-
fully-made nose-ring of bloodstone. Then, when the funds
for the work had been exhausted and the museum abandoned the site, another institution despatched an expedition to carry on excavations where I had left off. And

almost the first grave they opened—with many more thereafter, was literally filled with golden objects! Never, probabľy, in the whole history of archæological excavations in America, have such rich burials been found. There were golden breast-plates, arm-bands, leg-guards, shields, helmets and images; beads and ornaments of gold, carved bones covered with gold; gold wrought into endless forms and designs. The spot was a veritable treasure house, and I had missed it by a few hundred feet! Had I continued with my work for another week I would have found those wonderful graves so replete with golden objects. But such is luck, Fate or whatever you choose to call it. Neither should I complain, for on another occasion Lady Luck played into my hands in much the same manner.

For nearly five years I had been digging and delving in the prehistoric ruins and cities of Peru that were old before the first Pharaoh was born. I had mined mummies in the desert sands, had burrowed deeply into burial mounds and had opened the strange bottle-shaped graves on rock-strewn *punas*. I had been more fortunate than most. I had secured feather robes and head-dresses from long dead Moujik chieftains, truly marvelous ceramics from the mummy-bundles of the Nascan graves, wonderful portrait jars from the cell-like niches of the Chimu burial mounds; copper, bronze and silver ornaments, with here and there a bit of gold—in fact nearly every object known to or used by the Incan and pre-Incan races.

But never had I disinterred a mummy rich in gold and silver objects, and never had I found the mummy of a royal Inca. By that I do not mean the mummy of an Incan emperor, one of the true "Incas" or rulers, but the body of a person of royal blood—a noble, prince or general, a priest or the governor of a province; and for that matter I never expected to find one. Still, somewhere, buried in some tomb or grave or mound, there must be mummies of Incan nobility—even the mummies of the supreme reigning emperors themselves. And as the Incan nobility, and practically all officials, were members of the royal family and were most gloriously adorned and arrayed in the finest products of Incan looms, and decked with insignia and ornaments of precious metals, one of their mummies would have been an archæological treasure-trove. No one, however, had ever found one—unless some *huaquero* had brought one to light and had stripped the mummy and said nothing, and there was little really first-hand information as to just how the Incan nobles were attired, the old Spanish chroniclers having disagreed lamentably on such matters. Why no one had ever found a royal mummy was a mystery. But the fact remained, and it would have been a hopeless undertaking to have dug all or even a small portion of the Incan graves in the faint hopes of finding a noble's body—one of the "golden ears" as the Spaniards called them, because of the gold shells or ear-coverings worn by them. This custom, I might add, had a most curious origin. One of the sons of the Inca, Pacha-Kutik, lost an ear in battle, and to conceal the mutilation he wore shell-shaped gold coverings over his ears. In order that he might not be conspicuous, and to commemorate his bravery, the Incan princes all followed his example and wore the *huancos* which in time became the recognized insignia of the royal family. But as I said above, I never dreamed that I would be so supremely fortunate as to find a mummy with the golden ears. And then Lady Luck stepped in and played her little joke.

I had ceased field work and I was packing up my collections preparatory to shipping them to New York, when a friend arrived from Cuba. He was fascinated with the specimens and was most anxious to be present when a mummy was disinterred and unwrapped, and to please him I offered to dig up a mummy or two for his especial benefit. Near at hand, all about Lima and its suburbs, were numerous mounds. Many, I might almost say all, had been dug into more or less, yet so universally worthless were their contents that the *huaqueros* had long since abandoned all hopes of finding treasure in these burial places. However, my friend wished merely to help disinter a deceased member of the Incan race; one mound was as good as another for all contained mummies, and for his satisfaction the dried and shriveled body of a farmer, wrapped in the cheapest and coarsest of textiles, would answer all requirements. So for convenience I selected a small, obscure mound actually within the city limits. It was barely ten feet in height and not over fifty feet in diameter, and the few torn fragments of textiles and scattered bones, disinterred in years past, indicated that it was the burial place of the humblest caste of husbandmen.

Selecting a spot which looked promising and had not been disturbed, we set to work with picks and shovels. Dust flew in clouds, under the blazing sun perspiration ran in streams, and our nostrils, mouths and eyes were filled with the pulverized detritus of dead bodies, bones, earth, decayed textiles and the other ingredients of the mound. But presently a human skull was unearthed.

(169)

There was no sign of a mummy or even a wrapping, and it was obvious that the cranium had fallen from some body that had been buried near the surface and had weathered away during the course of centuries. Then, a few inches deeper down, we came upon a layer of leaves and reeds—sure indications of a burial beneath.

Carefully this was removed, revealing a few fragments of animals' skeletons, some bits of cloth and two or three pottery jars. Then two more skulls—one a woman's, the other an infant's—and a few bones. I was, as the children say in Hunt the Thimble, "getting warm." Somewhere below this stratum of leaves and trash was a mummy; but whether that of a man or a woman, a farmer or a person of high station, was impossible to guess.

To proceed farther with pick and shovel would have been to court disaster, so on hands and knees I commenced digging carefully with a trowel. Presently I came upon a small, tightly-wrapped bundle containing the mummified body of a little Incan dog. The next instant my trowel struck wood, and carefully scraping away the sand and dirt, I discovered four upright wooden stakes with carved tops, that were lashed together with fiber ropes to form a quadrangle packed tightly with fine dry fibers.

My interest was now thoroughly aroused. No ordinary peasant would have been buried so carefully and elaborately, I knew, yet never had I found a burial of the same sort, and with the utmost care I lifted out the fiber. A cry of delight and amazement escaped my lips. Beneath the fiber were brilliant yellow and scarlet feathers, and very cautiously and gently I lifted a gorgeous crown from its resting place on the mass of hair that covered the skull

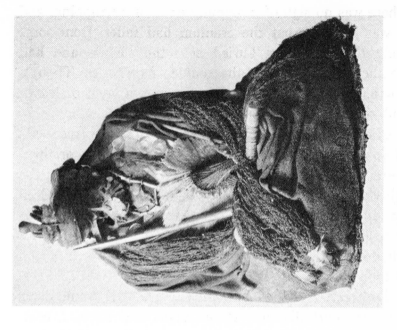

A PERUVIAN MUMMY DECKED WITH GOLD

THE GOLDEN REGALIA OF AN INCA'S MUMMY

beneath. It was a regal head-dress and in a perfect state of preservation. But even greater surprises were in store. Beside one of the upright posts was a carved and painted wooden shield; beside another a bronze-headed spear, while a magnificent bronze battle-ax with staff intact was beside a third post. Little by little I removed the masses of fiber that filled the grave, until at last the mummy could be seen—a shapeless bundle wrapped in heavy striped cloth.

But it scarcely could be called a mummy. Practically no skin or dried flesh adhered to the bones, and despite every care the skeleton dropped apart when the bundle was lifted from the grave. But the wrappings were intact and as I commenced unwrapping the bundle I hardly could believe my own eyes. Never had I seen such a mummy! There were textiles of the rarest and finest weaves and patterns; ornate pouches, bundles of quipos, woven sashes and belts. And as each strip of cloth or each garment was removed, more and finer objects were disclosed. There were implements of bronze and of wood, charms or amulets, a carved wooden scepter or staff, tipped and ornamented with gold, and about the bony wrists were wide golden bands with raised figures of birds and the sun god. Below the knees were golden bands or garters from which hung little silver jinglers tipped with scarlet feathers, and upon the skeleton's chest were three gold disks each embossed with the tiger-faced, bearded god or Wira Kocha. At the front of the head-dress of golden-yellow feathers, attached to a gorgeous *llantu* or head-band, was the golden symbol of the rainbow, the royal Incan standard, topped by a pompom of scarlet and black feathers, with a little gold sun hanging

(171)

over the forehead—the symbol of the *borla* or fringe worn only by the royal Incas. All or any of these objects and insignia would have proved the mummy that of a noble or a prince, but, best of all, there were the gold *huancos* that in life had covered the ears of the deceased. Their presence left no doubt of my astounding luck. I had actually unearthed the mummy of an Inca! And I had found him in a small insignificant mound which I had passed by scores of times and had not thought worth the digging.

To a professional *huaquero,* perhaps, my royal mummy would not have proved a great treasure, for like most Incan gold work, his ornaments were of thin beaten metal worth probably not more than a few hundred dollars as bullion. But scientifically speaking, he was a real treasure-trove and of far greater value archæologically than dozens of ingots or bars of solid gold.

Yet in some ways my gold-decked mummy was not so remarkable a find as the magnificent gold jars, carafes, plumes, pins and head ornaments on exhibition in the American Museum of Natural History in New York City.

Several years ago a Peruvian visited the museum and offered for sale a collection of ancient gold objects, which, according to his story, were unique and not only of great intrinsic value but of the greatest archæological interest. As the exportation of antiquities from Peru was prohibited, and as the government claims all gold taken from the graves, the Peruvian naturally was somewhat secretive and loath to divulge the manner in which the alleged collection had come into his possession. But finding that the museum authorities were not at all interested unless they learned the origin and history of the objects, he at last told them his story which, it must be confessed, sounded like some wild fictional tale.

Among the army of natives employed upon his hacienda there had been an old Indian who for many years had been a trusted retainer and was regarded more like a member of the family than a servant. And when the aged aborigine had been dying he had told his employer of a golden treasure in the distant hills and had given him minute directions as to how to find it.

The planter and his sons were not, however, in need of riches, they were far too wealthy to bother over hidden Inca treasures and, moreover, they felt that in all probability the old Indian had been wandering in his mind and that the treasure, if ever it had existed, had long since been found. So they paid no heed to the fellow's tale and forgot all about it.

Then, several years later, their fortunes took a sudden change. A new political party had arisen, rebellion had broken out, a new executive occupied the presidential chair in the ancient Pizarro Palace in Lima, and, almost overnight, the wealthy planter and his sons found themselves stripped of lands and almost penniless. It was then that they recalled the dying henchman's story and decided to search for the hoard of ancient gold whose hiding place he had revealed.

According to the Peruvian's story, the spot was a bare sandy hillside and there, protruding from the surface or half-covered with sand were golden jars, and vessels, plumes and gorgets of gold. But even with the gold in their possession the three were scarcely better off than before. They could not dispose of it in Peru. If it became known that they had it the government would seize it,

(173)

and their only hope of profiting by their find was to smuggle their treasure out of the country and sell it to some museum or scientific institution, for they realized that its archæological value would be four or five times as great as its value for bullion.

The amount asked for the collection was, however, far in excess of its real value, and the tale seemed much too romantic and far-fetched to be true, so the curator made a fair offer for the specimens on the condition that a representative of the museum should return to Peru and accompany the treasure finder to the spot and verify his story.

Arriving at the locality where the Peruvian claimed the golden objects had been obtained, the scientist found a bare sandy hillside, with here and there little piles of charcoal, but no signs of a former settlement, village, or even traces of burials. But as the party spread out and walked slowly along, one of the men discovered the edge of a gold plate protruding from the soil, and within a short time half a dozen golden objects had been picked up. Why the treasure should have been in such an unusual location was a puzzle. No one could offer a plausible theory to fit the case, and the matter remained an unsolved mystery. But several years later, while examining old documents in the archives of Peru I came upon an entry which, I am convinced, explained the presence of the Chimus' golden vessels. At the time when Pizarro and his men were ravishing the coastwise districts of Peru, a party of Spaniards looted a Chimu temple of its golden ceremonial objects, and while returning to the coast were attacked by a large party of the infuriated Indians. Realizing that hampered with their loot they could not escape, the Dons buried the treasure on a wooded hillside. But only a few of the raiders survived, and I could find no record of any having returned to disinter the golden vessels they had hidden.

No doubt, years later, the trees upon the hill were burned—leaving the piles of charcoal marking their stumps, and the surface of the earth, thus exposed to sun and wind, drifted away to reveal the buried gold. And as the locality where the little party of Spaniards concealed their booty agreed with that where the old Indian's tale revealed the hoard, I feel that there is little doubt that the golden vessels and ornaments in the New York museum are those filched from the Chimu temple centuries ago, and which were hastily buried by the Spaniards in a vain attempt to save their lives.

ⁱⁱⁱ

Truth That Is Stranger
Than Fiction

THE well known miners' slogan, that gold is where you find it, is equally applicable to buried or hidden treasures. And just as many of the world's richest mines have been located through chance or accident, so many, I might even say most, treasures found, have been discovered by mere chance.

Very often, too, the stories of the finding of these treasures, and the strange chain of events, the unusual occurrences or the incidents which led to their discovery, sound far more like fiction than fact. For that matter it would be a hard job for fiction writers to invent tales or plots to equal the reality, and if any author introduced in his yarns, some of the incidents, coincidences and mystical happenings which have actually taken place and have resulted in treasure being found, they would be scoffed at as incredible and impossible. Where, for example, could one find a pulp magazine story to equal that of:

The Treasure Found Through a Dream

Probably no part of the United States is so replete with tales of lost, hidden and sunken treasures as is Florida.

(176)

And I doubt if in any other portion of our country so many lost and hidden treasures actually have been found. There are very good reasons for this. Florida, before it was purchased from Spain by the United States, was a sparsely settled, almost unknown territory outside of the few larger towns. Its cays, coasts, bayous, swamps and rivers were the haunt of smugglers and pirates, and the frequent Indian wars and the raids by pirates and other gentlemen of fortune caused many a well-to-do Spaniard to bury or secrete his valuables. Even for years after Florida became a part of the Union, pirates found safe and secure refuges along its coast. In another chapter I have told the story of Billy Bowlegs' treasure. Then there is the treasure of Jose Gaspár, or Gasparilla, the king of the pirates, whose treasure-filled ship was sent to the bottom off Gasparilla Island by an American sloop of war in 1821. Near the mouth of the Suwanee River a schooner carrying five millions in gold, the indemnity to Spanish citizens paid by the United States, went to the bottom during a storm in 1820. Off Long Key a fleet of Spanish plate ships went down in a hurricane in 1715, and all along the coasts are other authentic treasure-filled wrecks. Considering all this, and the fact that for fifty years or more the inhabitants of Key West made not only their living but goodly fortunes by wrecking, it is not surprising that Florida should be the treasure state of our Union.

Moreover, many a man in Florida has a tidy fortune derived from some treasure trove he has found, although as a rule the finders have little to say as to where and how they found the hoards or the value of the same. This is the case with the man who found a fortune through a

(177)

dream. Only he knows how much was obtained, but as he gave his son $75,000 in cash with which to buy a garage, we can safely assume that it was no small treasure that he secured in one of the most incredible, and in fact mystical ways, ever recorded. And as he is a well known, respected and strictly honest gentleman, and holds a government position, there is no reason to discredit his story.

Oddly enough, too, he was not a hidden treasure fan nor had he ever, as far as is known, taken any interest in treasure hunting. Yet on a certain night a year or two ago, he had a most vivid dream of hidden treasure. Not far from Ft. Myers, on the Gulf coast of Florida, is an old stone dwelling known as Braden's Castle, which, during the time of war in days gone by, served as a refuge for the people for miles about. On the night I mention, the man dreamed of being in this building and of seeing a Spanish gentleman, dressed in old fashioned garments, descending a flight of stone stairs. Reaching the bottom, the wraith of the Don lifted a stone slab and vanished in a subterranean chamber. Presently he reappeared carrying a sack filled with gold, and exclaiming, "All the rest is yours," he vanished.

Mr. Carney, as we may call the dreamer, thought nothing of the matter, but when, two nights later, the same dream was repeated, he mentioned it to a friend who suggested that he should consult a clairvoyant. Mr. Carney, however, was a practical man and had no faith in mind-readers, fortune tellers or dreams and he scoffed at the idea.

Then, twice more he dreamed of the old Spaniard and the treasure, and just to satisfy himself that there was "nothing in it," as he expressed it, he decided to visit the old "castle" to see if there was a staircase such as he had visualized in his sleep. To his astonishment the place was exactly as he had seen it in his dreams, and descending the stairs, he recognized the stone slab which the ghostly Spaniard had lifted. Almost in a daze Carney grasped the stone and tugged, and to his utter amazement the slab moved to disclose a narrow flight of stone stairs leading into a vault below. Feeling as if he were still in a dream he descended and fairly gasped. Revealed by the light of his electric torch were chests and rotten sacks filled with ancient gold and silver coins!

For a space he could not credit the evidence of his own senses. It seemed too impossible, too incredible to be true. But the pieces of eight, the doubloons and *castellanos,* were real enough, even though their presence had been revealed by a dream. Neither he nor any one else can account for it. Why should a man dream of a hidden treasure in a spot miles from his own home, in a place he had never visited? And why should he dream, not once but repeatedly, of the Spaniard's ghost and the secret stone trap door? Call it coincidence, telepathy, chance, spiritualism or what you will, it still remains an inexplicable mystery.

But there was nothing mysterious about another treasure found in Florida, although it was mere chance that led to its discovery, even if Lady Luck was aided and abetted by a man's inherent laziness.

The Treasure That Bought a Department Store

The negro laborer, digging a drainage ditch across a patch of cleared land on a big estate, straightened his back and stretched his arms. Behind him the ditch ran straight and true, but a few feet ahead, a big pitch-pine stump was directly in line with the trench. The man shook his grizzled head dubiously and contemplated the charred butt of the tree.

"Yo' shooly is a hard gent'man," he apostrophised it. "'Pears like Ah gwine have a tough job movin' you' outen mah way. Yass, sah, gwine be plenty wo'k." Then, rubbing his chin: "Reckon Ah'll res' a spell an' tek consid'ation of tha bes'est manner fo' doin' it."

Seating himself on a nearby log, he filled his blackened pipe and puffed contentedly, as he pondered on the work before him. It would be a tough job to cut and dig the trench through the roots of the old tree, and, after all, he argued to himself, why should the trench be straight? If it were dug around the stump it would serve its purpose just as well, he decided, and his tobacco having burned out, he rose reluctantly, picked up his shovel and again bent to his task.

Presently, as he dug to one side of the old tree, his spade struck something solid and an exclamation of disgust and disappointment came from his thick lips. He hadn't expected the tree's roots to extend so far from the stump. Still, it must be a root, for there were no stones in the black, mucky soil. Bending over, the negro commenced scraping away the dirt in an endeavor to determine the size of the supposed root preparatory to cutting through it. The next instant he cast aside his shovel, dropped to his knees and began pawing furiously at the dirt, for the impediment he had struck was no root but a blackened wooden chest bound with rusty iron bands.

Feverishly he worked. Never before had he exerted

himself as he did now, while half-forgotten tales of buried treasure on the estate flashed through his mind. In a few moments he had cleared away the soil over the entire top of the ancient chest, and inserting his shovel blade below the lid, he pried upward. With a splintering of rotten wood the cover gave way, and the negro's jaw gaped and his eyes rolled wildly as he stared, dumbfounded, too amazed even to utter an ejaculation of wonder, at the gold and silver coins half-filling the old chest. Treasure! A fortune!

Nervously, apprehensively, he glanced about. Had any one seen him? Had one of the other laborers noticed his actions? Apparently not. All were working steadily, paying no attention to him. But, he realized, at any moment one of his fellows might approach and see the treasure chest. Also, he realized, he could not by any possibility transfer that mass of old coins to the pockets in his ragged overalls. Shaking with nervousness, in a blind terror of some one learning his secret, he seized his shovel and refilled the cavity with earth, not even stopping to take a single coin of the hoard he had found through his disinclination to work. Then, with the chest once more hidden he fell to attacking the old pine stump with an energy and vigor utterly foreign to his nature.

Borrowing a neighbor's handcart he returned late that night to the spot and safely transferred his treasure chest and its contents to his shack where he reinterred it beneath the floor. For a negro laborer he was an uncommonly shrewd and sensible chap, and early the next morning, donning his best clothes, he journeyed to Miami and paid a visit to a reliable lawyer. To him the lucky fellow told the entire story, exhibited several of the coins to prove his amazing tale, and asked legal advice as to how to dispose of the treasure-trove and how best to invest the proceeds.

For once the finder of a buried treasure did not go half-mad with the acquisition of sudden wealth and spend it recklessly. Instead, he invested his quarter of a million by purchasing a large block of stock in one of Miami's leading department stores, and, like the heroes of fairy tales, he has lived happily and in affluence ever since.

This treasure, literally the reward of laziness, was not, however, the only Florida treasure which had been wisely invested by its finders.

Some years ago a cache of buried pirates' loot was discovered quite by accident at Pensacola, and the finder made use of his lucky strike by employing the thousands he had found to erect the Thesian Building, one of the largest business and office buildings in Pensacola. Found by a more remarkable chance than the discovery of the chest of gold and silver by the black ditch digger, and perhaps the strangest of treasures, as far as its hiding place was concerned, was:

The Treasure of the Ancient Cannon

As I have said, the inhabitants of Key West and the other Florida cays made an excellent living by salvaging wrecks in days past, and throughout the long line of reefs and cays that stretch in a great semi-circle from the tip of the Florida peninsula to Key West, countless skeletons of foundered vessels rest upon the ocean floor. And often, gazing down through the crystal clear water, one may see the massive timbers of long-lost ships, or rusty anchors or corroded cannon, lying amid the sea-fans and coral growths. No doubt some of these old wrecks contain valuables, but the majority were merchant ships and long since were stripped of all their cargoes and fittings of any worth. But old-fashioned cannon, especially if of bronze, are worth salvaging, and when, a short time ago, a couple of fishermen discovered two ancient bronze guns caught among the coral on a reef not far from shore, they decided to get them up and add a few score dollars to their meager incomes.

It was not a difficult job; the cannon were lightered ashore, and the men proceeded to chip and clean away the encrustation of lime, coral, sea-weed and marine growths which covered them. This accomplished, they set to work to dig out the muck, sand, dead shells and other material which filled the bores to the muzzles. With knives and crowbars they dug into the tightly packed mass when, to their utter amazement, out came dozens of corroded, blackened silver coins! Each of the old guns was packed full of coins, mostly silver, but with many of gold, and by the time the bores of the cannon had been completely cleaned the lucky fishermen were the richer by some one hundred thousand dollars—surely a goodly reward for the fishing up of a couple of old bronze guns.

The Hog's Treasure Trove

Remarkable and unexpected as it was to find a goodly treasure packed into bores of ancient cannon, it was no stranger or more surprising a discovery than that made by a resident of the Isle of Pines a short time ago. In the first place, when one finds old, corroded guns lying on the

(183)

bottom of the sea one may reasonably suspect that there has been a wreck in the immediate vicinity and that valuables may be near at hand. And in the second place, the lucky finders of the cannon with their loads of coins were, in a way, treasure seekers, for they expected to realize a few dollars for salvaging the guns. But the man to whom I refer was no treasure hunter, he had no reason whatsoever to expect that there were valuables in the vicinity, and he was not planning to make money when Fate literally thrust a treasure upon him. On the contrary, he was engaged in the wholly unromantic and uninteresting task of finding a strayed hog. Discovering that the porker had managed to escape from its enclosure and had taken to the bush, the owner set out on the hog's trail. It was not a difficult trail to follow, for the boar, proceeding leisurely and with no definite objective in view, had stopped to root about and regale himself on roots and tubers, thus leaving most obvious evidences of his passing.

As the beast's owner pushed onward through the brush, stopping now and again to listen for the grunts and sounds of the slobbering jaws of his quarry, he came to a little open glade where the miniature hills and hollows of freshly-turned earth showed evidences of the hog having made a very thorough job of it. And as he glanced at the mucky soil he stood staring open-mouthed, scarcely able to believe the evidence of his own eyes, for there, exposed by the pig's rooting, was an overturned, cracked earthen oil jar or "garafon" filled with dull, yellow golden coins. Instantly the potential ham and bacon was forgotten, and falling on his knees, the excited man began scooping up the coins so strangely found and chuckling with delight as he chinked them in his hands. Then came another and if anything a greater surprise. Close to the first jar he discovered the top of a second, and as he feverishly dug and scraped away the mucky soil he came upon another and another, until at last he had disinterred five "garafons" filled to the brims with old Spanish doubloons, pieces of eight and objects of solid gold. No longer would he be compelled to farm and raise hogs for a livelihood. He was rich, not a millionaire, but possessing enough gold to make him independent if he invested it wisely. And he owed his amazing good fortune to a runaway hog! Let us hope that he was duly grateful to the porcine treasure finder, although in all probability he was not. But if ever a pig deserved to be glorified and honored this one did. In fact it would have been no more than the beast deserved if he had been housed in a marble pen, with the finest of viands to eat, with a valet to scrub and care for him; with a golden ring in his nose and with manicured and tinted hoofs for as long as he lived, and with a bronze casket and a mausoleum to perpetuate his memory when he died.

But to the lucky, suddenly-enriched man, pigs were pigs; the hog who was responsible for his amazing good fortune met the customary fate of all swine, and it is safe to assume that those who consumed his well-smoked hams or devoured his luscious bacon, never dreamed that they were dining on the flesh of a treasure hunter who actually found a treasure.

CHAPTER XIV

The Treasure Ship
That Vanished

IN the old days when hardy and daring adventurers were busily exploring and conquering the New World, and

"Plate ships high, with purple sails,
Taut to the trade-wind's strain,
Buried their bows in tumbling seas
On the homeward voyage to Spain,"

it was a most perilous and uncertain undertaking to sail American waters.

No one had surveyed or charted the reefs, shoals, bars, rocks and coasts of the mainland and the islands of the western world. Mariners knew nothing of the various currents, the winds and tides of the oceans, seas, gulfs, and bays on this side of the Atlantic, and what maps had been made were inaccurate, incomplete and almost worse than nothing as far as serving as guides was concerned. Navigation, also, was by no means the exact science it is today. The ships' captains' instruments were of the crudest sort, their compasses were not corrected for magnetic variation, and if an observation—followed by long and

(186)

laborious calculations, located the vessel within a radius of twenty miles, it was considered amazingly accurate navigation. For that matter comparatively few of the captains or "pilots," as the navigators were called, relied upon "shooting the sun," but preferred to work out their positions by means of dead reckoning, which was usually a far more accurate and dependable method than by taking observations. And some of the feats accomplished by dead reckoning were almost incredible. For example, when Captain Sharp, the buccaneer, was ravishing the west coast of South and Central America in the captured Spanish flagship *Most Blessed Trinity*, the ship was navigated by Basil Ringrose as "pilot" who had no knowledge of taking observations but depended wholly upon his dead reckoning corrected by landfalls from time to time. When, after two years of sailing up and down and back and forth along the coasts, the buccaneers decided to return to the West Indies by sailing around South America via the Straits of Magellan, Ringrose undertook to carry the battered old ship safely on her long voyage by means of dead reckoning alone. And he succeeded. More, they missed the Straits altogether, rounded Cape Horn and never sighted land from the time they left the coast of Chile until they reached the West Indies. Most amazing and incredible of all, so accurate were Ringrose's calculations that when, on a certain day, he ordered men aloft to keep a lookout for Barbados, they sighted that little island only *eight miles off their course!*

But this was of course an exceptional case, and, moreover, the buccaneers were by all odds the most skillful mariners in the entire world at that time. But considering the ignorance of reefs, currents, winds and shoals in those old days, as well as the clumsy, slow-sailing, high-pooped, pot-bellied ships utterly incapable of sailing anywhere near the wind, it is remarkable that so many vessels ever reached their destinations, rather than that so many left their timbers among the coral reefs and sand bars of the West Indies and adjacent waters.

No one will ever know how many vessels sailed from Europe for the New World, or squared away from America for home, and were never heard from again. Records were carelessly kept in those days. If a ship foundered far from land the crew were usually lost to the last man and the vessel merely disappeared. But the treasure-laden galleons and the plate ships of Spain were a different matter. Strict accounts were kept of the riches in gold, silver, dye woods, pearls, emeralds and other valuables that were sent from Mexico, Central and South America and the West Indies to Spain. And if, as often happened, a treasure ship was lost, the Spaniards recorded the fact. To be sure, it was sometimes unknown whether a missing plate ship had struck a reef, had been sunk by a hurricane or had fallen to buccaneers, pirates or war vessels of Spain's enemies. But, on the other hand, the fate of the majority of these treasure carrying ships was well known. If the buccaneers took a fine and valuable prize they were not the type to keep quiet about it, but boasted of their deeds. And as many of the lost galleons were driven onto reefs or ashore within comparatively easy reach of land, and there were survivors of the tragedies, the exact locations of the wrecks were known. Also, after the buccaneers had played such havoc with the Spanish shipping that a single vessel, no matter how heavily armed, had little chance of running the gauntlet of the Caribbean, the Spaniards strove to safeguard their treasures by having their galleons sail in fleets convoyed by heavily-armed, heavily-manned, swift frigates. While this method did prevent the ships from falling to the freebooters, for even the hardiest of buccaneers would scarcely dare attack a fleet of a dozen or more galleons reënforced by two or three great frigates, yet it was no protection from reefs or hurricanes, both of which took heavy toll of Spain's gorgeously-painted and gilded plate ships.

Today our mariners receive warnings of hurricanes when the tropical storms are hundreds of miles distant. They know from hour to hour the exact position of the hurricane's center, the speed and direction in which it is moving, and its intensity, and they can thus make port, or steam out of the track of the storm. But in the days of Spanish treasure flotillas no one possessed the least knowledge of hurricanes. Not until the terrific storms burst upon them with all their destructive fury were the mariners aware of their approach, and then it was too late to do anything. It was one of these fearful West Indian hurricanes that drove the fleet of sixteen galleons, carrying over sixty millions in treasures, upon the Silver Shoals, and it was another hurricane that, in the year 1595, burst upon the Spanish plate ship, *Santa Margarita*, just after she had passed through the Florida Straits carrying silver bullion worth at present prices about seven million dollars, as her cargo.

She was a stout, seaworthy ship, her captain was a skilled and brave, as well as an experienced man, and realizing that a hurricane was upon him he shortened sail to the limit and headed northward hoping to outrun the worst of the storm. Perhaps, had he stood farther out to sea, he might have saved his ship and her great treasure. But instead, he hugged the Florida coast too closely and

(189)

his ship was driven with terrific force upon a bar off the present site of Palm Beach. Battered and stove, with masts carried away by her impact, with many of her crew swept overboard and with her rudder disabled, the *Santa Margarita* was carried over the reef by a tremendous sea and sank like a plummet with her millions in bullion.

Three centuries passed and the *Santa Margarita* and her treasure were almost forgotten incidents of history. Along the sandy shore where there had been only dense untrodden jungle when the ship had gone down, palatial homes and thriving towns stood amid the groves of waving palm trees. Upon the beach, scores of bathers lolled on the sand or frolicked in the tepid water all unaware of the millions in silver lying upon the bottom almost within stone's throw. Great steamships churned back and forth above the skeleton of the old galleon, and close to where her battered hulk rested a telegraph cable had been laid upon the ocean's floor.

In all probability had it not been for the cable all memory of the *Santa Margarita* would have been lost and the only record of her ill-fated voyage and her cargo of treasure would have been the time-yellowed documents in the musty files of the archives of the Spanish Admiralty. But one day the cable failed to function. A break was located near Palm Beach, and a diver was sent down to find and repair it. As he moved about, following the cable that stretched like a gigantic serpent along the sandy bottom, he noticed a bulky mass looming dimly through the misty-green of the sea. Curious to learn what the object could be he moved nearer and to his surprise discovered it was the shell- and weed-encrusted wreck of a ship.

Hidden as it was by the accumulation of sea-growths,

(190)

and half-buried in the sand, yet, as the diver examined the hulk more closely, he knew it to be the remains of a very ancient ship, a ship such as he had never seen except in pictures, a vessel whose rotted broken timbers still showed traces of a lofty stern-castle and high bluff bows. And as he poked about he came upon two shell-covered ornate bronze cannon. There was no doubt that he had stumbled upon the wreck of a Spanish galleon, and half-forgotten traditions of a lost treasure ship off the coast flashed through his mind. Tearing away the masses of weeds and barnacles upon the timbers, he crawled between the massive ribs of the wreck and with bar and hands dug away the sand that half-filled the old hulk. And there, buried under a few inches of the fine shell sand, were tiers upon tiers of squarish metal bars, corroded and black from centuries of immersion in salt water, but showing the bright gleam of silver when the exultant diver scratched them with his knife. He had found a fortune. By mere chance he had discovered a treasure worth millions. He alone knew the secret of the lost galleon. But, he realized, he was there to repair a broken cable, not to salvage treasure, and consoling himself with the thought that as the wrecked galleon had remained there undiscovered for centuries it was not likely to vanish in a few weeks or months more, the diver moved from the wreck and busied himself at repairing the cable.

Being a practical and experienced man familiar with salvage work, the diver knew that it was not a one-man job to recover hundreds of tons of silver from the bottom of the sea. A wrecking barge or vessel with proper equipment and a reliable crew would be needed, and to secure these ample funds were required. But it was not such a simple matter to secure the necessary capital as he had

confidently supposed, and two years passed before he succeeded in finding some one to finance his treasure hunt.
There was no difficulty in relocating the wreck of the long-
lost *Santa Margarita*. He had taken accurate bearings
when he had come to the surface after his discovery of the
treasure, and soon the salvage barge was moored above
the sunken galleon and preparations were made to begin
recovering the tons of silver.

But fickle Fortune, or the jinx which ever seems to
guard lost treasures, had other plans. Though passing centuries had wrought great changes on the land, Old Devil
Sea had remained as treacherous and uncertain as in the
days when the *Santa Margarita* had gone down, and roaring up from the Caribbean came just such a hurricane as
had sent the galleon to her doom. Howling with demoni-
acal glee it overwhelmed the salvage ship and snuffed out
the lives of a number of her crew. The diver and a few
others barely escaped with their lives, but the entire
equipment that had cost so much time and money was a
total loss. But the worst was yet to come. When, after
the storm had passed and the sea again stretched blue
and calm beneath a sunny sky, the diver descended to the
ocean floor on the chance of salvaging some portion of his
lost gear, he could find no trace of the wrecked galleon.
On every side the bottom extended smooth and unbroken.
The terrific seas raised by the hurricane had completely
changed the topography of the bottom and had buried the
wreck and her treasure under many feet of shifting sand.
Although they searched for weeks no trace of the sunken
galleon could be found, and at last all efforts to relocate
the treasure hulk were abandoned. Perhaps, by now, the
ever-changing bottom of the sea has been so altered by
hurricane-lashed waves and currents that the skeleton of

the *Santa Margarita* lies fully exposed above the ocean floor, or on the other hand, she may rest deep beneath countless thousands of tons of sand, her millions in bullion buried far out of reach of all treasure seekers.

Bitterly disappointing and disheartening as it must have been for the diver and his partners to have lost a vast fortune just as it seemed within their grasp, yet Fate played an even worse trick on another party of treasure hunters in Florida.

Over one hundred years had passed since the *Santa Margarita* had been lost, but the perils of the sea that beset the treasure-laden ships of Spain had not lessened. On the contrary they were greater than ever, for added to the dangers of hurricanes and uncharted shoals and reefs and treacherous currents there had been the buccaneers. No matter how heavily manned and armed a galleon might be these dare-devil, reckless freebooters would attack and take the Spanish ships, and to safeguard the riches that flowed in a steady stream from the New World to Spain, the Spaniards no longer depended upon single ships to transport their treasures but arranged for whole fleets of galleons to sail forth convoyed by swift frigates, and it was such a flotilla that was gathered in the harbor of Havana in June, 1715. From the various ports of Mexico, Central and South America they had come. There were ships from Campeche and Vera Cruz laden with gold and silver bullion, logwood and spices; ships from Porto Bello and from Cartagena bearing fortunes in gold and emeralds in their strong rooms; vessels from Maracaibo and La Guayra, from Cumana and Hispaniola, and a single galleon from Margarita carrying the island's yearly shipment of priceless pearls. Fifteen fine staunch Spanish ships, with cargoes totaling over fifty million dollars in value in their holds and strong rooms; fifteen ships fairly bursting with treasure, bristling with guns and heavily manned, for although the dreaded buccaneers were a thing of the past, pirates still haunted the seas, and with Spain and England at loggerheads as usual, there was the added danger of cruising British frigates to be met. But with such a large and powerful fleet the Spaniards felt little fear of either pirates or British war vessels, and on the twenty-eighth of June, 1715, wind-lasses were manned, anchors were hoisted, sails were set, and with a thunder of saluting guns the fifteen stately galleons sailed out from Havana's harbor, and passing the Morro, curtseyed to the swell of the open sea.

Across the Straits of Florida they sailed. Far to the westward the shadowy outlines of Key West and the chain of palm-crowned cays shimmered upon the horizon. But the very clearness of the air, the brassiness of the sky, the puffs of hot wind that ruffled the oily sea should have warned the Spanish captains of what was in store for them. Any experienced seaman of modern times would have read in these signs the approach of a hurricane. But, the Spanish mariners must have been woefully lacking in weather-wisdom or else felt such supreme confidence in themselves and their ships that they had no dread of any storm which might arise, for instead of putting back to port they kept steadily on their course. And when the hurricane burst upon them the ships were in a most perilous position with the jagged reefs and coral-heads of the Florida Keys on their lee. With sails torn from their bolt-ropes, with spars carried away; battered and smashed by the terrific seas, the doomed ships were driven inexorably toward the foaming line of breakers. One by one they struck, and with timbers shattered and planking pierced by the coral fangs the ships went down off Cayo Largo. Of all the fifteen galleons only one escaped. A smaller, better sailer than the others, better handled and having been farther out from the lee shore when the storm roared down upon the fleet, this one vessel remained afloat. By some miracle she had not been dismasted; with rags of sail which withstood the fury of the hurricane her captain and crew managed to claw off shore, and with bulwarks smashed, with rigging half carried away, and leaking badly, she came limping into port with news of the loss of the fourteen treasure ships.

Had such a catastrophe taken place a century earlier the Spaniards would doubtless have taken the loss as an act of God and let it go at that, making no attempt to recover the millions in the wrecked ships. But the maritime world had advanced greatly since the day when sixteen galleons went down on Silver Shoals. Diving gear, although crude and unreliable, had been invented, and Spain decided to have a try at salvaging the treasure of the lost ships. A year after the fleet had gone down the salvage ship with its crew and divers arrived on the scene and a camp was established on a little palm-fringed cay within a short distance of the reef on which the galleons had been wrecked. There was no difficulty in finding their battered hulks. The water was not deep, it was as clear as glass, and only a year had passed, so that no growth of coral, shell or weeds had concealed the timbers and the hulls lying conspicuously between the reefs. But it was slow work salvaging the treasure. With the crude equipment of that era it was a difficult job breaking into the wrecks which, despite the terrible punishment they had received, were still fairly intact. But time was of no particular object, and surely if slowly the bullion was hoisted to the surface and was stored on the neighboring cay. And as the accumulation of gold and silver grew until the salvaged treasure amounted to over a million dollars in value, fifty men were put ashore as a guard. Not that the salvors expected any one to steal the bullion they had wrested from the sea. There was no fear of that, for the coast was uninhabited and they were far off the track of ships which gave the treacherous coast a wide berth. The only danger, the officers felt, was from their own men, for a million dollars in bullion was a big temptation, and it was to safeguard the salvaged treasure from the crew that the guard was placed on the cay. And when, one day, a dingy little turtling sloop hove in sight, and when the sun-blackened, shirtless crew of two stared curiously at the salvagers, and tacking close inshore, skirted the island with its store of silver, the Spaniards thought nothing of it, for what possible danger could lurk in a weather-beaten turtle boat and a couple of half-naked fishermen?

As it happened, however, the sloop and its occupants hailed from Jamaica and her tatterdemalion skipper was a certain Captain Jennings who was more of a pirate than fisherman. Having discovered what the Spaniards were about, and more particularly the fact that they had a goodly treasure conveniently piled on the islet with only fifty easy-going men to guard it, Captain Jennings shifted his course and as soon as he was out of sight of the Spaniards, crowded on all sail for Jamaica where he duly reported what he had seen.

Although Port Royal, the famous stronghold of the buccaneers, had been destroyed and submerged by an earthquake for a quarter of a century, piratical instincts still survived in the hearts of the islanders whose forbears had been Brethren of the Main and had sailed "on the ac-

WHERE THE SPANIARDS CACHED THEIR SALVAGED TREASURE

count" with Morgan, L'Ollonois, Sharp and many another famed buccaneer chieftain. Moreover, the Spaniards were legitimate prey and enemies of His Britannic Majesty, and Captain Jennings' news was received with almost delirious joy. To pirate—or as we would express it, hijack—the salvors was an undertaking exactly to the Jamaicans' liking; just such an adventure as would have delighted Sir Harry Morgan or any of his compeers, and within a few hours of Jennings' arrival an armed brig, swarming with three hundred men as reckless and daredevilish as ever trod the decks of a buccaneers' ship, set sail for the Florida Keys.

The result was just what might have been expected. Fifty Spaniards equipped only with side-arms were wholly incapable of offering any resistance to three hundred determined, heavily-armed rascals, not to mention the ship's cannon. And fully realizing this, and being sensible fellows, the Dons decided that saving their lives was preferable to attempting to save treasure which wasn't their own property but belonged to the King of Spain who could well afford to lose it. So guards and salvors hurriedly deserted the accumulated silver, and retreating to the security of the jungle left the British to help themselves to the store of salvaged bullion.

Quite naturally the Spaniards felt that it was not only a thankless but a dangerous task to recover treasure from the wrecked galleons, only to be set upon and robbed by their British foes. So as soon as the triumphant hijackers had vanished below the horizon, they packed their belongings upon the salvage ship, hoisted anchors and sailed away for Spain, leaving the sunken galleons and their unsalvaged millions at the bottom of the sea where they still remain.

⊥⊥

CHAPTER XV

The Lost Mine of
Tisingal

SOMEWHERE within the wild, un-mapped, jungle-covered mountainous country along the boundary between Panama and Costa Rica is the famous "lost" mine of Tisingal. Of all the fabulously rich gold mines worked by the old Spaniards in America, Tisingal was the richest. And of all the lost mines it has, perhaps, the most romantic history.

Clad in their steel armor, the Spanish conquerors came to the New World, ruthless, cruel, mad with the lust for gold and their fanatical determination to force their religion upon the Indians. But Christianity was scarcely more than a cloak with which to cover their inhuman deeds and hide their bloody swords, and acceptance of the so-called True Faith never saved the hapless aborigines from death and slavery, for those who were "converted" or were friendly were forced to labor like beasts or worse to enrich their "civilized" masters, while those who resisted the Cross or the invasion were tortured, put to death without mercy, and thereby met a more merciful fate.

Human mind can scarcely conceive of what those ruth-

(198)

less, cruel Dons endured in order to secure gold. Through jungles they hewed their way, over mountains they toiled, and in cumbersome, makeshift craft they conquered rivers and rapids, until at last they found Indians who possessed gold. Tropical sun, pestilential insects, venomous serpents, hostile tribes, torrential rains, starvation and fever, poisoned darts or stone-tipped arrows, meant nothing to them in their insatiable thirst for gold. Thus they forced their way into the fastnesses of the mighty, forest-covered ranges of what they later called Costa Rica (Rich Coast) because of the incredible quantities of gold in the land, until they reached a remote tribe of Indians wearing countless ornaments and objects of virgin gold. Innocent of the white men's purpose, regarding the mail-clad strangers as semi-deities, the Indians gladly revealed the source of the precious metal, and riches beyond belief came to the adventurous Spaniards. What mattered it to them that the great veins of brown, rotten quartz fairly bursting with gold lay many weary leagues from the sea? What mattered it if the jungle hemmed them in on all sides, if savages lurked in the forests? It was a simple matter to kill off all the tribesmen who resisted, and the others, cowed, starved, chained and enslaved, were forced to toil ceaselessly, hewing a trail through the jungles to the nearest navigable river, laying a corduroy road, hauling great logs to build stockades; dragging boulders from the rivers' beds and blocks of stone from the mountainsides to erect forts and bridge abutments; carrying on their shoulders enormous loads through the wilderness; burrowing like human moles into the gold-riddled earth.

By countless hundreds they died from ill-treatment, abuse and lack of food. But the supply of human cattle appeared inexhaustible, and slaves were always to be had for the taking.

Slowly the rough road was completed, forts and walls were built, and the mine with its winches and buckets, its crude mill and machinery came into existence. Houses, barracks, even a church arose in the heart of the wilderness, and to guard the richest of Spanish mines from possible invaders, such as the buccaneers, bronze cannon were hauled over miles of rough trails from the distant port and were mounted with their grim muzzles commanding the narrow pass that led to the mine whence, for many years, a steady stream of gold flowed overseas to Spain.

But at last came the day of retribution, when, unable to endure their burdens longer, to submit to the cruel lash and the tortures inflicted by the Spaniards, the Indians rose *en masse*. Taken completely by surprise, grown careless by years of the Indians' apparently brute-like submission, and vastly outnumbered by their erstwhile slaves and the still free savages of the forest, the Spaniards were massacred to the last man. Then, to prevent any other white men from reopening the mine which had been the cause of all their years of suffering and misery, the Indians burned the buildings to the ground, tore down the stone walls and forts and wrecked the machinery. For days, weeks, they toiled at the willing labor, until not a vestige of the mine remained, until the bridges had been destroyed, until even the roadway had been obliterated. Then again the forest swallowed the Indians, and the jungle soon hid all scars of man's occupancy. But for long months thereafter skulking naked figures maintained a constant vigil beside the trail and no white man lived to reach the ruins of the mine and carry back news of its fate to the settlements on the coast. And thus, in time, Tisingal became only a memory, a "lost" mine, with its exact location unknown to the world.

Years, centuries later, a Spaniard was taken prisoner by a tribe of Indians of the district, and the daughter of the chief, falling in love with the white captive, agreed to release him and guide him back to his friends and fellow Spaniards. As the two fugitives passed through the forest, they came upon the jungle-covered remains of ancient stone works and the Spaniard, remembering tales of Tisingal, realized that he had stumbled upon the lost mine. But death overtook him before he could profit by his knowledge. Avenging tribesmen killed the Indian girl and wounded her companion who, suffering untold agonies and near to death, struggled into a rubber-gatherers' camp, babbled a few incoherent words, and expired. Clutched in his fingers the *chicleros* found a lump of almost solid gold.

Since then many attempts have been made to find the ancient mine. But all have come to nothing, for the Indians saw to it that the searchers' bones were added to those of the butchered Spaniards and the fleeing princess. Dozens, scores of men have defied death, lured on by the records of fabulous wealth lying somewhere in the forests, but no man who has ever found the mine has lived to tell of it or to profit by his discovery. No one can even guess how many lives have paid the penalty of seeking for Tisingal; no one can say what toll the Indians have taken, for the silent jungle tells no tales and never gives up its dead.

Long had I been familiar with the story and history of the famous lost mine, and then, on one of my scientific expeditions, I found myself in the district where it was supposed to be. I was not searching for lost mines, how-

ever, but was engaged in making ethnological collections
and securing data from remote Indian tribes, and at the
time I was living in the house of the *cacique* of a little
known tribe—the Shayshans. They were friendly enough,
I had won a measure of their confidence, and Chief Polu
and I were on the best of terms. But when I asked him
about other tribes who were supposed to inhabit the in-
accessible mountains, Polu was evasive and professed the
greatest fear of them, although claiming that the Shayshans were at peace with all other Indians.

And when I proposed visiting the Doraks, as they were
called, the chief and his fellows showed the greatest con-
cern. They insisted it would mean my certain death, explaining that while a Shayshan might enter the Dorak
country no white man would be permitted to set foot
beyond the invisible boundaries of the Shayshan territory.

Somehow, from the chief's manner, I felt positive that
he was trying to conceal something from me, As I puzzled
over this I began to wonder if the Shayshans held the
secret of the Tisingal mine. Was it possible? Could it be
that the wily *cacique* was trying to avoid any possibility
of my stumbling upon the secret? Was I, as they say in
the game of "Hunt the Thimble," getting warm?

It was a rather fascinating, I might even say, amazing
idea, and it was by no means impossible or improbable
that the fabulously rich Tisingal might be very near to
Polu's village. But I had no intentions of searching for
treasure, either in lost mines or elsewhere. I was engaged
in scientific work and Indians and their customs interested me more than old Spanish mines and traditional
riches. Also, I realized that to show any deep interest in
the matter might well result in arousing the suspicions or
even resentment of the Shayshans, provided they did

know of the ancient mine and its history, and the failure of my mission. Nevertheless, the romantic aspect of the matter appealed to me; my exploring instinct had been aroused, and—well, I doubt if there is any one who would not be thrilled at the thought of being within bow-shot of a long-lost, incredibly rich mine which countless men had sought in vain, and whose history was one of tragedy, drama, bloodshed and mystery.

But the most carefully framed, guarded and adroit questioning failed to draw any definite information from Polu and his fellows, even though I felt sure I had convinced them that I was not searching for gold.

Perhaps, I decided, it might be that, as they said, the Doraks knew of the mine. That they themselves only knew what had been handed down in traditions for centuries. That they had heard from their fathers who had heard it from their fathers, that long ago the Spaniards had a mine somewhere in the mountains and that the Dons had forced the Indians to labor as slaves, until they had risen and killed the white men. But, so they declared, they knew nothing; they had no knowledge of gold (it was a fact that not one wore an ornament of the precious metal) that it was valueless to them, and that if they knew where the mine was they would gladly tell me, for I was their friend, I had given them presents, lived with them like a brother, and dwelt in their *cacique's* house.

So, deciding that my imagination had overridden my common sense, and that in all probability the Shayshans were as ignorant of Tisingal as myself, I busied myself with my notes and specimens and forgot all about the lost mine. Then, as so often happens, Fate intervened and opened the sealed lips of the *cacique*. His daughter, a chubby brown princess of eight, was seized with an ago-

(203)

nizing but far from dangerous fit of colic, the result of eating far too many oily piva-palm nuts.

Her screams and shrieks in the middle of the night aroused every one, and the Indians, firmly believing some evil spirit of the darkness had taken possession of her, added their wails, lamentations and incantations to the uproar.

At first Polu and his copper-colored queen would have none of the white man's medicine. But when the most potent charms and "medicine," the beating of drums, the slaying of a fowl, and the application of "magic" wood and fungus failed to exorcise the "devil," the Indians, as a last resort, appealed to me.

Very promptly the little princess' tummy responded to proper treatment, her screams of agony changed to sobs, the sobs to whimpers, and soon she was sleeping soundly and quietly on her mat of pounded bark-cloth beside the queen.

I doubt if Polu slept again that night. When I crawled into my hammock he was sitting motionless, staring fixedly into the black night, and when I awoke at dawn he was in precisely the same position, immobile as a bronze statue, his mind evidently concentrated on some very deep and important matter. In fact I could almost believe his spirit had left him and was wandering far away, and that only the shell of his body was seated there in the hammock.

Not until the invariable chocolate was passed to him did he return to earth. Then, having gulped down the steaming drink, he rose, took down a long powerful bow and a sheaf of wicked-looking arrows, and very carefully examined each one in turn. Evidently, I thought, the king was preparing to go on a hunt. And then, to my astonishment, he requested me to accompany him.

For a time he walked in silence. Not until we had passed beyond sight and hearing of the house did he speak. Then, halting, he turned, beckoned me to his side and grinned. His Spanish was limited and rather crude, and my recently acquired knowledge of the Shayshan dialect was even more rudimentary. But we always got on famously and there was no possibility of misunderstanding. Rubbing his stomach, he twisted his face into an expression of agony. "Wasit" (child), he exclaimed, "mala, mucho mala!" (sick, very sick). Then he closed his eyes and sighed contentedly. "Mekano shabi wasit bueno" (I am grateful, you were good to my child), he declared in his mixture of Shayshan and Spanish.

"Oron" (yes), I replied. "Wasit kaba warang" (I am glad the child is well), I continued, anxious to please him by using his own language.

Polu squinted his eyes and the half-quizzical expression I had often noted, an expression suggestive of crafty shrewdness, like the look in an elephant's eyes, came over his face. For fully a minute he studied me. Then he turned abruptly and pointed towards the green, forested mountains still streaked with shreds of morning mist, their shadows purple, mysterious, fathomless.

"Batagoa!" (come), he ejaculated. "Tisingal!"

I could scarcely believe my ears. I was absolutely dumbfounded. Polu *did* know the secret of the lost mine! He was about to reveal it to me, was taking me to it as proof of his gratitude for curing his daughter! For hours we climbed the mountains through a misty, penetrating drizzle. Mile after mile I followed the *cacique* through the shadows of the vast forest. I completely lost all sense

(205)

of direction, I was drenched to the skin, and was becoming heartily sick of it all, when the chief suddenly halted and beckoned me to his side. Carefully parting the drooping ferns and interlaced creepers, he pointed to a pile of rot-ting-moss-grown masonry rent asunder by the snake-like, twisted roots of great trees, and almost hidden in the accumulation of decaying vegetation.

Here, buried in jungle, was the ages-old handiwork of civilized men, and, unquestionably, as proved by the mor-tar, of Europeans. Polu walked a few yards farther, and stepping aside, showed me a stretch of roughly-paved roadway beside which were the almost vanished hardwood logs of what once, centuries before, might have been a massive gate or a stockade.

My mind was a chaos of sensations, for I was convinced that I actually was gazing at the remains of the ap-proaches to Tisingal. And if so, then very near at hand, was the long-lost, fabulously rich mine, the mine which so many men had sought for only to die, which no living white man had ever seen!

The *cacique,* looking about with furtive glances, as though desecrating a tomb, bent low, and pressing through a thicket, halted among the trees. Before him lay two large cylindrical objects half-buried in the earth. At first glance I thought them merely moss-covered logs, and then, with fast-beating heart, I bent over them. There was no doubt about it; they were cannon!

Bronze guns; ancient and with small bores, ornately-ringed, bell-mouthed and thick with the verdigris of cen-turies.

Carefully scraping away the corrosion and the growth upon them, I revealed letters and figures cut into the metal. Some were almost wholly obliterated, but here and there a letter or a number was decipherable, and the date, 1515, was clear and distinct upon one of the guns.

I had thought that lost mines, either real or imaginary, held only a passing interest, a mere curiosity for me. Yet, as I knelt there beside those centuries-old Spanish cannon in the heart of the jungle, I felt a thrill of excitement and exultation such as I seldom have known. Tired muscles, aching limbs, the weary tramp, reeking wet garments and countless intolerable ticks were forgotten. Beyond the shadow of a doubt, I was looking at objects which many a man would have given half his life, thousands of dollars to behold—the very guns that once guarded the way to the richest mine in the New World, long-lost almost mythical Tisingal! Strangest of all, I had been shown the relics by one of the tribesmen whose ancestors had risen in their despair and had destroyed all traces of the mine. And by some inscrutable whim of Fate, the open sesame had been an Indian youngster's tummy ache.

Had I dared to enter that section of the jungle alone, a silent arrow might have ended my curiosity and my scientific expedition then and there. But with Polu I was safe, and as I stood there in the dark ominous forest with the yelping barks of toucans and the chattering parrots breaking the oppressive silence, I was thankful that the secret of the mine had been and still was so effectively guarded. Gold and the white man's lust for wealth have always been the curse of the Indians, and had the location of Tisingal become known it would have spelled the doom of my friends, the Shayshans, and their neighbors.

Then I noticed that Polu appeared nervous. He was impatiently urging me to move on, speaking in whispers, peering about, searching the dense jungle growths as if in imminent fear of stealthy, hostile savages. It may have been my imagination, or possibly the *cacique's* fears were a bit contagious. At any rate I felt that we were being watched, that unseen eyes were fixed upon us, and that I was standing very close indeed to death.

So with a final glance at the mute guardians of Tisingal, I turned, and following in Polu's footsteps, threaded my way along the almost invisible trail that led to the domains of my silent companion.

At last we came forth from the jungle with the king's house in view, and instantly I halted in amazement. Gathered in a group before the thatched hut were half a dozen wild-looking, naked savages!

Had the hostile Doraks swept down upon the Shayshan village to demand retribution for betraying the secret of the lost mine to a white man? But before I could frame a question, the savages had seen us and, in the twinkling of an eye, had vanished.

Oddly enough, as it seemed to me, the *cacique* did not appear either disturbed or surprised at the presence of the shock-headed, feather-bedecked strangers. He could not or would not understand my questions, but merely grinned amiably as we hurried across the few rods of open grassland to his home. Then I understood. Seated in the house were the wild-looking savages, but now all wore ragged shirts and patched trousers. At sight of the white man they had hurriedly transformed themselves from savages to semi-civilized Indians—at least outwardly. But it was not until days later that I learned the whole truth. Not until I was preparing to leave for my long and thrilling journey down the river, did Polu, with a mischievous twinkle in his eyes, reveal the secret. Then, quite frankly,

A GUARDIAN OF THE LOST MINE

he informed me that the Doraks and the Shayshans were identical—a Jekyll and Hyde tribe, peaceful and friendly and with an external veneer of civilization, or wild, savage, hostile as conditions demanded. But in either case the sole guardians of the lost mine.

ʇʇ

Treasure Hunts in
Home Waters

ALTHOUGH mention of hidden treasure hoards and sunken treasure ships brings up visions of ancient galleons and palm-fringed, tropical shores, yet many a great treasure lies near at hand, resting in the remains of long-lost ships in northern waters. Perhaps the most famous of these—for it has had the most publicity, is the Ward Line steamship *Merida*, which was sunk in a collision with the *Admiral Farragut*, in 1911, off the Virginia Capes. As is so often the case, there was considerable mystery connected with the loss of the *Merida*, and stories and reports told by the passengers and crew, all of whom were saved, were rather conflicting. But all agreed that the ship remained afloat for nearly an hour and that the captain and some of the officers returned to the stricken ship, when they found she still floated, and secured papers, documents and valuables. Also, as is often the case, rumors of vast treasures aboard the *Merida* were circulated. It was reported that hidden somewhere upon her were millions of dollars in gold coin belonging to the refugee family of an ousted President of Mexico. Even more spectacular was the rumor to the effect that the ship had gone down carrying with her the crown jewels of the ill-fated Emperor Maximilian and the Empress Carlotta. But the vessel's manifests showed no such treasures aboard the *Merida*, which omission, so argued the sponsors of the tales, was quite to be expected as the crown jewels had been surreptitiously smuggled out of Mexico, and the exiled family's fortune would have been seized had the Mexican authorities known it was aboard the ship. But the *Merida's* papers *did* show that several tons of silver bullion and considerable specie were included in the ship's cargo, together with a number of mahogany logs, and of course there were a certain number of valuables—currency and jewelry, belonging to the passengers, which had been left aboard in their hurried exodus from the stricken vessel.

And although the Ward Line's records do not indicate that any great amount of insurance was paid on passengers' claims, or that any insurance had been taken out on the alleged millions in gold and the crown jewels, the tales of the *Merida's* vast treasures persisted and caught the popular fancy, as tales of the sort always do, for there is a romantic streak in most of us. And what could be more romantic than the long-lost jewels of Maximilian and his consort lying at the bottom of the Atlantic within the hulk of a sunken steamship?

Of course, efforts were made to locate and salvage the *Merida*. But the wreck was too deep for any practical salvage work by divers in ordinary gear, although Frank Crilley, who holds the world's record for deep diving, reached the wreck, examined her thoroughly and duly reported his findings. As a result of his report, the salvage company employing Crilley abandoned their efforts, having decided that it would cost more to recover the ship's valuables than they were worth.

The decision did not, however, discourage others, and from time to time, for a number of years, one expedition after another has set sail to salvage the mythical millions in the *Merida*. Most famous and prominent of these were the expeditions of the late Captain Bowdoin whose persistence and perseverance are worthy of all commendation even if, up to the time of his death (1935), he had not recovered or found a trace of treasure and has expended a good sized fortune on the work. Moreover, Captain Bowdoin must be given all credit for having been the first to employ successfully metal-armored diving suits in salvage work and for having not only brought up portions of the *Merida,* but in addition, securing underseas photographs of the hulk. From time to time newspapers have announced in bold headlines that the treasure of the *Merida* had been found, and about a year ago, excitement and expectations ran high when the shell-covered, mud-coated safe of the *Merida* was brought to the surface. All felt that the ship's massive safe would contain priceless jewels, bags of golden coin, perchance even the Maximilian jewels. But when at last the long submerged safe was forced open it was found empty—as bare of valuables as Mother Hubbard's cupboard was bare of bones.

Even more conveniently near at hand than the *Merida* is the sunken hulk of the British frigate *Hussar* which lies somewhere in the East River almost within stone's throw of busy, bustling New York City.

There is no doubt that the *Hussar* was wrecked in the East River in 1780 when, on her way to Newport, Rhode Island, she was caught in the treacherous currents of Hell Gate and struck a reef near Randall's Island. But there is considerable doubt as to whether or not she carried something over two million dollars in gold, silver and copper currency which was to be used in paying the long overdue wages of the Hessian troops, as has been claimed. Undoubtedly, when the *Hussar* set sail from England she *did* carry a very large sum in minted coin; but records, historians, log books and other documents are most confusing and contradictory when it comes to the matter of the *Hussar's* treasure. One chronicler says "Reaching New York from England, Sept. 13, 1780, came the famous *Hussar*, frigate, with a cargo of a large sum of money in copper, silver and gold coin. The British forces had not been paid for a long time and this money was to still their complaints." Yet the log of the *Hussar* does not make any reference to the treasure nor does that of the frigate *Mercury* which sailed from England about the same time and was supposed to be carrying 380,000 pounds sterling in coin. On the other hand, Fletcher Betts, an officer on the *Hussar*, in his report on the disaster, stated that twenty thousand pounds in coin, which was all that was on board the *Hussar*, had already been transferred to the Commissary General at New York.

Still another historian states that the British records show that the largest sum ever shipped to America during the Revolution was fifty thousand pounds sterling, yet in another paragraph he declares that the *Mercury* carried three hundred and eighty thousand pounds, despite his statement that her log did not mention any treasure. As it it impossible to reconcile these various contradictions, any one may believe, with equal reason, either that the lost *Hussar* went down with millions in her strong room or was sunk with no treasure worth mentioning.

Neither does any one know exactly where the *Hussar* now lies. As late as 1850 the wreck was buoyed as a menace to navigation, but she may have been carried far from the spot by the swift tides and currents of the East River since then. Of course many attempts have been made to salvage the *Hussar,* for even the chance of millions in treasure resting on the bottom of the river within a few hundred yards of shore is a lure too strong for any real treasure seeker to resist.

The first attempt was made in 1818, when the frigate's anchor and some of her guns were brought up, but with the crude diving gear in use at that time it was impossible to get into the wreck and secure the coin, if any, that was there. A few years later, another group of men had a try at salvaging the old *Hussar* by means of a diving bell. The wreck was located, but the bell proved useless and one of the party—a youth sixteen years of age and a powerful swimmer—dove out from the diving bell, swam into the cabin of the *Hussar* and secured a bronze plaque, pieces of table ware and other articles which are still preserved, some of the salvaged objects being in Columbia University and the others in possession of the grandson of the daring young man who salvaged them.

Since then, from time to time, the press has announced that some one was trying to secure the *Hussar's* almost legendary treasure. Only last year there were two salvage vessels with divers working in the East River off 132nd Street searching for the long-lost frigate. But the bottom of Hell Gate is strewn with wrecks, old junk and refuse; the soft slimy mud has covered the older hulks to a depth of ten feet or more, and to find and identify one particular wreck is an almost hopeless undertaking, especially as there is no certainty as to where the *Hussar* lies.

(214)

Possibly, had these last searchers been permitted to continue their work longer, they might have located the *Hussar*, but unfortunately, the United States Government has something to say in the matter. Not only do the Federal authorities control all dredging and salvaging operations in rivers and harbors, but in addition, the Government claims the *Hussar* and her contents, owing to the fact that she was an enemy warship sunk in American waters during a war. The only man who has official permission to salvage, or to attempt to salvage, the frigate, is Simon Lake, the famous inventor of submarines, who confidently hopes to succeed by means of his latest salvaging device. This consists of a captive miniature or "baby" submarine and a hinged steel suction tube somewhat like a gigantic vacuum-cleaner in principle. Within the submarine, which is connected with the salvage ship by cables, telephone wires, air hose, etc., a diver may examine the bottom, and when a wreck is found he can emerge from the tiny underseas craft by means of an air-lock, or if conditions demand, he can operate claws or grapples attached to the submarine. The purpose of the suction pipe is to suck up and remove the accumulated silt and also to draw up any valuables that may be found. At the present time, Mr. Lake feels that he has actually located the *Hussar*, but again and again salvagers have thought they had found the old frigate, and only time will tell whether Mr. Lake has succeeded or not. But even if it proves to be the *Hussar*, Mr. Lake is not over-optimistic as to securing treasure. "I wish it clearly understood," he says, "that I am not sure there is any treasure in the *Hussar* wreck. But we mean to find out. I have wanted to settle the question for fifty years." So until the wreck of the ill-fated frigate has been found and the many feet of silt that

(215)

covers her have been removed, and the old hulk explored from stem to stern, no one will know for a certainty whether she carried millions to the bottom or whether her reputed treasure is only a myth.

But there is no question whatever as to the treasures that still rest within the rotting hulk of another British frigate which is lying somewhere on the bottom of the East River not far from the spot where the *Hussar* went down.

This is the *Lexington,* which was sunk in the eighteenth century carrying with her an immense fortune in currency, said to amount to over a million dollars, in addition to a treasure consisting of gold and silver bullion, gold plate, and other precious objects which were taken from Vera Cruz, Mexico.

Yet such is fame, that few persons have ever heard of this treasure ship wrecked so close to New York City, and no serious attempts have been made to salvage her lost riches, whereas the *Hussar* is quite famous and a real fortune has been expended in efforts to recover a treasure which very probably exists only in tradition and in imagination.

ꞮꞮ

The Most Successful of all Treasure Hunts

ODDLY enough, the salvaging of vast sums in coin or cargo from modern ships sunk in northern waters in recent times, never arouses the same interest as the recovery of treasure from some old galleon beneath a tropical sea or some hoard of gold buried by pirates, smugglers or others on an islet under the palms. No doubt the reason for this is because so little true romance surrounds the foundering of a steamship and the recovery of its contents by organized matter-of-fact wrecking companies, whereas there is ever the halo of adventure and of romance about the old galleons, the swashbuckling, pirates and buccaneers, pieces of eight, golden doubloons, and visionary treasure-hunters faring forth to desert isles and shark-infested coral reefs.

Yet far greater treasures lie upon the bottom of northern seas than among the corals and sea-fans of the tropics, and far more of these sunken riches have been recovered than have ever been salvaged from galleons and plate ships.

When, a few years ago, the salvors, after long months of dangers, hardships and heartbreaking disappointments,

(217)

wrested the treasure from the sunken steamship *Egypt*, it caused scarcely a ripple of excitement or interest, whereas, had some one salvaged a few millions in golden doubloons and plate from the wreck of a Spanish galleon in the Caribbean, press and public would have clamored for the story and every one would have been thrilled.

Successful and remarkable as was the salvaging of the *Egypt's* treasure it was not the only fortune which has been recovered from sunken steamships in recent years without arousing any particular interest or notice.

In 1912, the P. & O. steamship *Oceana* collided with a German vessel off Beachy Head, England, and went to the bottom carrying with her a treasure in currency and bullion worth more than four million dollars. And although I doubt if one person in ten thousand ever heard of it, salvagers recovered every cent's worth of her cargo except two bars of raw silver worth two or three hundred dollars at the most.

It was a truly wonderful, as well as a most highly successful piece of salvage work, yet nothing by comparison with the salvaging of the steamship *Laurentic*, which stands out as the most remarkable as well as the most successful of all treasure hunts in the history of sunken treasure ships. Not only was her immense treasure recovered, but more remarkable still, the salvaging was carried on during the period of the World War and continued for seven years, and was so well and so economically conducted that the entire costs amounted to barely half a million dollars, a good sized sum to be sure, but a very small item by comparison with the twenty-five millions salvaged from the lost ship.

It was on January 25, 1917, that the *Laurentic* was sunk off Fanad Head by a German U-boat. Over three hundred human lives were snuffed out by the tragedy, and twenty-five millions in gold went to the bottom with the torpedoed steamship. Fortunately a little mine-sweeper was not far from the *Laurentic* at the time and her captain, Commander Geoffrey Unsworth, rushed his vessel at full speed to the scene of the disaster to succor passengers and members of the crew who still lived.

It was terrible weather, a southwest gale was howling across the sea and the huge combers broke in icy spray over the gallant little ship. But the Commander and his men were true British seamen, and for forty fearful hours they battled seas and gale, bitter cold and freezing spray, and by superhuman determination and grit rescued every survivor of the *Laurentic's* company. But the heroic officer very nearly sacrificed his own life, for the exposure and cold he had endured brought on pneumonia and he was hurried to a hospital.

He was the one man who knew the exact spot where the *Laurentic* had gone down, and when the Government had searched in vain for the sunken ship in order to salvage her millions, Commander Unsworth left his sick bed, and with a heroism seldom paralleled in the history of the sea, located the sunken ship and buoyed the spot. Had it not been for this one desperately ill man the chances are that the twenty-five millions in the *Laurentic's* strong room would still be lying at the bottom of the sea. Yet so lacking in sentiment and gratitude was his government that his services were never mentioned nor was he honored in any way by the British Admiralty, although the actual salvagers were handsomely rewarded.

Of course, in the salvaging of the *Laurentic*, the salvors had one great advantage over all others. The entire resources of the British Navy and the Government were backing the venture. The capital they could draw upon was unlimited, and they were equipped with every known device, invention and apparatus for deep sea salvage work. And bearing this in mind, we can better appreciate the difficulties to be met in recovering treasures from wrecks in deep water under stormy seas when we consider that despite the fact that active work was begun within a month from the time the *Laurentic* was sunk, seven years elapsed before the final load of treasure came dripping up from the depths.

Never in the history of salvage work have men gone about their undertaking under more adverse conditions. The World War was raging on land and sea, enemy submarines were all about, there was no shelter from storms, gales and waves, and the *Laurentic* was twenty-five fathoms beneath the surface. Moreover, the explosion of the torpedo that had sunk her and the bursting of her boilers had torn the liner to pieces and left her a mass of bent, warped and twisted metal, while at the depth where she rested the divers, using conventional suits (the present day armored suits had not been perfected) could work for only an hour or so at a time. Had the ship been undamaged above the decks it would not have been such a terrific job to have entered and reached her strong room. But as it was, it was necessary to remove hundreds of tons of broken and twisted steel and iron and blast a passage through five steel decks.

Also, of course, the divers were working in almost total darkness, and in order to aid them in their work of tearing away the wreck piecemeal the salvors had a scale model of the *Laurentic*, exact in every detail, and each day, as the divers blasted and ripped apart the sunken ship, the same portions of the miniature ship were removed from the model.

Again and again the salvage ship *Racer* was forced to slip cables and seek safety from tempestuous weather, and often weeks would pass with no possibility of salvage work being carried on. But at last the hardest of the work was done, the shattered plates, the torn and buckled bulkheads, the twisted stanchions and steel frames, and the wreckage of state rooms, saloons and cabins had been cleared away; a great gaping hole had been blasted through all five of the liner's decks, and the strong room had been reached. But so slowly had the work progressed, so often had bad weather interrupted the salvagers, that only eight bars of gold were recovered the first year. But in 1920 over six hundred ingots were salvaged, the following year three hundred were brought up; during 1922, the salvors recovered nine hundred bars of gold and in 1923 all records were broken by salvaging one thousand one hundred and fifty bars, the total when work was at last abandoned being three thousand and fifty-seven ingots of gold, leaving only one hundred and fifty-four bars unaccounted for. Truly the most remarkable, profitable and successful of all treasure hunts considering all the facts of the case.

No doubt, the question will arise in the minds of my readers as to why, if the British Government had such success in salvaging the *Laurentic*, the Admiralty did not also salvage the *Lusitania?*

There are several reasons. In the first place the *Laurentic* went down in twenty-five fathoms or one hundred and fifty feet of water, whereas the *Lusitania* sunk in more than one hundred fathoms or over six hundred feet, which is over three hundred feet deeper than any diver in a rubber suit ever descended, and it is only within the last few years that mechanically-operated, armored metal diving suits capable of withstanding the enormous pressures of deep water have been invented and perfected and have become practical. In the second place, the exact spot where the *Laurentic* sank was known, although if it had not been for Commander Unsworth, she might never have been found, whereas no one knows precisely where the *Lusitania* sank. Although the spot where she was torpedoed is known, the stricken ship drifted several miles before she went to the bottom, and as she undoubtedly sank very slowly she may have been carried a mile or more farther by the tides and currents before she reached the bottom six hundred feet and more beneath the surface of the sea. Also, there was no question that the *Laurentic* carried a cargo of gold worth twenty-five million dollars, whereas there is considerable doubt as to whether the *Lusitania* had on board enough treasure to cover the cost of salvaging her, despite the fact that newspaper accounts refer to her "millions in gold," sometimes conservatively mentioning a mere twenty millions, at other times boosting the total to two hundred millions. But largely the depth of water above the torpedoed *Lusitania* has been the stumbling block which has prevented serious efforts being made to salvage the most famous of steamships sunk by the Germans in their inhuman and relentless submarine campaign. But at the present time an expedition is actively engaged in attempting to locate and salvage the *Lusitania*.

With the salvage ship *Ophir,* provided with every up-to-date, scientific device, and aided by the British Admiralty and survivors of the *Lusitania's* crew, the treasure hunters on the *Ophir* stand a very good chance of being successful in their quest. Among the other highly perfected apparatus employed by the salvors on the *Ophir* is an electrical echo-sounding machine. Broadly speaking this is a device which sends sound waves from the ship to the bottom of the sea at the rate of one hundred and thirty per minute, and these sound waves, striking the bottom, "echo" or are returned upward to the ship where they are amplified and actuate a moving stylus which traces the varying depths upon a prepared sensitized roll of paper, thus giving a "graph" or profile of the ocean's floor. By slowly steaming over the sea the salvagers can see the outline of the bottom on the graph as clearly as though gazing upon it with their eyes, and any wreck or other object is instantly recorded. Already a number of sunken ships have been found and registered by the remarkable device and at any minute—before I have completed this paragraph, perhaps—word may be received that the *Lusitania* has been found. For descending to the wreck, the divers of the *Ophir* will use a highly perfected armored suit weighing nearly a ton, but so constructed that the man within can move about, use arms and legs and can grasp, move or lift objects by means of the steel claws or fingers which serve in place of hands. Safely ensconced within this suit the diver can descend to depths far out of reach of the ordinary rubber suit, and as he depends upon oxygen contained in a tank upon the back of the suit, instead of compressed air, he is not affected by the pressure and can breathe freely and normally.

Provided the *Lusitania* is located, there is no reason why the salvors should not recover everything of value within the sunken steamship. Perhaps she does hold a vast treasure. Perchance the total valuables recovered will not repay the costs of the expedition. But even if no treasure be found, if the *Lusitania* is located and the divers, as they surely will, descend to the wreck, the salvors will be well repaid and will have performed a service for which the civilized world should be grateful, for an examination of the sunken steamship will settle for once and forever whether or not the *Lusitania* carried arms and munitions of war and hence was legitimate prey for a U-boat, or whether the Germans by torpedoing her committed the most callous and inhuman of crimes, the most atrocious wholesale murder, when they sent the giant Cunarder to the bottom and sailed away, deliberately leaving thousands of men, women and children to drown.

ıllılılıllıllıllıllıllıllıllıllıllıllıllıllıllıllıll

The Greatest of all
Treasure Hunts

ALTHOUGH the salvaging of the *Laurentic* was unquestionably the most spectacular and successful of treasure hunts up to the present time, although the salvaging of the *Egypt* and the *Oceana* netted the salvors millions, and although sturdy old Captain Sir William Phipps holds the world's record for recovering treasures from long-lost Spanish galleons, yet, all of these together, with the salvaging of the *Lusitania*, if successful, in addition, would not equal, either in scope or in the value of treasures sought, the great treasure hunt that is now being organized in New York.

Ever since treasure ships went to the bottom of the sea there have been treasure seekers and salvors striving to recover the submerged gold. But in every case, irrespective of whether success or failure was the outcome, the treasure hunters have confined their efforts to some one treasure or some particular wreck. In a way this is a good deal like putting all of one's eggs in one basket, as the old saying goes. If the one wreck sought is not found, if storms or other circumstances prevent work on the one wreck, if it is found impossible to secure the treasure or if for any one of a dozen or more reasons the attempt is unsuccessful, then time and money have been lost with no chance of making good. But the expedition I refer to is to conduct operations on quite a different basis. Instead of setting out to salvage any one treasure ship, these salvors have scores of treasure-laden wrecks on their list. Indeed, it is planned to search the entire coastwise waters of the Atlantic seaboard of the United States from Florida to the Gulf of Maine, with some of the West Indian seas in addition, combing the reefs, shoals, bars and waters for the treasure-laden vessels which have gone to the bottom during the past three centuries or more, and salvaging all that may be found. It is a stupendous, a gigantic undertaking; beyond any question the greatest, most elaborate treasure hunt in the history of the sea. Also, it stands the greatest chances of being successful, for surely, among a score and more of wrecks which are known to hold treasure, it would be strange indeed if at least one were not found and salvaged. And any one of the many to be searched for would repay all costs of the expedition with a million or more over as dividends.

Moreover, even if no golden doubloons, no blackened silver coins, no long-lost gems or precious bullion are recovered, there is little chance of this salvage expedition being out of pocket, for aside from treasure ships there are countless wrecks, filled with valuable cargoes of merchandise, dotting the ocean's floor between Key West and Eastport.

While bales of silks and velvets, bundles of merchandise, cases of dry goods, and crated motor cars and machinery, are rendered worthless by immersion in salt water, there are many cargoes which suffer no harm through being sunk, even for years. Copper and tin, lead and zinc, case-oil and liquors, cabinet woods and minerals, even canned provisions and side leather are all salvageable. And to the salvor who is out to make a profit, all should be treasure which comes to his grapples, to paraphrase the trite old proverb. Even if there is a lure and a romance in gold and silver and precious stones, a few thousand tons of copper or tin, thousands of feet of mahogany or rosewood, hundreds of cases of choice imported liquors and other equally unromantic commodities all are worth good money, and a million dollars is a million dollars quite irrespective of whether it exists in the form of gold, silver, copper, lumber, brandy or champagne, or other merchandise.

Finally, this greatest of treasure hunts will be equipped with the most highly perfected, the most efficient and the most practical of modern devices. The armored suits to be used in diving are capable of permitting a diver to descend to depths of a thousand feet and have already been thoroughly and exhaustively tested as deep as six hundred feet with entire success. Although appearing like some grotesque, semi-human monster, gigantic, cumbersome and bizarre, yet the suit is so constructed that the diver has as much freedom of movement as if in an ordinary rubber suit even at extreme depths, for the all-metal joints are so designed that the greater the water pressure upon them the more mobile they become. When working at great depths the diver within the suit depends upon mechanical hands and fingers consisting of steel grips which are so delicately yet strongly adjusted that a single coin may be picked up or a section of heavy timber torn from its fastenings. But in fairly shoal water the diver may do away with these and use his own hands and arms like any diver in a conventional suit.

For breathing, the occupant of the suit depends upon oxygen contained in a tank within the suit itself, thus entirely obviating the danger of a leak releasing the precious gas and leaving the diver to suffocate before he can be drawn to the surface. Moreover, the diver ensconced in this remarkable gear is not cramped, but can move about freely. In fact there is abundant space for him to watch the dials and indicators within the suit, use the telephone or even read a paper. As the northern seas are ever murky and visibility poor, even in shoal water, and as the ocean is a dark, greenish-black void at great depths, entirely new and wonderful underseas lights have been provided which will illuminate the bottom of the sea for many square feet and will enable the divers to have as clear a view of the wrecks as though working at moderate depths in the crystal-clear, transparent waters of tropical seas.

Finally, one of the most interesting, the most novel and the most spectacular features of this greatest of all treasure hunts will be the radio broadcasting from under the sea. Each day, as the diver descends and moves about upon the ocean's floor, he will talk into a microphone within his helmet, telling what he sees, describing his surroundings, giving a graphic account of the grotesque forms of life about him—the strange fishes, the great gray sharks, the gigantic lobsters and enormous crabs lurking in ancient wrecks or reaching immense claws from crevices in subterranean cliffs. No living man has ever yet seen the inhabitants of the bottom one hundred fathoms or more below the surface of the Atlantic along our coasts. No one can say what unknown, strange, impossible monsters may inhabit these depths. But the diver in this wonderful new suit, with the powerful beams of the undersea

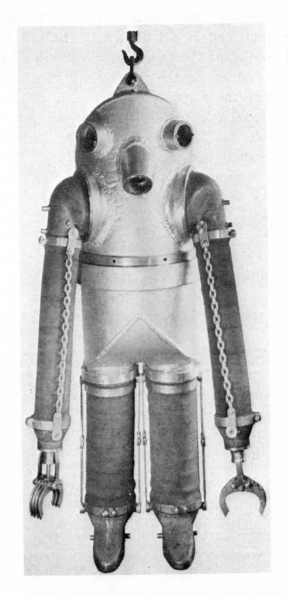

THE OGRE-LIKE SUIT TO BE USED IN
THE GREATEST TREASURE HUNT

lights illuminating the ocean's floor, will see and report to the world the wonders of marine life. And when a wreck is found tens of thousands of listeners will hear the voice of a human being, far beneath the surface of the sea, describing the appearance of the shell and algæ-coated hulk, the rotting timbers, the ancient guns, or if it be a more recent wreck, the corroded iron hull, the twisted and torn steel beams, the slime-covered decks will be described. Even after the diver in his grotesque armor has actually entered the wreck his voice will still be heard, coming through hundreds of feet of water, through hundreds of miles of space; uncanny, thrilling, amazing, as he tells of fearsome devil fish and octopi, of giant eels and huge crustaceans haunting the empty staterooms and cabins, or announces that he has entered the strong room of some ancient treasure ship and with his steel fingers is lifting bars of gold or silver or is pawing over mounds of black and encrusted metal disks that once were shining golden and silver coins.

So even if the expedition salvages no great treasure, even if no centuries-old galleons are found, it will be a success, for it is a many-sided undertaking with an egg in every basket, metaphorically speaking; a treasure hunt which even if on the sea will still be on the air.

Perchance, at the very first descent, the diver in his metal armor may find himself standing beside the wreckage of some once proud and stately galleon with a mound of gold marking the spot that once had been her strong room. Perhaps many a mystery of the sea may be solved. No one can say with certainty what new and wholly undreamed-of creatures may or may not be discovered during this exploration of the bottom of the Atlantic. But one thing is certain. Within the next few months countless thousands of persons throughout the world will be transported mentally to the bottom of the sea, and for the first time in history, divers, hundreds of feet beneath the surface of the ocean, will be talking to the world at large, broadcasting the story of what they see and find where no human being ever has been before; where no human eyes have ever gazed upon the strange inhabitants of the Atlantic's depths, where hundreds of shattered, forgotten wrecks lie scattered on the ocean's floor with incalculable treasures only awaiting the modern salvor in his fearsome armor—a far more grotesque monster than any denizen of the deep.

APPENDIX

Hints for Treasure Hunters

ɪɪɪ

Hints for Treasure Hunters

I HAVE often been asked why it is that so many treasure hunts fail if the treasures really exist and their locations are known?

There are many reasons why treasure hunts do not always result in finding and recovering treasure. Granted that the treasure hunters actually possess knowledge of the exact location of a hidden, buried or sunken hoard, the principal reasons for failure are: lack of adequate funds to carry on the work, improper equipment, inexperienced personnel and insufficient knowledge and experience in the work undertaken.

But far more treasure hunts are doomed to dismal failure because of inaccurate information, faith in traditions or legends, faked maps or charts, or ignorance of the laws of the countries where the treasures exist. Amateur treasure hunters are, as a rule, very credulous and will swallow as gospel truth almost any exciting tale of hidden or sunken treasures. Many a man has set out on a quest for some mythical treasure with only a few hundred dollars in capital and an alleged chart or map as his equipment. And here let me warn all prospective treasure hunters to beware of charts, maps, written directions or

(233)

similar documents purporting to reveal the precise spot where some old hoard has been cached. Nine times out of ten these are faked, or if genuine they were purposely made misleading, the owners of the treasures being the only persons who could understand them. In other words, they are a sort of code, and so many paces or feet to the north, for example, may mean the same number of yards in another direction. As a rule, however, maps and charts of buried treasures, despite their apparent age and their earmarks of being genuine, are modern and are made with the object of luring innocent treasure hunters on false quests. Take, for example, the alleged map of the Cocos Island treasure mentioned in the chapter on that famous treasure. It purported to have been made by Captain Thomson of the brig *Mary Dear;* but it would never have fooled a sailor or any one thoroughly familiar with the history of the Lima treasure hidden on Cocos. In the first place, Thomson's name is spelled "Thompson" on the document. In the second place, it reads "Captain of the *Mary Dear,*" although no master-mariner would ever sign a paper other than as "Master," while finally, the real Captain Thomson was quite illiterate and spelled the name of his brig *"Mary Dere."*

Another chart which I have seen, and which led an expedition on a wild goose chase and cost the dupes nearly ten thousand dollars, showed the cached treasure buried, "a fathom deep," in a spot which proved upon investigation to be bare, solid ledge. Still another "pirate's map" which was crackled and yellow as if of great age, and was written and drawn in a faded reddish ink (supposedly blood) gave the exact location of a sunken pirate ship fairly bursting with loot. Yet the spot where the ancient wreck was supposed to be resting in six fathoms of water was, in reality, over a mile from the sea!

I do not mean to assert that *all* treasure charts are fakes or that there may not be genuine treasure maps in existence. But if so, their owners would go hunting the treasure for themselves, instead of disposing of them for a few hundred dollars and a "share" in the treasures. Neither do I know of but two treasures which have ever been recovered by means of one of these supposedly old charts. I am convinced that it was very rarely that any one hiding treasure or who knew of the exact location of a sunken or hidden treasure, really made a chart disclosing the hoard's precise location. To have done so would have been to risk having it fall into the hands of some one else who would be in a position to recover the riches. Even Sir William Phipps took good care NOT to mention the exact location of the galleon whose cargo of treasure he salvaged. Nowhere in his journal or log was its position referred to, and his chart, which is still preserved, although clearly showing the reefs of Silver Shoals, does not indicate where the wreck was discovered. Only by a careful study of his notes telling the depth of water where he anchored, the general direction from his anchorage to the wreck, the time it required for his "pinnace" to make the trip, and other trivial matters, was I able to figure out the general position of the wreck. In the chapter on the Valverde treasure I have mentioned the old map, a copy of which is reproduced. Although Valverde intended—or supposedly intended—that his chart should enable others to locate the source of his riches, yet it is so indefinite and confused that no one yet has been able to follow the route to the treasure, with the single exception of Colonel Brooks. Perhaps Keating's original chart, showing the

(235)

treasure cache on Cocos Island, may still be in existence as is claimed by the present possessors of a map alleged to be his. But by far the greater portion of treasure charts are of no more value in a search for hidden hoards than the imaginary map of Treasure Island in Stevenson's well known book.

Another common fault with treasure seekers is their habit of starting on a hunt without first learning the conditions they are to face—the laws of the country, if out of the United States, concerning treasure trove; the character of the territory where the treasure lies, or the seas, bottom and reefs, if a sunken treasure; the difficulties to be encountered, and the engineering or salvaging problems to be solved. A ten-acre islet may appear a mere pin point even on a large scale chart; but ten acres of jagged coral rock and sand covered with dense, thorny jungle and razor-edged sawgrass, and infested with sand flies, mosquitoes and ticks, is a lot of territory to dig over. And even in the crystalline waters of the West Indies, where the bottom is visible thirty or forty feet below the surface, it is a long, costly, tiresome and disheartening undertaking to spot an old wreck. A sunken ship, even if a good-sized vessel, is a small object compared to the area of bottom, the cliff-like reefs, the great submarine caverns, the immense coral-trees and the jungles of sea-growths, and when coated with lime, coral, sea-fans and algæ a wreck is almost invisible. Even if the exact location—within a few square yards—of a buried treasure chest is known, the searcher should bear in mind that a million dollars' worth of gold occupies a space scarcely as large as an ordinary steamer-trunk, and that there is a lot more earth than chest even in a space a few yards square.

(236)

Also, recovering a treasure is not always a simple matter of pick and shovels and elbow grease, nor is it such an easy undertaking for an amateur in a makeshift diving gear to descend to a sunken ship and salvage her treasures.

The treasure seeker, if he is to have even a chance of success, must either possess engineering knowledge and be an experienced sailor and diver, or else employ men who are. And all this costs money. To attempt to salvage a sunken treasure or to recover treasures buried on land on the proverbial shoestring is a sheer waste of time and money. If the treasure seeker feels that he has reasonably definite knowledge of the location of hidden or sunken riches it should be a good enough gamble to risk adequate capital. And if not, then pass it up as too great a risk.

Treasure hunts, if properly conducted, are expensive propositions. In fact most persons will be amazed to learn how expensive they are. It is practically impossible to undertake a maritime treasure hunt with less than fifteen to thirty thousand dollars capital, and while a treasure hunt on land may cost less, if comparatively accessible and near at hand, yet it is surprising how quickly ten or fifteen thousand dollars may be legitimately expended. Why, it may be asked, is so much money required? Let us consider the expenses of an expedition to salvage an old treasure wreck in the West Indies. First, there is the boat to be purchased or chartered. A good, fast, seaworthy vessel with steam or Diesel power is necessary. A yacht is worse than useless for such work, a sailing vessel is worse yet, and a power-propelled ship large enough and seaworthy enough to make a long ocean voyage and stand Caribbean seas, squalls and a possible hurricane, will cost at least $3000 per month chartered. Unless she is a

(237)

wrecking or a salvage vessel she will require powerful hoists, reënforced derrick-booms, small boats, a diver's boat and extra heavy ground-tackle. The wages of her crew, consisting of captain, two mates, engineer, assistant engineer, oilers or firemen, cook, and at least two seamen will amount to over five hundred dollars a month. In addition there must be a diver who will receive a minimum salary of three hundred a month, and a diver's tender at two hundred. Next there is the diving equipment. If this is hired it will run into a lot of money, and nine times out of ten will be unsatisfactory. Some divers supply their own suits and gear, but as a rule these are supplied by the expedition. There must be two full suits, a shallow water helmet, several hundred feet of air hose, a powerful air compressor, plenty of new, high-grade hemp rope, repairing supplies, a diving ladder or stage and other incidentals which will run up the bill to a couple of thousand dollars. Enough provisions to supply twelve men and the treasure seekers for several months must be taken along, and it is astounding how much food a dozen husky seamen and a couple of divers will eat. Finally, there are the fuel and water, the costs of papers—clearances, manifests, consular documents; port charges, pilotage and other incidentals— to consider. In other words the operative costs will run to almost five thousand dollars a month or for a three-months' trip fifteen thousand dollars plus equipment, diving gear, food, etc., which will come to fully two thousand dollars additional. And as a reserve fund for unforeseen contingencies is essential, the capital required will be fully twenty thousand dollars. Of course a treasure-hunting expedition on land is far cheaper. But if the search is to be made in Latin America there will be the costs of securing a concession, the good-sized "presents" to be made to officials which are essential if long delays and opposition are to be avoided, the costs of travel, wages of laborers, food and equipment—all of which must be provided before starting on the expedition; tools and instruments, steamship fares, and usually a large sum of several thousand dollars to be deposited as a bond to insure the fulfillment of the treasure seekers' part in the concession. Neither should the prospective treasure seeker forget that it costs money to clear jungles and to dig holes. It would be a simple matter to disinter a treasure if one knew the *exact* spot where it was buried, but, unfortunately, this is rarely the case, and even if one is certain that the cache is located within a given area of a few hundred square feet a deal of time and cash will be expended before that area is thoroughly excavated. If the treasure seeker plans to dig ancient graves or mounds he will find a number of problems, aside from the expense, confronting him. In every country of Central and South America there are laws which prohibit the excavation of the old Indian tombs, graves and mounds without permission of the government, and then only when the work is done by representatives of some recognized scientific institution. Moreover, in such cases the government reserves the right to any and all specimens desired for the local museums or collections and, as a rule, claims all objects of gold, agreeing, however, to pay the finders the bullion value of such specimens. And as an official usually is appointed to accompany the expedition and supervise all excavations there is little chance of "getting away" with anything, quite aside from the ethics of such a procedure. I do not mean to state that it is impossible to dig ancient graves without a concession or permit. Neither is it impossible to secure a permit which allows the concessionaires to retain what treasures they find. But, in the first case, it is risky business, for the diggers, if apprehended, are liable to heavy fines or imprisonment, while one must expect to "pay through the nose" as the English express it, in order to secure a favorable concession or to blind the eyes of officials as to what is going on. Even assuming that the expedition locates and secures treasure from the ancient graves, there is still the problem of getting the objects out of the country, for in most cases the exportation of *huacos* is prohibited unless one has a permit, and Latin American customs officials have the right to open and inspect outgoing as well as incoming packages and luggage.

But let us assume that the expedition is going in search of some treasure which does not come under the law governing archæological specimens, and estimate the costs of such an undertaking. First, there is the camp and other equipment, including provisions and supplies, tools, fire arms, packs, clothing, etc. The cost of such will of course depend a great deal upon the number of persons forming the expedition, the distance to and the locality of the treasure trove, and the length of time to be devoted to the search. But assuming that there are but two men, that the objective is somewhere in the Andes—as the Valverde treasure, for example, and that it is planned to be gone for six months, the preliminary costs of outfitting will run into a thousand dollars at least. Then there are the steamship fares, say another thousand for the round trip, which is putting it rather low. Landing, freight, wharfage and customs charges on the outfit will spoil another couple of hundred dollars.

There will be hotel bills to meet while the party is being organized and permits, documents, etc., are being obtained, and by the time these essential papers are secured a third thousand will have been expended. Then comes the question of labor and of transportation. Horses, mules or llamas must be purchased or hired to convey the outfit into the mountains beyond the railways or motor roads, and a gang of native Indian or Cholo (mixed white and Indian) laborers must be hired. Labor, to be sure, is fairly cheap in Latin America, a day laborer receiving on the average a dollar a day or less; but don't forget that it takes four or five natives to do the work of one husky European laborer. At least ten natives must be employed if anything is to be accomplished, so that the labor bill alone will amount to fully fifteen hundred dollars, not counting the cost of pack-animals and their drivers. In other words, such an expedition might just as well be abandoned unless you are prepared to expend at least six to eight thousand dollars. And as totally unexpected and unforeseen contingencies almost invariably arise there should always be a reserve fund of several thousand dollars on hand.

Treasure hunting, whether on land or under the sea, is not a poor man's game. In fact it is not a game for anyone unless he or they look upon it *as* a game, an out-and-out gamble, and enter into it for the adventure, the thrill and the fun to be had for the investment. Regarded in such a light, treasure hunting is one of the most exciting and pleasurable of sports with prizes worth the proverbial king's ransom, for the lucky winners. But as a business proposition, treasure hunting, as a general rule, is about the poorest investment any one can make. There are, however, exceptions to that rule as to every other. When the location—within a reasonable distance—of a sunken treasure ship is known, and when the value or approxi-

(241)

mate value of her contents is established by historical or other documentary evidence, treasure hunting may be considered as a *bona fide* business proposition with more than even chances of paying immense dividends.

That more of the countless treasure-laden ships which dot the oceans' floors have not long ago been salvaged is largely because of obstacles and conditions which formerly could not be met and overcome. The ordinary diver in his rubber suit and bronze helmet is restricted as to the depth at which he can work, while the amount of work that he can do, even in fairly shallow water—say fifty feet, is limited. Any one who has ever descended in a diving suit appreciates the handicaps under which even the most skilled and experienced divers must work. One's movements and vision are both very limited. One must move slowly, as if in one of those nightmarish dreams where one is striving madly to dash from some peril and finds oneself incapable of moving rapidly, but must crawl laboriously and painfully forward. And as a man in a diving suit has little stability and less weight, any great exertion or effort is impossible. A diver may pry or lift *up* on a bar or some piece of wreckage, but the moment he presses *downward* the effort lifts him from his feet. To use a bar, pick or shovel for digging, or to wield an axe, maul or hammer effectively is impossible. One has only to immerse one's arm in water and try to use a hammer or a hatchet beneath the surface in order to realize how futile it is. As a result of all this it becomes obvious why so few of the sunken treasure wrecks have been salvaged, for the majority lie one hundred feet or more beneath the surface and in water so turgid or so dark that for a diver to locate them is an undersea game of blind-man's-buff. But within the past few years tremendous strides have been made in improving gear and apparatus for deep sea salvaging. The Williamson undersea tube was devised primarily for salvaging, but has proved of more value as a means of taking underseas motion pictures, although the depth to which this collapsible tube with its huge glass-windowed observation chamber may be lowered is limited to about fifty feet. More practical and ingenious than such devices, which are clumsy and restricted in their scope, are the armored, articulated diving-suits, several of which have been invented and used. These heavy all-metal suits, which resemble weird robots or monsters from some other sphere, are designed to be used at great depths and to withstand the terrific pressure of the water several hundred feet beneath the surface. Several of these armored suits were provided with leather, rubber or other flexible material at the movable joints of arms and legs, but proved worthless in deep water where the pressure so compressed the flexible material as to render it solid and immovable. As a result, the latest designs in metal suits have all-metal joints, some being provided with ball bearings and others with ball-and-socket joints. At least three different types of these have proved practical and have been tested out at depths utterly beyond the reach of divers in ordinary rubber suits. One such has been used in attempts to salvage the steamship *Merida,* another type is now being used in efforts to salvage the *Lusitania,* and a third form, which is probably the best and most promising, is to be used on the greatest of all treasure hunts now being organized (see Chapter XVIII).

With such modern apparatus, together with submarine lights which illuminate the bottom for an area of many square feet, there is no valid reason why many of the lost treasure ships should not be salvaged. But the expense

(243)

entailed in using them is very great. The suits alone cost hundreds of dollars, special electrical and other devices essential to them add to the cost, the underseas lights are expensive, and a specially fitted and equipped ship must be provided. Only a very wealthy man could afford to undertake a salvaging expedition of this sort on his own. In order to conduct such an expedition with any hopes of success a company or organization with ample capital is required, and the work should be planned and carried out on a hard and fast, matter-of-fact business basis as a salvage job pure and simple, depending upon the recovery of general cargoes, such as copper, coal, merchandise, case oil, canned goods, etc., for profits, and with treasure as a side line. Such an undertaking may destroy the romance, the thrill and the adventure of treasure hunting, but it also eliminates a great portion of the element of chance and is the only way in which treasure hunting will ever become a business proposition and not a gamble.

The majority of men, however, are inherently gamblers—in one form or another, and as long as human beings *are* human beings, as long as men find a thrill and excitement in taking a chance; as long as the love of adventure and the lure of romance exists in the hearts and minds of men, treasure hunting will hold its own and men will follow the will-o'-the-wisp of golden hoards whether buried under the palms on sea-girt tropic isles, hidden in secret caverns in the fastnesses of the mountains or lying amid the coral-encrusted, rotting hulks of ancient galleons beneath the sea.

Only those treasures the existence of which is borne out by historical or documentary evidence have been included.

NOVA SCOTIA. *Oak Island.* The origin of this mysterious treasure is unknown. It lies at the bottom of a shaft about 130 feet below the surface. At intervals of about ten feet, bulkheads of timber, matting or cement were placed in the shaft, and two side tunnels nearly five hundred feet in length were constructed with secret openings below the level of the sea so designed as to cause any excavation to be flooded with sea water. For nearly two hundred years various attempts have been made to recover the treasure, but so far without success. Borings, however, have proved its existence, for bits of gold and silver, a ring, parts of a gold chain and a fragment of parchment with writing upon it have been brought up by the drills. At the present time another effort is being made to

CHAPTER VII

(245)

secure this immense, mysterious hoard estimated to be worth several million dollars.

MAINE. *Machias.*

MASS. *Eastham.* The pirate, Bellamy, sought to establish a pirates' fort and colony on the Machias
River. Remains of his earthworks are still visible. At that time he had recently captured
a treasure ship, the *Whidaw,* with several millions in gold, gems and other valuables on
board. He may have buried much of the treasure here on the banks of the Machias River,
for his men, or rather the survivors, swore that
he never divided his loot. On the other hand it
may have been on board the vessel when she
was intentionally run upon a reef off Eastham,
Mass., by a whaleman whom Bellamy had
captured.

MASSACHUSETTS. *Cape Cod.* In 1898, the steamship *Portland* went down off Provincetown. She was reported to have had between one hundred and
two hundred thousand dollars on board in the
ship's safe, as well as valuables belonging to
the passengers. Some of her fittings have been
salvaged, but the safe has never been recovered.

CONNECTICUT. *Thimble Islands.* In 1785, a smuggling
sloop loaded with fine French brandy, while
endeavoring to escape from coast-guard ships,
ran onto a reef and went down. Although not
strictly treasure, the brandy today might well
be worth more than its weight in gold.

Connecticut. *Long Island Sound.* In 1779, the Connecticut privateer, *Defence,* under command of Capt. Samuel Smedley, while fleeing from a British corvette, struck a reef near Stonington and went down. She had already taken several British ships and carried a large sum in money and valuables taken from her prizes. The crew of the *Defence* reached shore in safety, and Captain Smedley requested that the Connecticut Government appoint a commission to inquire into the loss of his ship, and if he were found to blame, to courtmartial him. He was completely exonerated. The wreck has never been salvaged and would be of great historical value, quite apart from the thousands of dollars of treasure it contains.

New York. *New York City.* During the Revolutionary War, in 1780, the British frigate, *Hussar,* struck a reef in East River and went down. She was bound for Newport, R. I., to pay off the Hessian troops and is supposed to have been carrying between two and four million dollars in currency. She sank near Randall's Island within one hundred yards of the shore, and as late as 1850 her wreck was buoyed as a menace to navigation. In 1818, a diver working from a diving bell entered the wreck and secured a bronze plaque, tableware, ornaments, etc., which together with the ship's bell and anchors are still preserved. But so far no one has salvaged the money or other contents of the ship. Simon Lake and many others have made at-

(247)

tempts to salvage the *Hussar* and Mr. Lake is at present working on it.

NEW YORK. *Hell Gate.* Not far from the *Hussar,* the British frigate *Lexington* was lost in the treacherous Hell Gate in the eighteenth century. She carried an immense fortune in gold and silver bullion and other valuables taken from Vera Cruz, Mexico.

CHAPTER
XVI

DELAWARE. *Lewes.* On May 25, 1798, the British privateer, *De Braak,* sank in fifteen fathoms of water off the Delaware Capes. The *De Braak* was en route to Halifax from the Caribbean where she had captured the Spanish galleon, *St. Francis Xavier,* laden with gold and silver bullion valued at ten million dollars (probably one half that amount in reality). Several attempts have been made to locate and salvage this treasure, but so far without success, although several times it has been reported that the *De Braak* had been found. At the present time a party of New England treasure hunters are searching for the wreck.

CHAPTER
XVI

VIRGINIA. Perhaps the most famous of wrecked treasure ships in American waters is the Ward Line steamship, *Merida,* which was sunk off the Virginia Capes by collision with the *Admiral Farragut* in 1911. She was reputed to have carried a vast treasure including the crown jewels of the Emperor Maximilian of Mexico, and a million or more in gold coin belonging to the fleeing family of a deposed Mexican president.

CHAPTER
XVI

It is very doubtful if the *Merida* had anything of great value, aside from the ship's funds, some mahogany logs and several tons of silver bullion, for the records of the Ward Line (whose history I wrote several years ago) make no mention of unusual treasure on board, and the insurance paid on loss of cargo and contents of the ship would not indicate it. For several years salvaging expeditions have been making determined efforts to secure the *Merida's* alleged treasures, but so far have failed. Last year the Captain Bowdoin expedition secured the *Merida's* safe, supposed to contain a fortune in jewelry and specie, but when opened it was found empty.

It is reported that another attempt to salvage the wreck will be made this summer, 1935.*

CAPE HATTERAS. Among the countless vessels that have gone down off this famed and dreaded cape, was the two-thousand-ton steamer, *Central America*. The ship was homeward bound from California carrying raw gold to the value of over two million dollars. On September 12, 1857, she ran into a hurricane off Hatteras and foundered with a loss of four hundred lives. Never salvaged.

CALIFORNIA. On July 28, 1865, the side-wheel steamer, *Brother Jonathan,* sailed from San Francisco for Portland, Ore., with specie valued at three to five hundred thousand dollars. Two days

* Since writing the above Captain Bowdoin has died and it is doubtful if his operations will be resumed.

after leaving port she sprang a bad leak and when heading back for land struck a rock ten miles off Crescent City and sank within an hour. Never salvaged, although various attempts have been made to recover the treasure.

FLORIDA. *Palm Beach.* In 1595, the galleon, *Santa Margarita,* carrying silver worth seven million dollars, sank in a hurricane off the present site of Palm Beach. Several years ago a diver, while working on a broken submarine telegraph cable, located the galleon and found her practically intact.

Returning to New York, he secured funds and equipment and was about to salvage the old hulk when a hurricane compelled him to abandon the work. When the storm had passed it was found that the waves had so altered the shifting sandy bottom that the wreck could not be located. The *Santa Margarita* still remains where she went down.

FLORIDA. *Long Cay.* On June 30, 1715, fourteen Spanish plate ships went down in a hurricane near Long Cay. Their total cargoes were valued at sixty-five million dollars. In 1716, the Spanish Government sent a salvage ship and divers to recover the vast treasure. A million and a half dollars had been salvaged when a vessel from Jamaica arrived. Her crew overpowered the Spaniards and went off with the salvaged treasure. No further efforts were made to secure the balance of the treasure.

FLORIDA. *Key West*. The infamous pirate, Black Cæsar, is known to have secreted a large treasure either on Key West or on one of the neighboring cays.

FLORIDA. *Gasparilla Is*. In 1821, the ship of José Gaspár or Gasparilla, the "King of the Pirates," was sunk by an American sloop-of-war as the pirate chief
CHAPTER
II & XIII was attempting to escape from his den. He had already placed all his booty, amounting to at least a million dollars, upon the ship which went down with all the treasure. When Gasparilla found capture to be inevitable he committed suicide by wrapping chains about his body and leaping into the sea.

FLORIDA. *Suwannee River*. In 1820, the United States Government paid five millions in gold to Spain as an indemnity to Spanish citizens of Florida when
CHAPTER
XIII our country purchased the state. The specie was placed upon a schooner convoyed by a gunboat to be taken to Havana. During a storm the schooner sprang a leak, and in an endeavor to beach the vessel the captain ran her onto a reef off the mouth of the Suwannee River. She sank in about thirty feet of water, but has never been recovered.

FLORIDA. *Apalachicola*. While endeavoring to escape from a British corvette, Billy Bowlegs, the last of the Gulf pirates, ran his ship over the bar at
CHAPTER
II the entrance to a lagoon. She sank in shoal water but never has been salvaged. She was loaded with the booty from several captured

ships and had on board several tons of hand-picked gold ore as well as a fortune in specie. Billy Bowlegs also cached a vast fortune in the sands of the beaches of western Florida. None of his lost or hidden treasure has been recovered as far as known.

CUBA. *Matanzas*. In September, 1628, the Dutch, under Admiral Heyn, attacked and captured a fleet of Spanish galleons in Matanzas harbor.

To prevent their treasure from falling into the hands of the Dutch, the Spaniards threw overboard a large part of the three million dollars' worth of currency and church plate aboard their vessels. Never recovered.

CUBA. *South Coast*. In 1812, the Spanish ship, *Don Carlos III*, was sunk after striking a reef. Many of her guns and several thousand dollars in coins have been recovered from the wreck, but the bulk of her treasure has not been salvaged.

SANTO DOMINGO. In the year 1500, the ship of Bobadilla, the retiring governor of Hispaniola, went down off Santo Domingo City during a storm. She had on board nearly two millions in gold coin and plate, as well as the famous "Golden Pig," an immense nugget weighing 3370 pounds; the largest gold nugget ever found. Never salvaged.

SANTO DOMINGO. *Samana Bay*. The island of Cayo Levantado in Samana Bay was at one time a stronghold of the buccaneers, and according to historical records a large treasure was secreted on the island at the time when the buccaneers were finally driven off.

SILVER SHOALS. On these dangerous mid-ocean reefs, about one hundred miles north of Santo Domingo, the Spanish plate fleet of sixteen galleons struck in a hurricane in 1637. Nearly one hundred million dollars in gold, silver, pearls, emeralds and other treasures were lost, as well as every man. In 1687, Captain Wm. Phipps, later Sir Wm. Phipps, Governor of Mass., salvaged nearly two millions from one of the wrecks.

CHAPTERS IX & X

In 1933-34, the author conducted two expeditions to the reefs. One of the wrecks was located and much of her fittings and armament was salvaged. But bad weather, unforeseen circumstances, accidents and other causes prevented the salvaging of the treasure. Not far from this wreck the wreck of a privateer of 1812 was found and many arms, much equipment, etc., were recovered.

BAHAMAS. *Great Inagua.* On this island the Haitien Emperor, Christophe, had a summer palace, and it is universally believed that he concealed a vast sum in gold currency in the vicinity.

BAHAMAS. *New Providence.* When Sir Woodes Rogers took over Nassau the town was a famous and notorious pirate settlement. Prominent among the freebooters was the famous Captain Turnley who openly boasted of having a fortune cached near his fort-like home "on the hill above the parade." He met a violent death and if he had the buried treasure it is still there.

(253)

BAHAMAS. *Gorda Cay.* Early in the sixteenth century a Spanish ship struck a reef off this cay. In order to lighten the vessel the crew jettisoned the cannon. The vessel then rode over the reef and went down in four fathoms. The bronze guns have been salvaged and are now at Government House in Nassau. The remains of the wreck are plainly visible upon the bottom, and from time to time several thousand dollars worth of old gold and silver coins have been picked up on the nearby shore.

JAMAICA. *Kingston.* In 1692 the pirate city of Port Royal, noted as the "richest and wickedest city on earth," was shaken by a terrible earthquake and most of the town sank into the sea, carrying with it vast treasures. About fifty years ago a British expedition attempted to salvage the valuables in the submerged city. They secured many relics, including a large quantity of bricks some of which were used in making the pavement at the Royal Victoria Hotel in Nassau; but lack of proper diving equipment prevented them from securing any treasure (as far as reported by them). In clear, calm weather the outlines of the old city may still be seen under the sea.

NEVIS. *Jamestown.* Like Port Royal, Jamestown, the former capital of Nevis, was destroyed and submerged by an earthquake in 1680. No attempts to recover its treasures have been made, although the outlines of walls and buildings may be seen in calm weather.

(254)

DOMINICA. *Roseau.* Off the town of Roseau the flagship of De Grasse was sunk by Admiral Rodney in 1782. In addition to the French Admiral's plate and other valuables, the vessel had on board gold and silver currency to the value of about half a million dollars. No attempts have been made to salvage the treasure.

MARGARITA ISLAND. In 1670, the Spanish galleon, *Santisima Concepcion,* was sunk by the Dutch buccaneer "Wooden Leg" about half a league from the harbor. The ship carried a vast treasure from Panama, Peru and elsewhere. Never recovered.

VENEZUELA. *Cumana Bay.* During the Venezuelan War of Liberation, the Spanish ship, *San Pedro de Alcantara,* was blown up and sunk by the Venezuelans in the channel between the islands of Coche and Cubaque. She had on board about four million dollars' worth of currency, jewels, gold and silver and church plate. Several unsuccessful attempts to salvage her treasure have been made.

VENEZUELA. *Maracaibo.* During his raid on the Spanish towns on the shores of Lake Maracaibo, Sir Henry Morgan, the buccaneer, sank six Spanish ships, including the Spanish flagship, with over a million dollars' worth of currency, as well as much gold and silver plate on board. Never salvaged.

COLOMBIA. *Gulf of Uraba.* In 1610, a Spanish plate ship with five million dollars in gold and silver went down in this gulf. No known attempt to recover the treasure has ever been made.

COLOMBIA. *Lake Guatavita.* The old legend of El Dorado had, as its foundation, the custom of the Chibcha Indians whose king was annually coated with gold dust and was ferried to the center of this lake where he plunged into the water and washed the gold from his body. Also, at that time, numbers of objects of gold and platinum were cast into the lake as offerings to the Indians' gods. As this had been going on for unknown numbers of centuries, the total treasures in the lake must be stupendous. In 1903, a British company undertook to drain the lake and recover the valuables, but owing to inadequate equipment and lack of engineering ability only a few feet of water were drawn off. A great number of gold and platinum objects were recovered, but the bulk of the vast treasure still rests at the bottom of the lake. With modern machinery and devices it would not be a difficult feat to drain the lake and salvage the treasure.

PANAMA. In 1595, Sir Francis Drake held up a mule-train laden with treasure as it was passing along the old "Gold Road" from Panama City to Porto Bello. When a force of Spanish soldiers attacked the British the latter hastily buried most of the treasure in land-crab holes and under uprooted trees. Only a very small part of this was recovered, and fully ten tons of precious

CHAPTER XII

(256)

metals must still remain hidden beside the old Gold Road in the jungle.

It is a well known and historical fact that a good sized treasure is hidden in, under, or near the church at Natá which is the oldest church still in use in America.

According to tradition, the old church at San Francisco, in Veraguas Province, has twenty pounds of raw gold under each of its supporting columns.

In northwestern Panama the ancient Indian graves or "huacas" often contain a great deal of gold.

When Sir Henry Morgan sacked and burned Old Panama, many of the inhabitants hid their valuables in cisterns, wells and other spots. Many of the owners were killed or were carried away as captives, and there is good reason to believe that large quantities of valuables still are hidden at the site of the old city. A few years ago an attempt was made to find these by means of a radio detector; but the only object recovered was a gold rosary. Owing to disagreements with the government of Panama, and to the claims of private owners of the land, the search was abandoned.

Also, at the time when Morgan attacked the city, many of the people managed to escape in ships, taking with them their riches. Several of these vessels put in at Taboga Island where the treasures were buried. None have ever been recovered as far as known.

COSTA RICA. Close to the border of Panama, if not actually within the latter country, is the fabulously rich "lost" mine of Tisingal. Although many attempts have been made to find the mine since the time when the Indians massacred the Spaniards and destroyed all evidence of the workings, no one has ever located it and returned alive. Several years ago, while I was living among a tribe of little-known Indians, I rendered a service to the chief by curing his sick daughter. Out of gratitude the chief led me to the old abandoned road leading to the "lost" mine and showed me the ancient cannon which had once been mounted upon the stockade surrounding the mine.

CHAPTER XV

Many of the innumerable ancient Indian graves or "huacas" of Costa Rica contain numerous golden images, bells and other objects.

COCOS ISLAND. There are several large treasures on this most famous of all treasure islands. Davis, the buccaneer, hid several lots of treasure here, as did other buccaneers and pirates; but the largest treasure was that of Lima, mainly the valuables from the Lima Cathedral. At the time when Bolívar was marching on Peru, the loyal Spaniards and the priests sought safety for themselves and their riches in the Felipe Rey fortress at Callao. All who could do so secured ships and sailed away. Among the vessels in port was the British brig, *Mary Dear,* in command of a Captain Thomson. His ship was

CHAPTER VIII

chartered to carry the treasures of the cathedral
to Mexico, but the temptation proving too
much for him, he turned pirate, killed the
Spaniards, and hid the cargo of treasure on
Cocos Island. Later, he joined Benito Benito, a
notorious Spanish pirate, and for several years
the two looted Spanish and other ships and
cached their booty on Cocos. Eventually the
pirate ship was taken by a British war vessel
and most of the pirates were hanged, but Captain Thomson managed to escape. Several years
later, he made the acquaintance of a Mr. Keating of Newfoundland, and revealing his identity,
told of the Cocos Island hoard. An expedition
was fitted out but Thomson died before it set
sail. Keating and Captain Bogue landed at
Cocos and actually found the treasure. But the
crew mutinied and the two men endeavored to
carry away as much as they could before being
compelled to reveal the cache to the crew. Their
boat was capsized, Bogue was drowned, and
Keating was picked up by a Costa Rican vessel. He returned to Newfoundland but died
shortly afterwards. Since then countless expeditions have searched in vain for the Cocos Island
treasures. But scientists have established the
fact that landslides have occurred since Keating
and Bogue found the cache and the treasure is
buried under many feet of débris. As far as
known the only treasure ever recovered on
Cocos was a single gold doubloon picked up by
a German hermit named Geissler who lived on

the island and searched for the treasures for thirty years.

ECUADOR. *Plate Is.* In 1573, Sir Francis Drake put into this island, which was then known as Cano, and finding that the *Golden Hind* could not safely carry all the treasure he had looted from the Spaniards, Drake jettisoned about forty-five tons of silver. Later, Davis, the buccaneer, spent Christmas Day at the island, and his crew fished up several hundred pieces of eight by means of tallowed leads. Several years ago a man dredged up eighteen tons of the silver which Drake threw overboard, but fully thirty tons must still remain on the bottom in fairly shallow water.

CHAPTER XI

ECUADOR. *Guayaquil.* During the time of the Cromwellian wars in England the Spanish Government ordered the Viceroy of Peru to send about ten million dollars in gold and silver to aid in placing King Charles upon the throne. The ship struck a reef not far from Santa Elena, a short distance from the harbor of Guayaquil, and went down with all its treasure. In the eighteenth century an attempt was made to salvage the millions, but after a few thousand dollars had been recovered the native divers refused to go on with the work because of the number of sharks. After every severe storm, gold and silver coins from the wreck are picked up on the nearby beach. No recent attempts have been made to salvage the vast treasure.

ECUADOR. Somewhere among the Andes of eastern Ecuador there is a crater valley and lake where an immense treasure in ancient pre-Incan gold and silver images, ceremonial objects, etc., is cached. For many years a Spaniard named Valverde, who was married to an Incan woman, made frequent visits to the spot and returned laden with gold. The map which Valverde left at the time of his death shows the route and location of the hoard, but no one has ever succeeded in finding it, although the late Col. E. C. Brooks reached the crater. He was forced to leave owing to a cloudburst and the desertion of his Indians before he had a chance to reach the treasure. At the present time (August 1935) an expedition is being fitted out in New York to search for this famous treasure.

CHAPTER VI

PERU. *Paita.* A short distance from the present town of Paita, the Sieur Raveneau de Lussan, buccaneer, sank a Spanish vessel, the *Todos Santos,* with over a million dollars' worth of gold and silver bullion and specie. No known attempt to locate or salvage the wreck has been made.

PERU. *Ancient graves.* The ancient Incan and pre-Incan tombs, mounds and graves or "huacas" are often rich in gold and silver objects. In 1576, a Spaniard, Garcia Gutierrez, secured over one million dollars from a single mound near the present town of Salavery, and in 1592, he took over $675,550 more. No one can estimate the millions that still remain in these ancient graves.

CHAPTER XII

(261)

PERU. *Interior*. When Atahualpa was a prisoner of the Spaniards under Pizarro, he agreed to fill the room wherein he was confined with gold for his ransom, and ordered his people to bring all the gold from palaces and temples of the Incan Empire to Cajamarca where he was being held. The Spaniards, however, became impatient and put the Inca to death before the room had been half filled. Learning of Atahualpa's death, the Indians bringing the treasures for the Inca's ransom, secreted them in the Andes. Among other treasures was the gold chain, weighing over ten tons, of the Inca Huascar; the gold and silver ceremonial objects and ornaments of the Temple of the Sun in Cuzco; the twelve life-sized gold statues of the dead Incas, and raw gold weighing 75,000 pounds which was being carried by one thousand porters, each with a load of seventy-five pounds, the whole amounting to more than one hundred million dollars in value. No one ever has found any of this vast hidden treasure, although its location, within an area of ten miles square, is fairly well established.

CHAPTER XII

PERU. *Callao*. At the time of Bolívar's insurrection, when the various South American countries were seeking their freedom from Spain, the inhabitants of Lima (then the richest city in all (America) sought safety for themselves and their treasures in the Felípe Rey fortress at Callao. It was a part of this treasure that was concealed on Cocos Island; but a large amount

CHAPTER VIII

was hidden in the citadel and never has been recovered.

PERU. *Lake Titicaca*. For countless centuries before the conquest of Peru, the Incas and the pre-Incas had been making sacrifices to their deities by casting gold and silver images and other objects into the lake. These offerings were thrown from the Temple of the Sun on the Island of the Sun, and although the lake is exceedingly deep, yet at this point the shore slopes gradually and is rough and rocky, so that any object thrown from the temple could not sink far. No attempt has ever been made to recover this stupendous accumulation of treasure.

PERU. *Lurin*. Before the Spanish conquest, the ancient, holy city of Pachakamak (about eight miles from Lima) contained vast treasures. The doors of the Temple of the Sun were plated with gold and studded with pearls and emeralds, the woodwork of the temple was fastened together with golden nails, there were many life sized gold images in niches about the walls, and the inner shrine was ablaze with gold and jewels. The temple of the Virgins of the Sun was almost as rich in gold and gems, as were the lesser temples and shrines. When the people learned that Hernando Pizarro (brother of Francisco) was approaching, the priests and officials hid the treasures in the neighboring valley of Lurin. A single emerald and a few plates of gold were picked up by the Spaniards who burned the woodwork of the temple and secured thousands of dollars' worth of the gold spikes. They also found a store of several tons of silver and used some of this for shoeing their horses. Even the most fearful tortures could not wring the secret of the hidden treasures from the priests, and to this day it still lies, either buried or secreted in a cave, in the little valley of Lurin.

BOLIVIA. *Tiahuanaco.* Originally the gigantic blocks of stone of which this immeasurably ancient city was built, were fastened together by means of huge silver staples or "keys." Many of these were torn out by the Spaniards, and from time to time a few have been found about the ruins. But immense numbers must still remain buried under the fallen walls. Also, there is little doubt that somewhere in the ruined city there are marvelous golden utensils and other objects.

CHILE. In April, 1902, the Kosmos Line steamship, *Sakkarah,* went down off the west coast of Hamblin Island, one hundred miles south of the Chilean mainland. According to the ship's manifest, she carried a cargo of nitrates and also gold bullion worth $330,000. Never salvaged.

ﻟﻟ

List of Treasures Actually Known to Have Been Recovered or Salvaged in Recent Years

BAHAMAS. *Grand Bahama Bank*. A blockade runner's safe was salvaged from a wreck three years ago. It CHAPTER I contained several hundred thousand dollars in worthless British paper money and eighty-six thousand dollars in gold sovereigns.

ISLE OF PINES. Four or five years ago an American resident of this island located a cave wherein the loot of Vera Cruz was hidden. When he re-CHAPTER XIII turned to secure the treasure he found the local officials had taken it. Another treasure was found by a man searching for a lost hog.

ISLAND OF PLATE. Three years ago the owner of a tow-boat on the west coast of South America, CHAPTER XI dredged up eighteen tons of the silver thrown overboard at this island by Sir Francis Drake.

FLORIDA. *Florida Keys*. A short time ago two fishermen found several thousand dollars in gold and sil-CHAPTER XIII ver coins in the bores of two old cannon they had salvaged from the reefs.

Florida. *Miami.* A few years ago a negro laborer while digging a ditch unearthed treasure amounting to about $300,000. He invested it in stock in a big department store.

CHAPTER XIII

Florida. *Pensacola.* With a large treasure unearthed while excavating for a street, a resident of Pensacola erected the Thesian Building.

CHAPTER XIII

Florida. *Braden's Castle.* In this old fortress-like house a man found a cache of gold worth over seventy-five thousand dollars. Incredible as it may seem he found the hoard through a dream.

CHAPTER XIII

California. In 1931, the Panama Mail steamship, *Colombia,* was wrecked at Cape Tosca, Lower California. It was currently reported that she carried $850,000 in gold bullion from Central America. The steamship company, however, declared she had only $200,000 on board. The Merritt-Chapman & Scott Co. undertook to salvage the treasure, but when their wrecking vessels reached the spot they found the *Colombia* had gone to pieces and was in ten fathoms of water. The strong room had broken open and the gold coins had vanished in the mud and sand of the bottom. Tubes were lowered into the mud which was sucked up and run through screens and $190,000 of the treasure was recovered.

Europe. *France.* A few years ago the press contained frequent accounts of the salvaging of the S.S. *Egypt.* In the face of every obstacle, including sabotage, storms, deep water, etc., the Italian salvors recovered several millions in gold from the wreck.

Europe. *Great Britain.* During the World War, the S.S. *Laurentic* was sunk by a German submarine. Despite the war, rough weather and many other obstacles, the British Government recovered three thousand and fifty-seven bars of gold (valued at nearly twenty-five million dollars) out of the ship's total of three thousand two hundred and eleven.

CHAPTER XVII

Europe. *England.* In 1912, the P. & O. steamship *Oceana* was sunk in collision with a German vessel off Beachy Head. She had on board currency and bullion worth over four million dollars all of which, with the exception of two bars of silver, was salvaged.

CHAPTER XVII